HOSEA
THE PROPHET, THE PROSTITUTE, AND GOD'S UNRELENTING LOVE

The Proclaim Commentary Series

THE PROCLAIM COMMENTARY SERIES

HOSEA
THE PROPHET, THE PROSTITUTE, AND GOD'S UNRELENTING LOVE

VOLUME 28

MATTHEW STEVEN BLACK

WENATCHEE, WASHINGTON

Hosea: The Prophet, the Prostitute, and God's Unrelenting Love
(The Proclaim Commentary Series)
Copyright © 2020 by Matthew Black
ISBN: 978-1-954858-10-7 (Print Book)
        978-1-954858-11-4 (eBook)

Proclaim Publications
PO Box 2082 Wenatchee, WA 98807
proclaimpublishers.com

Cover art: *Hosea purchases Gomer*
Source: Unknown

Unless otherwise quoted, Scripture quotations are from the ESV® Bible (The Holy Bible, English Standard Version®), copyright © 2001, 2016 by Crossway, a publishing ministry of Good News Publishers. Used by permission. All rights reserved.

Scripture quotations marked NASB are taken from the New American Standard Bible®, Copyright © 1960, 1962, 1963, 1968, 1971, 1972, 1973, 1975, 1977, 1995 by The Lockman Foundation. Used by permission.

Scripture quotations marked NKJV are taken from the New King James Version®. Copyright © 1982 by Thomas Nelson. Used by permission. All rights reserved.

Scripture quotations marked NIV are taken from The Holy Bible New International Version®, NIV® Copyright © 1973, 1978, 1984, 2011 by Biblica, Inc.® Used by permission. All rights reserved worldwide.

Scripture quotations marked CSB are taken from the Christian Standard Bible®, Used by permission. All rights reserved. CSB ©2017 Holman Bible Publishers.

Scripture quotations marked NLT are taken from the Holy Bible, New Living Translation, copyright ©1996, 2004, 2007 by Tyndale House Foundation. Used by permission of Tyndale House Publishers, Inc., Carol Stream, Illinois 60188. All rights reserved.

Scripture quotations marked CJB are taken from the Complete Jewish Bible by David H. Stern. Copyright © 1998. Used by permission of Messianic Jewish Publishers, 6120 Day Long Lane, Clarksville, MD 21029. All rights reserved.

Scripture quotations marked KJV are taken from the King James Version of the Bible.

Typesetting by Laurie Hilsabeck Miller

All rights reserved. No part of this publication may be reproduced, stored in a retrieval system or transmitted in any form by any means, electronic, mechanical, photocopy, recording or otherwise, without the prior permission of the publisher, except as provided by USA copyright law.

First Printing, April 2020

Manufactured in the United States of America

To my dear elders and deacons at Living Hope of Roselle, Illinois – you are my beloved fathers and brothers in the faith who have shown me what it is to walk in the relentless love of our great Redeemer-King.

CONTENTS

INTRODUCTION: A RELENTLESS LOVE 17
  Perestroika 17
  The Story of Hosea and Gomer 18

1 | HOSEA 1:1-2:1 THE PROPHET AND THE PROSTITUTE 23
  The Author: Introducing Hosea 24
  God's Love is Undeserving (1:1-3a) 25
    What's in a Name? 26
    Why Marry a Prostitute? 27
    Why Did God Choose Israel & You? 28
  God's Love is Urgently Needed (1:3-9) 29
    Urgent Because Judgment is Coming 30
    Urgent Because Salvation is Available 31
    Urgent Because Eternity is at Stake 32
  God's Love is Unrelenting (1:10-2:1) 34
    Unrelenting in His Promise 35
    Unrelenting in Jesus 35

2 | HOSEA 2:2-23 THE EMPTY PROMISES OF ADDICTION 39
  All Good Things Come from God 40
  What Do These Idols Look Like? 40
  It's Good to Seek Pleasure in God 41
  We were Made to Worship God Alone 41
  Introducing Gomer 42
  The Price of Idolatry (2:2-5a) 42
    You Could Lose Your Family (2:2) 42
    You Could Lose Your Money (2:3) 43
    You Could Lose Your Children (2:4) 44
    You Could Lose Your Dignity (2:5a) 45
  The Power of Idolatry (2:5b-8) 46
    The Promise of Idols is Powerful (2:5b) 46
    God's Love is More Powerful than Idols (2:6-7) 47
    God, not idols, is the source of all our blessing (2:8) 48
    Idols have the power to destroy your life (2:9-13) 48
  The Pathway Out of Idolatry (2:14-23) 50

We Need to Experience a Greater Love (2:14-15) 50
We Need to Experience a Greater Redeemer (2:16-17) 51
We Need to Experience a Greater Rest (2:18) 51
We Need to Experience a Greater Romance (2:19-23) 52

3 | HOSEA 3:1-5 THE SLAVE MARKET OF SIN 55

The Place of Redemption: the Slave Market (3:1) 56
   A Place of Slavery 56
   A Place of Sin 58
   A Place of Salvation 58
The Price of Redemption: 30 Pieces (3:2) 59
   The Price of a Slave 59
   The Purchase of Gomer 60
   The Price of Your Redemption 61
The Power of Redemption: Transformation (3:3) 62
   The Power of Love 62
   The Power of Renewal 63
The Person of Redemption: Jesus (3:4-5) 65
   Messiah's Preparation 65
   Messiah's Incarnation 66

4 | HOSEA 4 DIVORCE COURT 69

The Summons for Divorce (4:1) 71
The Singling Out of Leaders (4:2-14) 73
   Godly Leaders Expose Sin (4:2) 74
   Godly Leaders Recognize Signs of Judgment (4:3) 76
   Godly Leaders Accept Accountability (4:4-9) 77
   Godly Leaders Unplug from the World (4:10-12) 82
   Godly Leaders Lead Others (4:13-14) 83
The Steps Back to God (4:15-19) 85
   The Warning: Repent 86
   The Wandering: Examples 86
   The Wind 88
   The Awakening 89

5 | HOSEA 5 COME BACK AND SEEK ME 91

God's Knowledge (5:1-7) 93
   God Knows Their Neglect (5:1) 93

God Knows Their Exploitation (5:2) 94
God Knows Their Unfaithfulness (5:3) 96
God Knows Their Enslavement (5:4) 98
God Knows Their Delusion (5:4b-7) 99
God's Mercy (5:8-11) 103
The Mercy of Courage (5:8) 104
The Mercy of Correction (5:9-10) 105
The Mercy of God's Crushing (5:11) 107
God's Invitation (5:12-15) 107
An Invitation to Reflect (5:12, 14) 108
An Invitation to Rest (5:13) 109
An Invitation to Repent (5:15) 110

6 | HOSEA 6 RESURRECTED ON THE THIRD DAY 113

The Pathway to Resurrection (6:1-3) 114
Hear the Invitation to Live (6:1) 114
Meet the Author of Life (6:2) 117
Experience Life with the Lord (6:3) 119
The Instruments of Resurrection (6:4-6) 121
We Need Awakening (6:4) 122
God's Word Awakens Us (6:5) 122
God's Love Awakens Us (6:6) 124
Our Hope for Resurrection (6:7-11) 125
We Need Hope, like Adam in Eden (6:7) 126
We Need Hope, like Jacob's in Gilead (6:8) 126
We Need Hope, like Abraham at Shechem (6:9) 127
Jesus: Our Only Hope for Resurrection (6:10-11) 128

7 | HOSEA 7 THE NET OF GOD'S LOVE 131

Pictures of Sin's Misery (7:1-10) 132
Dying in the Hospital (7:1-2) 132
Mocked at a Party (7:3) 134
Burning in the Bakery (7:4-8) 135
Forgetful in Old Age (7:9-10) 138
Promises of God's Love (7:11-16) 140
A Promise of Capture (7:11-12) 140
A Promise of Compassion (7:13-15) 142
A Promise of Change (7:16) 144

8 | HOSEA 8-9 THE SINFULNESS OF SIN 147

Sin's Deceit (8:1-14) 148
- Blow the Trumpet (8:1) 148
- Sin Makes God's Enemies your Friends (8:2-4) 149
- Sin Gives False Peace (4b-6) 151
- Sin Promises Good, but Delivers Hurt (8:7-10) 152
- Sin Tries to Replace God (8:11-14) 153

Sin's Destruction (9:1-17) 154
- A Loss of True Joy (9:1-2) 155
- A Loss of God's Protection (9:3-6) 156
- A Loss of Spiritual Sight (9:7-9) 158
- A Loss of Your Livelihood (9:10-14) 159
- A Loss of God's Blessing (9:15-17) 162

Sin's Defeat (Col 2:14) 165

9 | HOSEA 10:1-15 THE TRUE VINE 167

Distracted by Idols and Disconnected (10:1-11) 169
- The Perception (10:1) 169
- The Problem (10:2) 169
- The Platitudes (10:3) 170
- The Pattern of Empty Worship (10:4-8) 172
- The Paradox (10:9-11) 177

Connected to Jesus and Content (10:12-15) 179
- Plow Your Heart (10:12) 179
- Or Pay the Price (10:13-15) 181

10 | HOSEA 11 GOD'S LOVE IN CHRIST 187

God's Love is Found in Christ (11:1-4) 188
- An Unexpected Love 189
- An Undeserved Love 189
- A Tender Love 191
- God's Love Found in Christ Alone... 193

God's Love is Experienced in the Heart (11:5-7) 193
- The Price of Not Knowing God 193
- The Blessing of Knowing God... 194

God's Love is Relentless (11:8-12) 194
- God's Compassion (11:8) 195
- God's Mercy (11:9)... 196

God's Roar (11:10-11) 196
God's View (11:12) 197

11 | HOSEA 12 PRESSING INTO GOD 199

Why Press Into God (11:12; 12:1-2) 200
   A Warning from God 201
Why Pray? 202
   1. Some things come about only by prayer and fasting. 202
   2. We're commanded to pray! 202
   3. Prayer shows you haven't forgotten who really has the power. . . 203
   4. Because when you live for Christ you're going to war! 203
   5. Prayer gives you a holy boldness and the very words to say. 203
   6. Prayer gives you discernment. 204
   7. Prayer breaks through strongholds. 204
How to Press Into God (12:3-6) 205
   The Wrestling Match 205
   How Do We Get There? 208
How can you as a Christian tap into prayer? 208
   1. You should walk with God daily. 208
   2. Pray for people in your circle of close spiritual influence. 209
   3. Pray for those around you each day. 209
   4. Pray during every life situation. 209
   5. Pray when you are saying goodbye to people. 209
What's Stopping You from Pressing into God (12:7-9) 210
   Comfort Might Be Stopping You 210
   It's Not God Stopping You 211
The Prize of Prayer (12:10-14) 212
   God's Word and Spirit 212
   God's Awesome Power in Our Weakness 212

12 | HOSEA 13 THE DEATH OF DEATH 215

The Death of a Nation (13:1-3) 216
   An Autopsy Report 216
   Cause of Death: Idols 217
God Loves Saving People from Death (13:4-6) 218
   He Saved His People in the Exodus 218
   He Saved His People in the Wilderness 219
Death is Worse than You Think (13:7-13; 15-16) 220

- God's Warning..220
- Man's Responsibility..221
- Israel's Death..222
- The Death of Death (13:14)..223
  - The Old Testament Promise...223
  - The New Testament Redeemer 223

13 | HOSEA 14 GOD'S GARDEN OF LOVE..................................227

- Return to the Lord (14:1-3)..229
  - The Call to Return (14:1)..229
  - The Words to Return (14:2a)..229
  - The Cost of Returning to God (14:2b).................................230
  - Reject False Saviors (14:3)..231
- Rejoice in God's Garden (14:4-8)..232
  - The God of the Garden Returns to Us.................................232
  - The Beauty of the Garden Is Restored 234
  - The Protection of God's Garden (14:7)...............................236
  - The Source of Fruitfulness (14:8)......................................237
- Rehearse God's Promises (14:9)...237
  - The Humble are Established 237
  - The Proud Stumble! 238

ABBREVIATIONS

Common

cf – Latin "conferatur", compare, or see, or see also
ff – and following (pages or verses)
i.e. – Latin "id est", that is
e.g. – Latin "exempli gratia", for example

Books of the Bible

OLD TESTAMENT

Genesis	Gen	2 Chronicles	2 Chr
Exodus	Exo	Ezra	Ezr
Leviticus	Lev	Nehemiah	Neh
Numbers	Num	Esther	Est
Deuteronomy	Deut	Job	Job
Joshua	Josh	Psalms	Psa
Judges	Jdg	Proverbs	Pro
Ruth	Rth	Ecclesiastes	Ecc
1 Samuel	1 Sam	Song of Solomon	Song
2 Samuel	2 Sam	Isaiah	Isa
1 Kings	1 Kgs	Jeremiah	Jer
2 Kings	2 Kgs	Lamentations	Lam
1 Chronicles	1 Chr	Ezekiel	Eze

Daniel	Dan	Nahum	Nah
Hosea	Hos	Habakkuk	Hab
Joel	Joel	Zephaniah	Zeph
Amos	Amos	Haggai	Hag
Obadiah	Oba	Zechariah	Zech
Jonah	Jonah	Malachi	Mal
Micah	Mic		

NEW TESTAMENT

Matthew	Mt	Philippians	Phil
Mark	Mk	Colossians	Col
Luke	Lk	1 Thessalonians	1 Thess
John	Jn	2 Thessalonians	2 Thess
Acts	Acts	1 Timothy	1 Tim
Romans	Rom	2 Timothy	2 Tim
1 Corinthians	1 Cor	Titus	Titus
2 Corinthians	2 Cor	Philemon	Phm
Galatians	Gal	Hebrews	Heb
Ephesians	Eph	James	Jas

1 Peter	1 Pet
2 Peter	2 Pet
1 John	1 Jn
2 John	2 Jn
3 John	3 Jn

INTRODUCTION: A RELENTLESS LOVE

Come, let us return to the LORD. He has torn us to pieces but he will heal us; he has injured us but he will bind up our wounds.
HOSEA 6:1

The believer in Jesus Christ is constantly growing. We are not in any way sinless, but we ought to be sinning less. If you find yourself not sinning less, then chastening is coming your way. God will do what it takes to bring you to your knees not because he is cruel, but because he is the most tender compassionate Being in the universe. He wants you to be what he saved you to be. He wants you to confront sin in your life and be conformed into the image of Christ (Rom 8:29).

PERESTROIKA

Mention the word "perestroika" in Russia today, and you will be greeted with cynicism. The reason is quite obvious. In his book, then Russian President Mikhail Gorbachev made frequent reference to the credibility gap between words and deeds. He insisted that people did not want political slogans that failed to square with reality. "Perestroika" means "the unity of words and deeds," and on that basis Gorbachev attempted to reform the Soviet system. It was a noble aim, but for the Russian people, its failure was painfully evident. The unity between political promises and social reality was a myth; therein, bringing the downfall of Gorbachev's administration.

Every day we watch inconsistency lived out before us on the world's stage. We hear people say one thing; and, then, watch people do another thing. All sorts of promises are given, but not many promises are kept. That is how corporate ladders are climbed, positions are gained, and elections are won.

The sad reality is that the same is at times true of the lives of many struggling Christians. There are times in our lives when because we are not confronting sin urgently and honestly in our lives, that the Word of God seems to lose its power, and the voice of the Holy Spirit seems dull and distant. I want to urge you as you study the book of Hosea to confront problems in your life head on. A small area of stubbornness in your life right now may one day ruin your marriage. It may cause you to dry up spiritually. It may lead you to other sins. We need to stay tender and humble daily before the Lord.

THE STORY OF HOSEA AND GOMER

The book of Hosea is a story of the amazing love of God for us. It is also a salvation story. Hosea was asked by God to marry a woman who would prove to be unfaithful to him later on. He was to use his marriage as an object lesson for Israel because they were deep into sin and far, far away from God. Hosea was to play the part of God. His wife, Gomer would play the part of God's people. Gomer bore him three children. God named his first child, a son, Jezreel which means "scattered seed." His second child, a daughter, God named Lo-Ruhamah which means "no mercy". For his third child, another son, God named him Lo-Ammi which means "not my people" (1:2-9). Through the three children's names, God warned Israel that he would cast them away and be scattered. He would no longer have mercy upon them and no longer show them love. However, in spite of Israel's rebelliousness, there would come a time when God would restore them (1:10). Instead of casting them away, God would plant them. He would have mercy on them and love them and call them 'children of the living God'. Why? Because God promised Abraham, to "multiply your descendants beyond number, like the stars in the sky and the sand on the seashore" (Gen 22:17).

We see this covenant love of God played out in Hosea's marriage. In spite of Gomer's unfaithfulness, Hosea continued to care and provide for her to the extent that he went to buy her back from the slave market (3:1-2). The Hebrew word for God's covenant love is *"hesed."* Walter Kaiser comments: "In no prophet is the love of God more clearly demarcated and illustrated than in Hosea. His marital experience was the key to both his ministry and his theology. It was the picture of the holiness of God righteously standing firm while the heart of God tenderly loved that which was utterly abhorrent."[1]

Hesed refers to a lifelong love based on a covenantal relationship. It is a steadfast, rock-solid faithfulness that endures to eternity. It is also a love that is so enduring that it persists beyond any sin or betrayal to mend brokenness and graciously extend forgiveness. It speaks of a completely undeserved kindness and generosity done by a person who is in a position of power. *Hesed* is a love which cannot let you go – it is God's pursuing love for you and me. Remember Isaiah 54:10: "Though the mountains be shaken and the hills be removed, yet my unfailing love (*hesed*) for you will not be shaken."

The gospel of Hosea is this: No matter what we do, no matter how sinful we are, God pursues us, romances us, stalks us, and stakes us out in a radical grace based in himself. When we run away from him, God still pursues us. God pursues us because he does not want "anyone to perish, but everyone to come to repentance" (2 Pet 3:9). As we look back on our lives and how we came to salvation, many of us would have sensed the feeling that God pursued us. And just as God pursues us, we are compelled to pursue others too.

THE AUTHOR

We are introduced to this prophet, Hosea. Although it is not expressly stated in the book of Hosea, it is apparent from the level of detail and familiarity focused on northern geography, that Hosea conducted his prophetic ministries in the northern Israel (Samaria) of which he was a native.

> **Hosea 1:1** | The word of the Lord that came to Hosea, the son of Beeri, in the days of Uzziah, Jotham, Ahaz, and Hezekiah, kings of Judah, and in the days of Jeroboam the son of Joash, king of Israel.

What do we know about the prophet Hosea? Hosea was a prophet who lived and prophesied just before the destruction of Israel in 722 BC. He preached to the northern kingdom. The prophet's name means "salvation," likely a reference to Hosea's position in Israel as a beacon

---

[1] Walter Kaiser, *Toward an Old Testament Theology*. (Grand Rapids, MI, Zondervan, 1978) 197 – Kaiser renders the word hesed as "loyal love" incorporating the concept of covenantal love, which in the case of Hosea seems to be very appropriate.

of hope to those who would repent and turn to God because of his message.[2] Following the command of God, Hosea married Gomer, a bride God described as "a wife of harlotry" (Hosea 1:2) and a woman who bore Hosea three children, two sons and a daughter (1:4, 6, 9). God used the names of Hosea's children, along with his wife's unfaithfulness, to send specific messages to the people of Israel.

THE MESSAGE OF HOSEA: THE SACRED ROMANCE

The message of Hosea is vital to understanding the theology of the New Testament. Paul's treatment of marriage in Ephesians 5 is taken directly from Hosea and other prophets who connect the analogy of marriage to the relationship between God and his people in what Richard Lints calls the "sacred romance".

> "Picturing God as the bridegroom and Israel as his bride allowed the history of Israel to be construed as a sacred romance. The bridegroom searched out the bride and redeemed her from troubles she had brought on herself that had been thrust upon her by outside forces. The bride was not always careful to keep interlopers out of the marriage bed. She too often played the harlot."[3]

Practically speaking, we apply this truth of the sacred romance to God as the Bridegroom with an undying, unrelenting love for his bride. In practical terms, it is clear from Hosea's prophecy that God does not love you or hear you because you are good. There are none good. God loves you because he wants to magnify his mercy and unrelenting love for his bride. He does not love you because you are good. He loves you because he is *good*! Because he is good and kind, he brings discipline instead of destruction. God promised that if Israel obeyed him, they would be blessed, but if they rebelled, they would be taken by other nations for a time in order to sanctify them. That is exactly what happened. They broke God's commandments and broke their fellowship with God, but God went after them and rescued them.

In spite of our disobedience, God loves sinners! You cannot imagine or comprehend how much God loves undeserving sinners. God

---

[2] Francis Brown, S. R. Driver, and Charles A. Briggs, *The Brown-Driver-Briggs Hebrew and English Lexicon* (Peabody, Mass.: Hendrickson, 2006), 448.

[3] Richard Lints, *Identity and Idolatry* (New Studies in Biblical Theology) (Carol Stream, IL: InterVarsity Press, 2015), 98-99.

draws undeserving sinners! This is the message of Hosea. Jesus Christ is the Lamb slain from the foundation of the world (Rev 13:8). He has always had you in his mind. He has always loved you. His hands prove it (Isa 49:16).

Charles Wesley wrote a hymn about this verse:
Arise, my soul, arise.
Shake off thy guilty fears.
The bleeding sacrifice
In my behalf appears.
Before the throne my Surety stands,
Before the throne my Surety stands;
My name is written on His hands.

THE INTERPRETATION OF HOSEA

One of the most difficult objectives to attain in reading the Bible is a right interpretation and application of Hosea. Certainly, this is a book about a people who know about the Lord but many do not actually know him. The culture of God's people is luxurious and worldly. It is a hard-hitting book to apply in the twenty-first century in which I am currently living. How should we apply the book of Hosea today?

First, the message to the nation of Israel is that Jesus is coming. Jesus is the ultimate Bridegroom who pursues his unfaithful bride (ch 1-3). Messiah will be put to death and rise again (6:1). Messiah is the true vine (10:1, 12; *cf* Jn 15). Like Israel, he will be cast off to Egypt for a time, and then be called back (11:1). Messiah's death will conquer death (13:14).

Then, there is a strong message to lost people in the church. God loves you. Knowledge is not enough. Attending worship is not enough. God wants a personal and exclusive love relationship with you that requires you to turn from the idols and addictions and distractions of this world. The message to lost people in the church is that God still loves you, but there will be a point of no return. After judgment day comes, there is no more mercy. Turn to God while you can. If you do, he will take you back, just like Hosea took Gomer back.

Finally, to there are several messages to the faithful remnant in the church. (1) Stay faithful in the midst of a hostile, wicked generation. Don't let the world have its effect on you. (2) Get back up if you have backslidden. You may have fallen into a pattern of sin in your life. But

God will never leave the child of God in sin. He will always bring loving correction. (3) Be amazed at God's unrelenting love. Though you fall, you will not be utterly cast down since the Lord carries you forward. He is able to keep you from falling away.

A one sentence summary of Hosea might be: "I love you with an unrelenting love so turn to me with all your heart, and I will not disappoint you like the world but will satisfy you with the ultimate romance, which is best displayed in the ultimate Bridegroom: Jesus Christ."

1 | HOSEA 1:1-2:1

THE PROPHET AND THE PROSTITUTE

Go, take to yourself a wife of whoredom and have children of whoredom, for the land commits great whoredom by forsaking the Lord.
HOSEA 1:2

Have you ever been unfaithful to God? Have you ever backslidden as a believer in Christ? Do you ever feel like a failure? In Hosea 1, we see how the Lord disciplines every one of his children. He will not let us continue in sin. His love is relentless, and he always comes after his straying child.

Early in my ministry I did a marriage vow renewal ceremony for nine elderly couples. Several of the couples were married more than sixty years. Some of the couples couldn't hold hands anymore. One of the couples, the man couldn't say "I do," but everyone in that room said it for him. One of the couples, the man had a stroke, and the lady was still very mobile and attractive, but she did not forsake him. What a joy to see that! It's rare in our country.

Marriage is a picture of God's love for his church. Christ will never leave his bride. God's love is relentless. That's what we are going to find out in the book of Hosea. But marriage is a picture of something greater than us. It's about the greatest love story ever: God's love for us. The Bible story is that God vows to never leave you – whether you are rich or poor, whether you are sick or healthy – He promises to love you and care for you unconditionally. His love is unrelenting in his love to undeserving sinners.

Do you remember when you were a child? When children are small they run to their mother's arms. We have little children all around here. Those arms of mama and daddy are strong arms. They are a refuge. God's arms are our refuge. I love Deuteronomy 33:27, "The eternal God is your dwelling place, and underneath are the everlasting arms."

Where do you turn when you are tired? Where do you go when you are bored? What do you turn to when you find yourself in financial need? Financial pressure is boring down on you. Where do you go? Where do you go when the pressure of illness and health problems come when you are already exhausted with work? What do you do when you are really happy? Where do you turn? What is your refuge? What is your encouragement in the dark? That's your god. God wants us to turn away from

We come to a scandalous portion of the Word of God. Here we have a man, a prophet named Hosea. He's part of the school of the prophets. He's from northern Israel, in fact, he's the only prophet outside of Amos to have a message for apostate northern Israel. Things are good in Israel. They are in a time of unprecedented prosperity.

The Author: Introducing Hosea

We are introduced to this prophet, Hosea. Although it is not expressly stated in the book of Hosea, it is apparent from the level of detail and familiarity focused on northern geography, that Hosea conducted his prophetic ministries in the northern Israel (Samaria) of which he was a native.

> **Hosea 1:1** | The word of the Lord that came to Hosea, the son of Beeri, in the days of Uzziah, Jotham, Ahaz, and Hezekiah, kings of Judah, and in the days of Jeroboam the son of Joash, king of Israel.

What do we know about the prophet Hosea? Hosea was a prophet who lived and prophesied just before the destruction of Israel in 722 BC. He preached to the northern kingdom. The prophet's name means "salvation," likely a reference to Hosea's position in Israel as a beacon of hope to those who would repent and turn to God because of his message.[4] He begins his ministry during the same time as the prophet Isaiah, from the prophet Uzziah all the way to Hezekiah. He has a very long and powerful ministry. He's gifted. He's bringing a powerful message.

He's a prophet. He's a great prophet. He's a mighty prophet. The Word of the LORD comes to this great prophet (1:1). God spoke directly to Hosea. Wow. That's pretty intense. What's God say? God asks Hosea to marry a prostitute in order to show how deeply he loves Israel, who was committing spiritual adultery, and breaking the covenant. God says in this book, "You tell Israel, I still love them. I love them and my love is powerful. My love is strong. My love is infinite. I love you with an everlasting love. I've written your name on the palms of my hands. I love you." What a message!

Isn't it ironic 2000 years after the coming of Christ, the Bible has been translated into thousands of languages, movies have been made about the life of Christ, and yet the world still is divided and does not seem to have a clue about the love of Christ? But go back to this parsonage and consider these three truths as they unfold. The first truth is this:

GOD'S LOVE IS UNDESERVING (1:1-3A)

Here we learn about the man, Hosea. What we find is that he is relentless in his love to an undeserving wife. That love is really the story of the entire Bible. The Bible is God's love story to us, undeserving and unfaithful sinners.

Somebody's Getting Married!

God tells Hosea: "I've got a wife for you." I can imagine Hosea: "Great news!" "I'd love to get married. I have been thinking about that LORD. I'm living up here in this northern unbelieving kingdom, and I've got just the girl, LORD. She's a very godly girl." God says, "Oh, I've got a girl for you."

"Yes? Who is she?" asks Hosea.

Listen to the story in verse 2.

---

[4] Francis Brown, S. R. Driver, and Charles A. Briggs, *The Brown-Driver-Briggs Hebrew and English Lexicon* (Peabody, Mass.: Hendrickson, 2006), 448.

Hosea 1:2 | When the LORD first spoke through Hosea, the LORD said to Hosea, 'Go, take to yourself a wife of whoredom and have children of whoredom, for the land commits great whoredom by forsaking the LORD'.

Hosea was one of only two writing prophets who ministered to the northern kingdom of Israel (Amos was the other). During the same time period Isaiah and Micah prophesied to the southern kingdom of Judah. At the beginning of Hosea's ministry, the northern kingdom was quite prosperous under the reign of Jeroboam II. But though things appeared to be calm on the surface, underneath the torrents of the kingdom's destruction were swirling. The nation had forsaken the Lord. Though they retained allegiance to the Lord with their lips, their hearts were far from him.

They had begun to mingle elements of the Canaanites' fertility religion with the Lord's worship by engaging in sexual rites and drunken orgies which were thought to secure the giving of rain and the fertility of the land for their crops, and even the fertility of their women in childbirth. During these days of political and religious upheaval there prophesied a man whose very name, Hosea, means "salvation." His name was a glimmer of hope in the midst of a message of destruction.

What's in a Name?

But the LORD had a different idea. "I've got a girl for you," says the Lord. "Oh wonderful" says Hosea, "Lord, I can't wait! Who is she?"

"You mean 'What is she.' She's a prostitute."

"What?" says Hosea, confused. "What will the other prophets say?"

The Lord replies: "I want you to marry a prostitute to show how Israel has committed adultery on me."

"What's her name?" asks Hosea. "Her name is Gomer," replies the Lord.

What kind of a name is Gomer? Gomer in Hebrew means "satiated", i.e. "full of lust". It's like the Lord is saying: "Her name suits her. Her name is Lust because she is a woman of whoredom, just like my people Israel." We read about her family in verse 3.

Hosea 1:3a | So he went and took Gomer, the daughter of Diblaim...

She's "Gomer, the daughter of Diblaim" (1:3), which means "fig-cake," a common aphrodisiac. Normally the father is listed, but it seems instead it's her mother, who according to Jewish tradition was of the same profession (whoredom). I can imagine Hosea. "What? What are you asking me to do Lord? I'm supposed to marry a woman whose family business is in a brothel?"

The Lord says: "I'm asking you to marry a prostitute for a good reason. My people Israel have committed whoredom." Shocking. Controversial. Even scandalous. That's how grace is. God's love is really scandalous. We need to read this book of Hosea.

I want to show you the extreme case of God's unrelenting love in Hosea. Hosea is a tiny little book. You can read it in its entirety in about half an hour. There are fourteen short chapters, autobiographically written by a prophet called Hosea married to a prostitute named Gomer. He was living 700 years before Christ. He is preaching to Northern Israel that is about to be crushed and carried away by the Assyrian Kingdom. Let's read about it in Hosea 1. It is here we read about the unrelenting love of God for Israel and for us.

HOSEA'S EVENINGS

Hosea and his wife Gomer had three children, but tragedy struck that home even before the children came. For some unexplainable reason deep within the confines of Gomer's fallen heart, Gomer decided to thwart that love, and seduced by the allurements of the night life, she walked out of her home and started to sell herself in harlotry.

Many an evening this prophet who would be seen by people in the day preaching God's Word, would be seen in the streets at night in his beloved city looking for Gomer. At times we can imagine he'd be standing outside the brothel, just waiting for a moment to talk with her, to express his love to her, and to win her back. In the prophet Hosea's home, God display's his love for us in such extraordinary terms. And if you will give me your attention, I want to take you through three profoundly moving truths. I promise you if we understand these truths it will be the most revolutionary thing in your life because from these truths, everything we know about love is defined.

Why Marry a Prostitute?

We find this truth as we observe Hosea looking for his wife whose broken her bond of commitment to him. The first message Hosea received from Yahweh was that the prophet should go out and marry a prostitute. God says to Hosea, "Go, take to yourself a wife of whoredom" (1:2a). Somebody probably stands in the street and says, "We love you; we respect you; we honor you. You're a man of integrity. But we do have a question for you. *How can a holy man of God like you be in love with a filthy adulterous harlot like that?*" And Hosea says – "I'm really glad you asked, and I have an answer for you. Now I'm beginning to wonder *how a holy God like that could love such an adulterous nation like us.*" Hosea raises that question in his own mind. God told him to marry a prostitute because "the land commits great whoredom by forsaking the Lord" (1:2).

Hosea was called to "have children of whoredom" with Gomer. What does this mean? He's to marry a whore and have children with her. The next verse tells us that Hosea was to "take Gomer" and she was to bear him children even while she was a prostitute.

Why Did God Choose Israel & You?

There was nothing exceptional in Israel for God to choose her, in fact, it was precisely the opposite.

> It was not because you were more in number than any other people that the Lord set his love on you and chose you, for you were the fewest of all peoples, **8** but it is because the Lord loves you (Deut 7:7-8a).

God chose Israel because they were completely undeserving, just like you. This is an ancient allegory not just about Israel, but about you. You are Gomer. Are you prosperous like northern Israel? Do you think you deserve it?

> ...he chose us in him before the foundation of the world, that we should be holy and blameless before him. In love **5** he predestined us for adoption to himself as sons through Jesus Christ, according to the purpose of his will, **6** to the praise of his glorious grace, with which he has blessed us in the Beloved (Eph 1:4-6).

We deserve none of God's gifts. Where would you be right now in your life if God gave you what you deserve. Look over all the blessings in your life. Why do you have them? It's the sheer mercy of God. Do you see the mercy of God flowing in your life?

Why would God tell the prestigious prophet to marry a stained and sullied street walker? Brothers and sisters, this is an allegory not only about Israel, but about you. The real question is why would a holy God choose an filthy unworthy sinner like you? Are you aware of your great need for God's love? Are you aware that you are Gomer in this passage?

GOD'S LOVE IS URGENTLY NEEDED (1:3-9)

Have you ever needed a wakeup call? Sometimes we need to warning siren to tell us what's coming. I can remember as a kid in Oak Forest, IL, whenever a funnel cloud was spotted nearby, the tornado warning sirens would go off. Why were those important? Because years before, a tornado came through that area and wiped out a school. The siren is there to tell us: wake up! Get to safety. Jesus' love is our place of refuge. Admit your sin. Get to the place of refuge. Wake up! Wake up! The siren in this text is a list of the names of Hosea and Gomer's children.

In Hosea's day, God's people were living in prosperity and carnal ease, and God had to awaken them to the need of his love. Bottom line: we can't trust in anything else, but Christ and his love. So God tells Hosea to go out and marry a prostitute and have children with her. God wanted to awaken Israel to their dire situation, so he tells Gomer to name her children some very strange names. God uses these names to personify the people of Israel. He's using their names to get their attention. They needed a wake-up call!

When I was a kid, and I did something wrong, my siblings would say, "Your name is mud!" What did that mean? It was a way of getting my attention and calling me to account. God is getting the attention of his people. He does that by personally naming Hosea and Gomer's children. Israel wasn't listening! God had to get their attention. He wanted to awaken them to the urgency of his judgment. They were not changing because they were comfortable in great prosperity and luxury.

A Son Named Jezreel

Gomer says, "Hosea, I'm pregnant." Gomer gives birth, and it's a boy. It's a time of celebration. So God gives the boy a name after a wonderful, victorious battle. The battle of Jezreel, where the dynasty of Ahab and Jezebel was put to a final end.

Urgent Because Judgment is Coming

Yet we're going to read that the name Jezreel was not about victory, but about compromise. It was at that time that Israel had the opportunity to turn back to God, but instead they went right back to their idolatry. Jezreel is synonymous with superficial repentance. Hang with me and we'll read about it.

> **Hosea 1:3-5** | So he went and took Gomer, the daughter of Diblaim, and she conceived and bore him a son. **⁴** And the Lord said to him, "Call his name Jezreel, for in just a little while I will punish the house of Jehu for the blood of Jezreel, and I will put an end to the kingdom of the house of Israel. **⁵** And on that day I will break the bow of Israel in the Valley of Jezreel."

It is significant that the first child is named Jezreel, because God is going to bring the northern kingdom of Israel to an end in the Valley of Jezreel, right by Nazareth in the north. This will be the location of their ultimate defeat and God would "break the bow" of the northern kingdom of Israel. As luxurious as the culture was, God was going to bring it to a swift end. Hosea records what happened.

The Valley of Jezreel (Armageddon) was synonymous with bloodshed. They may have used 'Jezreel' like we might say 'Gettysburg'. Jehu ruthlessly slaughtered the previous dynasty, chief of whom were Ahab and Jezebel. Sounds good right? But God says: you northern Israel will have the same end. In 722 BC, the Assyrians invade and put an end to the kingdom of the house of northern Israel. Why does God punish the house of Jehu? Because he continued on in Baal worship. He had the opportunity to stop it. But he kept it going.

Jehu and his household went on to repeat the same idolatry of the Ahab and Jezebel and their predecessors (2 Kgs 10:31; 13:1). Since Jehu didn't go far enough, God would end the kingdom of northern Israel. Yet the end would not be the ultimate end. Northern Israel would never recover; they would never be brought back into the land; they would forever be forgotten as a people and become known as the Samaritans.

Yet in the new covenant, we know the story of Jesus and the Samaritan woman at the well who would have her eyes opened and become an early evangelist of the true Gospel. It is in northern Israel, in Galilee, that the Son of God would call eleven of his twelve disciples. It is in this land that the light of the Son of God would shine so brightly, just as the prophet Isaiah had proclaimed:

But there will be no gloom for her who was in anguish. In the former time he brought into contempt the land of Zebulun and the land of Naphtali, but in the latter time he has made glorious the way of the sea, the land beyond the Jordan, Galilee of the nations (Isa 9:2).

Judgment is coming if we don't fully repent. Jehu and all the other kings after him had the opportunity to turn things around. They didn't.

A Daughter Named: No Mercy

Gomer (Lady Lust) conceives another child. Gomer says to Hosea: "I'm pregnant again." And when the baby is born, they find out: it's a girl! What should we name her? Now this is curious. What a curious name. God says, "Call her No Mercy" (1:6).

Urgent Because Salvation is Available

God is sending a warning sign to northern Israel through the name God gives this daughter.

> **Hosea 1:6-7** | She conceived again and bore a daughter. And the Lord said to him, "Call her name No Mercy, for I will no more have mercy on the house of Israel, to forgive them at all. **7** But I will have mercy on the house of Judah, and I will save them by the Lord their God. I will not save them by bow or by sword or by war or by horses or by horsemen."

The first child had been Hosea's own: his wife 'bore him a son' (1:3). The second and third are not said to have been his: the 'by him' of verse 3 is missing in verses 6 and 8. So the joy of fatherhood was deeply clouded, and the children were living proofs of the infidelity of the marriage.[5]

Just like Gomer was unfaithful, Israel was unfaithful. Instead of trusting in God, Israel was trusting in the wealth of her neighbors, who worshipped the prosperity god named Baal. They had erected golden calf altars to Baal in Dan and Bethel. Assyria and Egypt are so rich and they provide protection through armies and swords and horses. Israel feels safe because of their prosperity.

---

[5] Derek Kidner, *The Message of Hosea: Love to the Loveless*, ed. J. Alec Motyer and Derek Tidball, The Bible Speaks Today (England: Inter-Varsity Press, 1976), 22.

God does not save by bow or by sword, by war or horses or horsemen. The northern kingdom was intoxicated with money. They were intoxicated with money. Anytime they had a need they turned to the pagan nations around them for more money: hiring armies for their own prosperity.

It was the best of times in Israel. Materialism was reigning. The more money they had, the more they worshipped the Baal idols, in this case in the form of a golden calf. There seemed to be no end to the prosperity of Israel. But God was going to bring it all to an end. "Woe to those who are at ease in Zion" (Amos 6:1a). They were soon going to lose all their wealth. God warns those who "feel secure" that the Assyrian armies are coming to bring the northern kingdom's materialism to an end. Today's Baal idols are the wealth and prosperity of Christians who squander their wealth. Let's admit it. We are all guilty.

Materialism or fixation on earthly possessions is one mankind's greatest temptations. Wealth in itself is not condemned in the Scriptures. In fact, it is often considered a gift or blessing. But the Bible warns against the dangers of wealth and gives instruction about its proper use. We are called to be content like Paul, "I have learned to be content in whatever circumstances I am" (Phil 4:11).

What a strange name for a child: No Mercy! Yet God is demonstrating what we all really deserve. We deserve *no mercy*. We deserve to be cut off from God's family. Isn't that what we deserve? Where does this leave us? God lays down the law with the name of this girl: you deserve judgment, no mercy, to be cut off from God. That's why God is saying all these extreme things to his people. They deserve judgment, but they are going to get love. They urgently need God's love. We deserve God's wrath, but we get his love.

A Son Named Not My People

The third child born to Gomer is a boy! How exciting! What's the name of this strapping little baby boy? God says: "Call him 'Not my People.'"

Urgent Because Eternity is at Stake

Hosea 1:8-9 | When she had weaned No Mercy, she conceived and bore a son. ⁹ And the Lord said, "Call his name Not My People, for you are not my people, and I am not your God."

We see in this name that there's an urgency because eternity is at stake! If you worship other gods, God says to Israel, you are "Not My People." What a name for a child.

How shocking! Isn't Israel God's chosen people? Yes! But Paul tells us that not everyone who is born as an Israelite "belong to Israel" as the true people of God (Rom 9:6). Paul tells us that takes faith.

God requires our faith in him exclusively, or we cannot rightly be called his people. Eternity is at stake! You are not God's people if you worship other gods. That's what he warns Israel of old. They had to break down their idols. They had tear down their Baal altars and their golden calf temples.

They were no longer God's people. They didn't do it outright. They kept adding other gods and idols until the true God was just one among many. We call that syncretism.

WHAT IS SYNCRETISM?

What is syncretism? The incorporation into religious faith and practice of elements from other religions, resulting in a loss of integrity and assimilation to the surrounding culture.[6]

Let me put it plainly. "Salvation is found in no one else, for there is no other name under heaven given to mankind by which we must be saved" (Acts 4:12). Eternity is at stake. No one else can secure your eternity.

God's people in Hosea's day were satisfied with their syncretistic worship of Baal and Jehovah. Baal worship was a type of fertility and prosperity worship of the bull and was common in many cultures: from Egypt to the Canaanites, the bull fertility god was worshipped everywhere. Sadly, throughout their history, Israel tried to syncretize the worship of Baal and Jehovah. It just doesn't work.

The very nature of idolatry is to worship a created thing as if it were God. [7] D.L. Moody said, "You don't have to go to heathen lands today to find false gods. America is full of them. Whatever you love more than God is your idol." Today the most common form of syncretism is to try to love the world and Christ.

---

[6] Martin H. Manser, *Dictionary of Bible Themes: The Accessible and Comprehensive Tool for Topical Studies* (London: Martin Manser, 2009).

[7] John M. Frame, *Systematic Theology: An Introduction to Christian Belief* (Phillipsburg, NJ: P&R Publishing, 2013), 36.

> You adulterous people! Do you not know that friendship with the world is enmity with God? Therefore whoever wishes to be a friend of the world makes himself an enemy of God (Jas 4:4).

Jesus says to the church at Laodicea:

> I know your works: you are neither cold nor hot. Would that you were either cold or hot! ¹⁶ So, because you are lukewarm, and neither hot nor cold, I will spit you out of my mouth (Rev 3:15-16).

The reason the apostasy of Israel is so dangerous is because they still act like they love God. They've got a temple. They've got an altar. I was over at the very place that the people of Hosea's day worshipped. In the city of Dan up in the northernmost part of Israel, it's still there: the altar to the golden calf.

Listen, there's no idol that can satisfy you like the love of God. You can't serve two masters. Christ must have all of your heart. What idol is it that is keeping you from the fullness of God's love? What idol has taken the place of Jesus so that you no longer treasure his love? I'm so amazed by the love of God. I urgently and desperately need it. I don't deserve it! But I'm so thankful that God is pursuing me! He's unrelenting.

GOD'S LOVE IS UNRELENTING (1:10-2:1)

God will stop at nothing to reverse your curse. In Hosea 1:9, God gives the greatest curse possible to this people and says, "I am not your God" (1:9). Gomer is unreconciled with Hosea, living in harlotry. In Hosea 3:1-2, God commands Hosea to buy Gomer back, and the prophet pays for her life. We see the promise of God's love for his people foreshadowed in the living parable of chapter 1.

> **Hosea 1:8-9** | When she had weaned No Mercy, she conceived and bore a son. ⁹ And the Lord said, "Call his name Not My People, for you are not my people, and I am not your God."

After Gomer weans the third child, God gives the tells us why he would warn them (and us). He's got a plan to redeem us. "He took our sins and our sorrow and made them his very own." He's got a plan!

Unrelenting in His Promise

The people he said would be cut off and have no mercy and not be his people don't get what they deserve. We see a reversal of the curse. To prove God's intention in reversing Israel's curse, he quotes his original promise to Abraham in Genesis 13:16.

> **Hosea 1:10** | Yet the number of the children of Israel shall be like the sand of the sea, which cannot be measured or numbered.

THE ABRAHAMIC COVENANT

This is the glorious Abrahamic Covenant spoken of in Genesis 15. God tells Abraham: "Count the stars" and "Number the sand" (Gen 13). Can you do it? Abraham couldn't either. Paul says in Galatians that in Christ we all become part of that promise. God's blessing is coming to all people because of the true Seed of Abraham: Jesus Christ.

> And he brought him outside and said, "Look toward heaven, and number the stars, if you are able to number them." Then he said to him, "So shall your offspring be." ⁶ And he believed the Lord, and he counted it to him as righteousness (Gen 15:5-6)

This is the glorious Abrahamic Covenant is for you! All who come to Christ get the promise!

> And if you are Christ's, then you are Abraham's offspring, heirs according to promise (Gal 3:29).

Hosea is saying in 1:10, "Christ is coming!" That was God's promise to the Old Testament believers. Don't worry, Christ is coming. We find that he's the king that's coming to bring his people under him. Aren't you glad he has come in this New Testament age?

Unrelenting in Jesus

We see the words of the curse upon Israel are reversed and words of hope are issued. The children are renamed!

NO LONGER SCATTERED, BUT GATHERED UNDER CHRIST

All the names are reversed to show Jesus. Jezreel means "scattered." The children of Israel would be scattered across the nations. They would be put into captivity in 722BC at the very end of Hosea's ministry. Hosea would see his own people scattered. But wait! Hosea 1:11 says that instead of being scattered...

> **Hosea 1:11** | And the children of Judah and the children of Israel shall be gathered together, and they shall appoint for themselves one head. And they shall go up from the land, for great shall be the day of Jezreel.

The hope centers on a Person under whom both Judah and Israel will be united. Who is this Person and what does this promise mean? Christ is appointed as the Head of the church! Christ is directly mentioned here: "they shall appoint for themselves one head" (2:11). This reminds us of many of the glorious New Testament proclamations, like the one in Ephesians 1:22-23, "And he [God] put all things under his feet and gave him as head over all things to the church, which is his body, the fullness of him who fills all in all."

The ultimate rescue of Hosea's children, according to the apostles, occurs in the times of the New Testament Church. The inspired authors of the New Testament saw the play on the names of Hosea's children as being ultimately fulfilled in Christ and his Church of both Jews and Gentiles. Note the following references to Hosea 1 in the New Testament. There are two (1 Pet 2:9-10 and Rom 9:25-26). Both apply these promises to Jesus and his church. We are no longer Jezreel – scattered, but we are gathered under Christ.

No Longer Under God's Wrath

Jesus is our No Mercy and our Not My People. He took God's wrath for me and you.

> **Hosea 2:1** | Say to your brothers, "You are my people," and to your sisters, "You have received mercy."

Christ took my curse on the tree. Christ bore my sins and my sorrows and presents me faultless, justified before an Almighty God. We who have come by faith to Christ, both Jew and Gentile, fulfill the promise of Hosea. Because of Christ are the beloved sons and daughters of the living God! We were once not his people, but now we God's beloved children! God stopped at nothing to purchase Israel back. The events of Hosea 1 are actually Gospel promises that come to pass when God, through the Jews, reaches the Gentiles. Both Jews and Gentiles are called by grace through faith to become the true people of God.

Conclusion

What a shocking love story that ultimately points to the greatest love story in God's Son laying down his life on the cross for an unworthy and unfaithful bride. In the symbolism of Hosea, God is the Prophet and we are the prostitute. In a very real sense, I am Gomer and so are you! We are unfaithful people who deserve God's wrath, not his mercy.

What a joy that Jesus loves his bride. We are all Gomers. He's come to redeem us from this life of spiritual prostitution. Do you believe that Jesus is the answer? He's the only way. You cannot be truly transformed through any other way.

But Jesus has become our Jezreel when he was judged by Almighty God, his Father. He took the wrath of God and won the victory against sin, Satan, death, and hell! I was under that curse. My name was Jezreel, awaiting judgment. My names were No Mercy and Not My People. He who knew no sin became sin for me that I might be made the righteousness of God in him (2 Cor 5:21). Jesus took my wrath and gave me mercy. Jesus took my judgment and gave me love. And now I can say I am a child of the living God. What a testimony. All because of Jesus!

2 | HOSEA 2:2-23

THE EMPTY PROMISES OF ADDICTION

She shall pursue her lovers but not overtake them,
and she shall seek them but shall not find them... Therefore,
behold, I will allure her, and bring her into the wilderness,
and speak tenderly to her.
HOSEA 2:7,14

What is idolatry? Webster's Dictionary defines it as: 1. The worship of idols, images, or anything made by hands, or which is not God. And 2. an immoderate attachment or devotion to something in the place of God. D. L. Moody put it this way:

> Whatever you love more than God is your idol. Rich and poor, learned and unlearned, all classes of men and women are guilty of this sin.[8]

Idolatry is a worship disorder. We were made to worship God and be satisfied by him. An idol is anything that you turn to that takes the place of God. An idol is normally something that dominates your life. These idols of the heart may be an unhealthy desire for control, pleasure, materialism, or pride. It may be subtle, like the need to always get

---

[8] William Revell Moody, ed.. *Record of Christian Work*, vol 40 (East Northfield, MA: Record of Christian Work, 1921), 539.

your way or the need to always be right, etc. It could be a life dominating sin, like anger, lust, or

All Good Things Come from God

I want to be clear. It is not a sin to seek godly pleasure. God invented pleasure. Aren't you glad he invented all good things? God created laughter, joy, freedom, sex, art, music, and everything delightful for your good and his glory. James says, "Every good gift and every perfect gift is from above, coming down from the Father of lights with whom there is no variation or shadow due to change" (Jas 1:17). We are to enjoy all things as we glorify God. But it is a sin to seek pleasure in any created thing, no matter how wonderful it is. God alone deserves our worship and trust.

Our problem is that when we seek anything in an unhealthy or ungodly way, we are breaking the first commandment: we are to never worship idols. An idol takes the place of God in your life. We must "flee from idolatry" (1 Cor 10:14). The apostle John says, "Dear children, keep away from anything that might take God's place in your hearts" (1 Jn 5:21, NLT). That means we must never give worship and glory to any other, which is due to God alone. We are called to worship and "love the Lord your God with all your heart, with all your soul, and with all your strength" (Deut 6:4). When you turn away from this in the slightest way, you are worshipping idols. God wants your whole heart, your whole mind, your whole body. Are you worshipping him that way?

What Do These Idols Look Like?

Idolatry is pervasive. It's the constant lie of the flesh. We try to stuff all kinds of people and stuff where God alone belongs. John Calvin said, "The heart is an idol making factory."[9] It could be an emotional idol. You could be addicted to control and having your way, and you are good at manipulation. It could be a behavioral idol, like pornography or gambling or lying – something that makes you feel better. It could be a substance idol, like alcohol or drugs or food. It could be a media idol, like compulsive web surfing or use of social media on your PC or phone. It could be an idol to materialism and the accumulation of more stuff. It could be people idol: like co-dependence, or fear of man, of seeking the

---

[9] John Calvin, *Institutes of the Christian Religion*, Ch XI, Para 8.

praise and popularity of others. It could be a thousand other things that take the place of God.

It's Good to Seek Pleasure in God

Our sinful heart has the ability to create thousands of idols. The root of all idols is the desire to please yourself above God. Pleasure is not a sin. We are called to "delight in the Lord" (Psa 37:4) and to have "joy unspeakable and full of glory" (1 Pet 1:8). It is not wrong to seek pleasure. It is wrong to seek it outside of God and his plan for our lives. All people seek pleasure. The question is, how do we seek it? Blaise Pascal said it this way.

> All men seek happiness. This is without exception. Whatever different means they employ, they all tend to this end. The cause of some going to war, and of others avoiding it, is the same desire in both.... The will never takes the least step but to this goal. This is the motive of every action of every man, even of those who hang themselves.[10]

The one thing that all of addictions have in common is idols promise to take away the immediate pains and pressures of life. Idolaters are described as "lovers of pleasure rather than lovers of God" (2 Tim 3:4). Any idol is a spiritual adultery for the child of God. James describes it this way.

> You adulterous people! Do you not know that friendship with the world is enmity with God? (Jas 4:4a).

We were Made to Worship God Alone

The truth is, we were made to worship God alone. He alone can satisfy all our desires. The Westminster shorter catechism asks: "What is the chief end of man?" The answer is: "Man's chief end is to glorify God and to enjoy him forever." David enunciated it beautifully: "Delight yourself in the LORD, and he will give you the desires of your heart" (Psa 37:4).

We were made to seek pleasure in God. We were made to worship him. So then, when we come right down to it, we all have a *worship disorder*. We were created to have pleasure in God, but we seek pleasure in a thousand other places. As we consider a woman in the book of

---

[10] Blaise Pascal, *Pascal's Pensees*, trans. W. F. Trotter (New York: E. P. Dutton, 1958), 113, thought #42.

Hosea who was an adulterer, let's consider how God can deliver all of us out of our idols and the things that take the place of God in our lives.

Introducing Gomer

There was a woman we met last week in the book of Hosea that understood what it meant to leave her husband for other lovers. The Lord teaches us a lesson through her life. Her name is Gomer. Remember her name means "Satiated [with lust]". We can call her "Lady Lust". She is an adulterous woman married to the prophet Hosea. Her addiction is the pleasure and luxury of this world. Interestingly, we learn in Hosea 2, that her addiction is not to sex itself, but to the rich lifestyle that she can obtain by selling herself. She is not so much addicted to sex, but to material things.

The sad thing is that her addiction to materialism costs her everything. Remember as well that this is not just about Gomer, but about the entire nation of Israel who had become materialistic. And this could be a letter just as well written to you personally about any number of idols in your heart and life.

THE PRICE OF IDOLATRY (2:2-5A)

Hosea cries out: "Plead with your mother, plead..." (2:2a). There is a play on words here. Hosea is telling his children to beg their mother to return to the family, but it is truly a message for adulterous Israel to return to God.

There is a high price for spiritual adultery for the child of God. The Lord is willing to chasten us because he loves us. Often chastening means loss. "For the Lord disciplines the one he loves, and chastises every son whom he receives" (Heb 12:6). God is willing to take away your comfort if you give your heart to idols. He wants to draw you back to himself.

You Could Lose Your Family (2:2)

Idolatry could make you lose your family. Listen to Hosea:

> **Hosea 2:2** | Plead with your mother, plead— for she is not my wife, and I am not her husband— that she put away her whoring from her face, and her adultery from between her breasts.

Hosea gathers his three children around: "Plead with your mom. Beg her to stay. She's not acting like my wife and your mother." Here we see Hosea pleading with Gomer when he could divorce her. Isn't it amazing that this is a story about us? God could divorce us and send us to perdition, but in love he pursues us! Despite Gomer's adultery, Hosea pleads with her to stay. The idea is that Gomer has broken the marriage. Divorce is inevitable. But Hosea is still pleading. Because of Gomer's "addiction" to worldly goods, she was willing to forsake her family and desert her husband. Idols have the potential to ruin your family too. Are you enslaved to an idol when you are meant only to serve God? It could cost you your family.

Living with life an overwhelming idol can put family members under unusual stress. Normal routines are constantly being interrupted by unexpected or even frightening kinds of experiences that are part of living with enslaving habits. What is being said often doesn't match up with what family members see right in front of their eyes. The enslaved person as well as family members may bend, manipulate and deny reality in their attempt to maintain a family order that they see gradually slipping away. The entire system becomes absorbed by a problem that is slowly spinning out of control. Little things become big, and big things get minimized as pain is denied and responsibility is shifted. Many a family has been sacrificed on the altar of anger, pleasure, materialism, lust, or an unsuccessful search for a happiness that never seems to appear.

I remember in the early 80s when no fault divorce became a thing. My mother thought she'd be happier with another man. There went our family. People are willing to sacrifice their family on the altar of career, romance, alcohol and substance abuse. Some are willing to leave just because they can't get their way. Idols about in our hearts, and sometimes our own dear family is on the altar.

You Could Lose Your Money (2:3)

Idols can make you lose your livelihood. God says Israel needs to put away her spiritual adultery or else God will cause her to be penniless like a beggar.

> **Hosea 2:3** | ...lest I strip her naked and make her as in the day she was born, and make her like a wilderness, and make her like a parched land, and kill her with thirst.

Here is a picture now of Israel without proper clothes or shelter (naked and thirsty). Israel's livelihood is soon to be lost altogether when they are carried away to Assyria. Their trust in the nations robs them not only of worshipping God, but also of their livelihood and money. Israel was whoring after the world for satisfaction. Things seemed fine. This was one of the most prosperous times in her history, but it was soon to be ripped away. We are called to "seek first" God's kingdom, and he promises that "all things will be added unto you" (Mt 6:33). Here we see Hosea pleading with Gomer to stop her adultery, because she will lose her family and her livelihood. Isn't it good that God warns us as well? If we as Christians backslide and turn to the world, God may well need to strip us of our jobs, our incomes, or our bank accounts. And of course, it would be worth it wouldn't it?

You Could Lose Your Children (2:4)

Idols could even make you lose your own children. Listen to the warning the Lord gives Hosea:

> **Hosea 2:4** | Upon her children also I will have no mercy, because they are children of whoredom.

God's people in Hosea's day has given birth to a generation that had no right to call Yahweh their Father.[11] And so it is, that those who put idols above their relationship with God often lose their children to the world, like Israel of old.

How often do we hear of a self-centered marriage breaking apart, and then what becomes of the children? The children are never taken into account when parents put happiness above holiness. Where is the time in the Scriptures for the children? Where is the time in prayer with the children? No time. Good things like jobs and overtime are turned into idols. Money and houses cannot replace the spiritual richness of God's Word and prayer applied to our children's hearts. Life goes by so fast, and before you know it, we've lost our children. Are they serving God? Are they loving him? Young parents, forsake your idols before it is too late for your kids.

Idols look like convenience, consumerism, social media and a culture that is entertaining themselves to death is what can steal the hearts of our children if we aren't watching. These kinds of idols can keep us from God and his Word and keep us from applying the Word to our lives as well as our children's lives in a meaningful and sincere way.

---

[11] Garrett. *Hosea*, 79.

How many kids have been lost due to a parent's idolatry of self and neglect of kids? A parent's idolatry can be as simple as having time to binge watch TV or (fill in the blank) yet you have not time to care for your children's souls. Your kids know if you love God. If you don't love God wholeheartedly, why should your kids? Is there anything you can name right now that is taking God's place? Be honest. The quickest way to repentance, forgiveness and restoration is sincere confession and forsaking of your idols (1 Jn 1:9). No idol is worth losing your kids.

You Could Lose Your Dignity (2:5a)

Idols could even make you lose your dignity.

> **Hosea 2:5a** | For their mother has played the whore; she who conceived them has acted shamefully.

Have you seen a Christian who you loved and respected fall into sin and suddenly, their blameless reputation is now gone? Their testimony is harmed because of an act of foolishness. I've seen godly people lose their testimony and their ministry because they wanted their way so bad, they stopped maintaining their marriage. They stopped discipling their kids. They stopped reading the Bible. They stopped praying. People who stop worshipping God start worshipping other things and it leads them to do shameful things. They lose their marriage, their kids, their livelihood, and eventually, their dignity.

Losing one's dignity is not an overnight quest. Year after year, they practice until this loss of dignity occurs. If a child of God "falls" into sin, you know it wasn't a long fall. It was a long process of getting to that edge, but it was a very short fall. Tim Keller in his book "Counterfeit gods" said this:

> Most people spend their lives trying to make their heart's fondest dreams come true. Isn't that what life is all about, 'the pursuit of happiness'? We search endlessly for ways to acquire the things we desire, and we are willing to sacrifice much to achieve them. We never imagine that getting our heart's deepest desires might be the worst thing that can ever happen to us. [12]

The truth is, getting the desire of your heart, if that desire is not put there by God, is always disastrous. Without God we — "the creature in place of the Creator..." (Rom 1:25). No created thing can satisfy our

---

[12] Timothy Keller. *Counterfeit gods* (Dutton: London, 2009), 1.

hearts. Our hearts are made to be filled with the infinite God. Without God, we fashion all things we have into idols! The need for God is so insatiable, that without him, our hearts become "idol making factories." Can we now recognize the depravity of our own idolatrous hearts? The greatest and best thing that could happen to us most of the time is to *not* get our "heart's desire" unless that desire is the Lord.

What a high price we all pay for idolatry. But there is a way out. Jesus is the way (Jn 14:6)! Peter says: "He himself bore our sins in his body on the tree, that we might die to sin and live to righteousness. By his wounds you have been healed" (1 Pet 2:24). The beautiful thing about the Gospel is that no matter what you've lost, you gain it all back in Jesus. Whatever price you have paid, you get it all back in Jesus. However sin has mangled you, it's "by his wounds you have been healed." Jesus has paid your debt in full if you repent and turn to him in faith! That's Jesus' message. He said: "Repent and believe" in me (Mk 1:15).

THE POWER OF IDOLATRY (2:5B-8).

It seems like everything in Hosea's life is out of control. Gomer has left him and is pursuing her lovers. She believes that her lovers can bring her all she wants. Her husband and children are pleading with her. But thankfully, God has put it in Hosea's heart to go after his wife. And God in the same way will go after his children. He will not let us pursue sin. He is pursuing us!

The Promise of Idols is Powerful (2:5b)

Consider the allure of idols. Why is it so powerful? What would make Gomer, Israel, and us be willing to lose all or some of our family, livelihood, our children, or our dignity? What is worth losing everything? Listen to Hosea's account of Gomer's words.

> **Hosea 2:5b** | For she said, 'I will go after my lovers, who give me my bread and my water, my wool and my flax, my oil and my drink.'

Our hearts can never be satisfied by earthly things. What is it that drives addictions, idols, and adultery against God? It is the promise of instant gratification. Gomer's lovers instantly gave her the wool and flax for clothing she wanted and the oil and drink to satisfy her desire to eat and drink lavishly. Bread and water are good in and of themselves, but our hearts want more than earthly pleasures. "The pleasures of sin" are only "for a season" (Heb 11:25). Our hearts can never be satisfied by earthly things. Look at Gomer. She's willing to leave her family and go after her lovers. But she can never be satisfied.

> "Hell and destruction are never satisfied; so the eyes of man are never satisfied" (Pro 27:20).

The flesh can never be satisfied. You can try to fill it and fill it, but it will never be full. That's why we must "put on the Lord Jesus Christ, and make no provision for the flesh, to gratify its desires" (Rom 13:14). Don't try to satisfy with the flesh what only the Lord can satisfy. God "has put eternity into man's heart" (Eccl 3:11). Earth is too small to satisfy our God-size desires. Your heart longs for the infinite love of God. No earthly thing: no relationship, no pleasure, no success, or amount of money can fill the place of God in your heart. Your heart was made to worship God, not stuff or people or power. At the end of the day, Jesus is the bread and my water my soul longs for.

God's Love is More Powerful than Idols (2:6-7)

Isn't this beautiful? God is will to put every obstacle in Israel's way so that sin and idolatry does not destroy his Bride.

> **Hosea 2:6-7** | Therefore I will hedge up her way with thorns, and I will build a wall against her, so that she cannot find her paths. ⁷ She shall pursue her lovers but not overtake them, and she shall seek them but shall not find them. Then she shall say, 'I will go and return to my first husband, for it was better for me then than now.'

Gomer pursued her lovers, but she couldn't overtake them. In other words, the pagan nations delivered to Israel for a while, but then they stopped taking her phone calls.

God's Walls and Hedges of Love

God says, I promise to put every obstacle in the way of your worship of idols so they don't dominate you. God says, "I'll hedge you in with thorns of love and build walls of grace and mercy around you. My walls of grace are so high you'll never be able to find your worldly lovers." God's love is so great, he hedges us in by his love. He may bring intense suffering or sorrow in your life to keep you far away from idols.

Sometimes the pain and loss we experience in choosing sin draws the child of God back to the Lord. The child of God can never be successful in pursuing idols because God is pursing the child of God. God's purposes are positive and gracious, no matter how vexing it may have seemed to Israel. God's goal was to thwart Israel's heated pursuits of the Baals that she would change her heart and return to the Lord.[13]

God, not idols, is the source of all our blessing (2:8)

The sad thing is God is willing to give us far more than our idols promise. He says of Gomer:

> **Hosea 2:8** | She did not know that it was I who gave her the grain, the wine, and the oil, and who lavished on her silver and gold, which they used for Baal.

God says, "Everything you thought you got from idols, I gave that to you." Every good gift comes from the Father in heaven (Jas 1:17). When we go after idols, we don't realize that it's God who invented pleasure, food, sex, joy, love, and contentment. We can have all those things and so much more in the infinite God. David reminds there is more joy in God than in the world. "You have put more joy in my heart than they have when their grain and wine abound" (Psa 4:7). God is the source of all blessing. Consider the words of modern Biblical counselor David Powlison (now with the Lord):

> "We are meant to long supremely for the Lord himself, for the Giver, not his gifts. The absence of blessings – rejection, vanity, reviling, illness, poverty – often is the crucible in which we learn to love God for who he is. In our idolatry we make gifts out to be supreme goods, and make the Giver into the errand boy of our desires."[14]

Idols have the power to destroy your life (2:9-13)

You always reap what you sow. Sow to the flesh you reap destruction. Sow to the Spirit, you reap life. Because of Israel's addiction to the pleasure of idols, God gives them a reverse harvest. They lose everything they were looking for.

---

[13] David A. Hubbard, *Hosea: An Introduction and Commentary*, vol. 24, Tyndale Old Testament Commentaries (Downers Grove, IL: InterVarsity Press, 1989), 82–83.

[14] David Powlison. *Seeing With New Eyes* (Phillipsburg, NJ: P&R Publishers, 2003), 134-135.

2:9-11 | Therefore I will take back my grain in its time, and my wine in its season, and I will take away my wool and my flax, which were to cover her nakedness. ¹⁰ Now I will uncover her lewdness in the sight of her lovers, and no one shall rescue her out of my hand. ¹¹ And I will put an end to all her mirth, her feasts, her new moons, her Sabbaths, and all her appointed feasts. ¹² And I will lay waste her vines and her fig trees, of which she said, 'These are my wages, which my lovers have given me.' I will make them a forest, and the beasts of the field shall devour them. ¹³ And I will punish her for the feast days of the Baals when she burned offerings to them and adorned herself with her ring and jewelry, and went after her lovers and forgot me, declares the LORD.

God takes back their food (their grain and wine). He takes back their wool and flax that would give them nice clothing (2:9). God sends the people of Israel into the hands of her lovers (2:10). They will be taken out of the land by the Assyrians who had provided protection for them. But in 722BC King Tiglath-Pileser III (Pul) of the Assyrians leads the ten northern tribes into captivity (2 Kgs 15:29). They lose the land and all the yearly celebrations because she "went after her lovers and forgot me" (2:13). The pain of idolatry is that satisfaction in anything earthly is always *temporary* at best. They can come to an end (2:11), they can be laid waste (2:12), and beasts of the field can devour them.

There are times when God has to strip his children of everything. They may have to lose all of earth so they don't lose all of heaven. We may have to feel the hard hit of his walls of love and thorn hedges of grace (2:6). God is willing to bring us to the lowest point of life on earth so that we no longer forget him (2:13).

Not Condemnation but Correction

"I will punish her" for worshipping the Baal gods (2:13). This is not *condemnation* but *correction*. God's punishment is to do whatever it takes to get Israel out of the land and away from the idols so that she can experience the love of her true Husband. Idols bring such pain. The good gifts of God are not to be worshipped. They can all be taken away in an instant. It's painful. But God never fails. He never wastes away. He is always infinite and fully satisfying! But how can a person be delivered from idolatry?

THE PATHWAY OUT OF IDOLATRY (2:14-23).

How do we defeat idolatry in our hearts? Hosea says that there needs to be a greater hope (a door of hope) that is greater than the false hope idols give us. Thomas Chalmers called it "the expulsive power of a new affection." He said,

> The heart is not so constituted, and the only way to dispossess it of an old affection is by the expulsive power of a new one.[15]

The pathway out of any idolatrous affection is to find a greater, more overwhelming affection. There is, as this passage teaches, a door of hope in the Valley of Achor. Achor is the valley where Achan was judged for his sin near Jericho. And the only pathway out of all addiction and idolatry is to worship the one true God. An addiction to God is when we are so filled with him that we display his glory and love, and power and delight. We are so satisfied with him, we want to please him. Rather than try to stop worshiping, we need to turn to Jesus and worship him. Your heart will not be at rest until you find rest in him.

We Need to Experience a Greater Love (2:14-15)

In Hosea 2, the prophet speaks of this wilderness as a door of hope.

> **Hosea 2:14-15** | Therefore, behold, I will allure her, and bring her into the wilderness, and speak tenderly to her. **15** And there I will give her her vineyards and make the Valley of Achor a door of hope. And there she shall answer as in the days of her youth, as at the time when she came out of the land of Egypt.

God begins by saying "I will allure her" or literally, "I will win her back." The word "allure" means to "draw, entice, persuade, seduce, or charm." You get the idea. God draws Israel and us with his love. He has the power of a greater joy than anything in the world. God says "A day is coming when I'll open a door of hope in the wilderness." I'll not leave you in Egypt or in the Valley of Achor where Achan died outside of Jericho. I'll be your true Moses. I'll bring you out out of Egypt! I'm bringing you to the wilderness to make a covenant, like a marriage contract, with you. I want you to be my people.

---

[15] Thomas Chalmers. *The Expulsive Power of a New Affection* (Crossway Short Classics) . (Wheaton, IL: Crossway, 2020), 19.

How do we turn our heart from any sin that enslaves us or dominates us? By turning to Jesus and finding a greater joy and allurement in his love. Can you "understand the greatness of Christ's love—how wide, how long, how high, and how deep that love is" (Eph 3:18)?

We Need to Experience a Greater Redeemer (2:16-17)

> Hosea 2:16-17 | And in that day, declares the Lord, you will call me 'My Husband,' and no longer will you call me 'My Baal.' **17** For I will remove the names of the Baals from her mouth, and they shall be remembered by name no more.

The Israelites called God "My Baal" which is how pagans referred to their gods. Only God can "remove the names of Baal" and idolatry from us. We need his amazing transformation. Jesus is the only Savior that can bring meaningful and lasting transformation in our lives. From the very beginning Israel prostituted herself with foreign gods. So rather than praying for rain for a crop, she prayed to the Canaanite Baals. Or rather than praying for health and help in the home, she prayed to Chemosh, the detestable god of Moab. Rather than wanting God as their father, Israel ran after the Sydonian goddess Asherah. Rather than flee to the true and living God for protection, she fled to Molech and to Milkim, the gods of Ammon. All these Israel call "My Baal." They turned to the world for provision instead of Yahweh who was a divine Husband to Israel.

When you come right down to it, the heart of Israel's idolatry was a mixture of *fear* and *pleasure*. They were afraid and wanted safety. They wanted comfort and pleasure. They were afraid they would lose these things. They sought worldly relief instead of heavenly connection and communion with God.

We Need to Experience a Greater Rest (2:18)

> Hosea 2:18 | And I will make for them a covenant on that day with the beasts of the field, the birds of the heavens, and the creeping things of the ground. And I will abolish the bow, the sword, and war from the land, and I will make you lie down in safety.

An intervention must be formed by the strongest partner, who in this case is God. It must be agreed to by the addict or idol worshipper. As always, God has to make for us a covenant. God promises to eliminate any threat of war and gently encourages them: I will make you lie down in safety. Sometimes addicts go to a twelve-step program. God is a one-step program. God is our safety. When we surrender to him in trust, he will keep us safe.

We Need to Experience a Greater Romance (2:19-23)

Now God uses the language of romance. He says, "I will betroth you forever" (2:19). It is here that God offers to renew his marriage vows to Israel.

A Personal Romance

God's betrothal has four qualities: righteousness, justice, love, and mercy.

> **Hosea 2:19-20** | And I will betroth you to me forever. [20] I will betroth you to me in righteousness and in justice, in steadfast love and in mercy. I will betroth you to me in faithfulness. And you shall know the LORD.

God says, "I will betroth you forever" (2:19). Isn't it amazing that "nothing can separate you from the love of Christ" (Rom 8:38)? Righteousness is God's integrity. He will do what he says. You are forever betrothed and united to God through Christ. Justice is God's leadership. He promises to guide us. Love (Heb, *hesed*) is God's unrelenting love or covenant faithfulness. He'll never let go of you. Mercy is the word for God's forgiveness. There is no aspect of God's restoration of us that is incomplete. We are fully reconciled to God. He makes all the provisions. This is God's pledge of marriage. The result of God's covenant is breathtaking: you shall know the LORD (2:20).

While a Christian can no longer continue in sin as a life's pattern (1 Jn 3), we do sin. Yet our righteousness is not bound up in our own record. We are robed in Christ's righteousness. We are betrothed to a perfect Bridegroom forever and ever and ever.

An Eternal Romance

God promises to provide material prosperity far and above the idols of the nations. This is referring to the way God as a divine husband will provide for his people. It's beautiful that the heavens and earth answer God's request to provide for his Bride.

> **Hosea 2:21-23a** | And in that day I will answer, declares the LORD, I will answer the heavens, and they shall answer the earth, [22] and

> the earth shall answer the grain, the wine, and the oil, and they shall answer Jezreel, **23** and I will sow her for myself in the land…

This is a romance on an eternal scale. He's very likely talking about the new heaven and the new earth. Since God controls the harvest, he will call on the earth to answer: the earth shall answer the grain, the wine, and the oil (2:22). But material blessing is a picture of a far greater spiritual blessing: God says, "I will sow her for myself in the land. And I will have mercy on No Mercy…" (2:23a).

There will be a response to this wonderful request for his people. We hear the conversation God has with Israel: "I will say to Not My People, 'You are my people'; and he shall say, 'You are my God' (2:23). This is the ultimate confession of salvation. We are God's people, and he is our God. This brings the joy and pleasure that no drug, success, relationship, job, or lottery ticket can bring.

A Worldwide Romance

Paul quotes Hosea 2:23b in Romans 9:25-26 to prove that God will have mercy not only on Israel, but that he will graft Gentiles into the covenant people. That means you and me!

> **Hosea 2:23b** | …And I will have mercy on No Mercy, and I will say to Not My People, 'You are my people'; and he shall say, 'You are my God.'

God desires to have mercy on the undeserving. God says in essence, *Stop committing adultery with the other nations around you. I will give you a romance of divine proportions*. Though I'm a sinner, he looks into my eyes and your eyes, and say, "You are my people" even though we are the least deserving. God can romance us infinitely better than the lost world!

Come to God, and he will be all you need to satisfy your deepest hunger. It is only by *pleasing God that we will experience the highest level of satisfaction in life*. It is only by experiencing the mercy, grace, love, and sovereign hand of God in your life that your soul will have "peace that passes understanding" and "joy unspeakable and full of glory." It is only when we realize that that we can say with the Psalmist: "As a deer pants for flowing streams, so pants my soul for you, O God. My soul thirsts for God, for the living God…" (Psa 42:1-2a).

Conclusion

Let me close with the words again of Blaise Pascal:

> "There once was in man a true happiness of which now remains in him only the cavity and empty space. He in vain tries to fill it from all his surroundings.... But all his trying is inadequate, because the infinite abyss of his being can only be filled by an infinite and immutable object, that is to say, only by God himself."[16]

Pascal is right. There is a void in the heart of man that only God can fill. For isn't the Lord's love "better than" anything this life could give (Psa 63:3)? We say with Paul, "I count everything as loss because of the surpassing worth of knowing Christ Jesus my Lord. For his sake I have suffered the loss of all things and count them as rubbish, in order that I may gain Christ" (Phil 3:8). We long for a joy and a satisfaction that God alone is able to give us in and through Jesus Christ.

---

[16] Pascal, *Pensees*, 113.

3 | HOSEA 3:1-5
THE SLAVE MARKET OF SIN

The Lord said to me, "Go again, love a woman who is loved by another man and is an adulteress, even as the Lord loves the children of Israel."
HOSEA 3:1

Do you understand how great God's love is to a sinner like you? Do you know what you were saved from? Do you remember that each of us is "a brand plucked from the burning" (Zech 3:2)? The only thing that separates us from an eternity in hell is the love of God so beautifully displayed in Hosea 3. James Montgomery Boice, the onetime pastor of Tenth Presbyterian Church in Philadelphia said this about Hosea chapter 3:

> The third chapter of Hosea is, in my judgment, the greatest chapter in the Bible, because it portrays the greatest story in the Bible—the death of the Lord Jesus Christ for his people—in the most concise and poignant form to be found anywhere.[17]

---

[17] James Montgomery Boice. *The Minor Prophets: An Expositional Commentary* (Grand Rapids, Mich.: Baker Books, 2002), 31-40.

Hosea 3 shows us God's work of redemption—the work by which the Lord Jesus Christ delivered us from sin's bondage at the cost of his own life—portrayed in Hosea's purchase of his fallen wife from slavery.

THE PLACE OF REDEMPTION: THE SLAVE MARKET (3:1)

In Hosea 3 we read of how our relationship with God is compared to a marriage. We see how God illustrates how he feels about our sin by the story of the Prophet Hosea and his adulterous wife Gomer. When God's people sin, he equates his feelings to that of a husband broken by his precious wife's adultery. God's heart is, in a sense, torn to pieces when we sin. Oh, how our Father in heaven loves us.

Hosea's wife Gomer has left her prophet husband to live with one lover after another. Finally, however, they all rejected her, and she found herself alone, possessing nothing and in so much debt that she is being sold into slavery. Here we can see her standing in the marketplace to be sold as a slave.

A Place of Slavery

> **Hosea 3:1a** | And the LORD said to me, 'Go again, love a woman who is loved by another man and is an adulteress...

"Go again," God says.

"Go where?" replies the prophet Hosea.

"Go again to the slave market. Your wife is up for sale. Her lovers have rejected her. No one will have her. Go again and love her even though she has been a prostitute. Go Hosea. Love that girl like I love my people Israel."

Gomer had left Hosea, as we have already seen, and she had sunk lower and lower in the social scale of the day. Now, at the last, she became a slave and was sold in the capital city of Samaria.

Gomer's for sale. How'd that happen? It's very possible the other lover has put her up for sale. Perhaps she has fallen into debt. That's one of the reasons you get sold into slavery. Or it could be the new lover was a pimp, and she had lost her marketability, and he was cutting his losses. It's bad. It's as far down as a person could fall. It's as bad as it can be. It's as broken as it can be. It's as miserable as it can be.

God describes his relationship with Israel in Hosea, like a bad marriage. So here is Hosea's really bad marriage. God says, "That is an image of what my relationship with human beings is like." He commands Hosea to go and search for his wife, looking everywhere, even in the arms of another man.

Hosea arrives the marketplace where the slaves were being sold. In those days, slaves were brought, stripped naked, and put on display so the buyers could evaluate their bodies. They needed to see whether they were strong or weak, emaciated or fat, because they were spending money on these slaves. Hosea's wife Gomer stood naked, on display with the rest of the slaves. Hosea was going to have to buy back his wife. He bought her, clothed her, fed her, and brought her home. Oh, what love that will not let us go![18] God loves his people though they turned to idols. Hosea pursues his adulterous wife no matter what. It's what God does for us. He pursues us.

SLAVERY IN THE ANCIENT WORLD

There were different ways in which a person could become a slave in antiquity. [19] Usually through war, slave, debt, or voluntarily.

A person could become a slave voluntarily. A person might want to work for the security of room, board and being under a person's protection. A person could become a slave through war – if another country invaded, it was possible you would be separated from your family and sold into slavery in the conquering country. Slavery occurred through birth – if your parents were slaves, and you were born to them, you automatically became a slave. Also, one could become a slave most often through poverty and debt. If you couldn't pay your bills, you would be sold into slavery. This is likely where Gomer was. God commands Hosea: Go again, love a woman, your wife, who is a prostitute (3:1a). Go back. Go to the slave market. Buy her back. What a devastating command.

We are all slaves of sin. We are all born and raised in the slave market of sin. Paul tells us this in Ephesians 2.

> And you were dead in the trespasses and sins ² in which you once walked, following the course of this world, following the prince

---

[18] PG Matthew. *"Love That Will Not Let Me Go"*. Online Sermon and commentary Hosea 3.

[19] Boice, 34.

of the power of the air, the spirit that is now at work in the sons of disobedience— 3 among whom we all once lived in the passions of our flesh, carrying out the desires of the body and the mind, and were by nature children of wrath, like the rest of mankind (Eph 2:1-3).

A Place of Sin

The slave market was a place to illustrate the ugliness of our sin. Sin strips us of everything valuable: our dignity, our purity, and most important, our standing with God. Sin is the "transgression of God's law." It breaks his covenant. Jesus said, "everyone who practices sin is a slave to sin" (Jn 8:34). Someone said,

Sin will take you farther than you want to go
Slowly but wholly taking control
Sin will leave you longer than you want to stay
Sin will cost you far more than you want to pay

When a Christian sins, they lose their peace. In place of the sweet peace of the Holy Spirit, there is a gnawing conviction of sin and emptiness. Joy is lost and unrest and depression settle in. Saint of God, you can never live comfortably in sin.

A Place of Salvation

In the midst of all this mess, Hosea humbles himself and goes after Gomer. He loves her like God loves Israel. We have to go to the slave market to see how much Hosea loves Gomer. And God says, that's a picture of my love for you, my people.

> **Hosea 3:1b** | even as the LORD loves the children of Israel, though they turn to other gods and love cakes of raisins...

Raisin cakes are ancient aphrodisiacs. God loves his people though they turn to spiritual aphrodisiacs. He would rescue them though they are deep into idolatry.

The pagan religions that Israel was involved in had to do very much with fertility and immorality. The cakes of raisins were referring to what they thought was an aphrodisiac (cf Song 2:5; Gen 30:14; Song 7:13). It was used in the Canaanite love rituals in which they committed gross immorality in their "worship" of the Canaanite deities. All idolatry is like an aphrodisiac. Idols promise so much but deliver only emptiness and shame.

The cakes of raisin were the delicacies that were served at the idol feasts.[20] Who knows what Gomer was involved with or how far she had gone, but the Prophet Hosea was willing to go to the ends of the earth to find her.

Despite Israel's idolatry, he loves them and pursues them. He's a God with a broken heart. We read, "the LORD loves the children of Israel, though they turn to other gods and love cakes of raisins" (3:1b). The Lord loves you despite your idols and your sin. He loves you enough to do whatever it takes to redeem you from that slave market.

God says, "Imagine you have a bad marriage, and you experience the worst betrayal you can think of. Your wife goes and puts herself in the arms of other lovers. That's exactly what happens when I love my people and I love human beings, and they put other things before me, and they worship other gods before me."

Part of the sinfulness of sin is that your sin is not against a God who hates you, but who loves you and is pursing you. You do not understand the impact of wrongdoing on your God until you understand this image. When the person you love most in your life is putting him or herself in the arms of another lover, that's agonizing. Some of you have been through that. There's nothing like that pain, and God says, "Until you've been through that, you don't understand the impact of your wrongdoing, your coldness and your waywardness upon me."[21] God's love is astounding here in this chapter isn't it?

We learn something amazing in John 8. Jesus says, "Truly, truly, I say to you, everyone who practices sin is a slave to sin…. So if the Son sets you free, you will be free indeed." Can anyone here testify today that this is true in your life?

THE PRICE OF REDEMPTION: 30 PIECES (3:2)

The Price of a Slave

When God says, "Go again, love a woman who is loved by another man" (3:1a), he's saying, "Go to the slave market. Go back and love the woman who was used up by other men."

---

[20] Timothy J. Keller. *The Timothy Keller Sermon Archive.* "The True Bridegroom" (New York City: Redeemer Presbyterian Church, 2013).

[21] Ibid.

Hosea 3:2 | So I bought her for fifteen shekels of silver and a homer and a lethech of barley.

There was an auction, and Hosea would not be outbid the others. He didn't have thirty shekels of silver, which was the full price of a slave, so he said, "I will give you fifteen shekels of silver for her and the rest in grain." Hosea offered 15 pieces of silver and a homer or lethech of barley. A lethech of barley is nine bushels, which is another 15 shekels, and so basically, she was bought for 30 shekels. What does this mean? All we know is 30 shekels is how much it costs to buy a slave in Israel in those days. That must mean she had sunk down to the place where maybe her lovers were just sending her around. Maybe they were pimping for her. Finally, she ends up so poor that she's at the slave market, on the auction block. She is up for sale. She's in the marketplace. What a terrible thing that was. We know she was probably standing there, stripped naked, because the people who were about to buy wanted to see what their merchandise looked like.[22]

What a picture we have. "Silver" is what nobility and those who were more well off would have used to purchase things. "Barley" is what the poor would barter with. And so, we see a shadow of Christ here. Christ gave the silver of his deity and the barley of his humanity for our redemption. Let's not forget that it was Christ who was betrayed for 30 pieces of silver (Mt 26:15). He was sold for 30 pieces of silver in order to purchase our redemption.

The Purchase of Gomer

"So, I bought her ..." (3:2). Do you know what that must mean? From what we can tell, Israel in the eighth century BC, which is when Hosea and Amos were prophesying, had really decayed spiritually and culturally and was pretty much like all the other pagan nations around it. She had adopted many of the customs of the pagan nations around it. Therefore, there's a very, very good chance this was a public auction, that Gomer was being auctioned as a slave in a public marketplace. Israel was forbidden to have these markets, but they had them anyway. She was likely put up for sale in the capital city of Samaria.

---

[22] Ibid.

The custom in the pagan markets was to unclothe the slaves. Gomer lost her dignity. Hosea, a holy prophet, humbled himself to pursue Gomer. There's Gomer, up for sale. The bidding starts. It's not hard to imagine that she probably would have had her eyes closed, because it's not much to do, but it's about the only thing she had left to shield herself just a little bit from the moment of her greatest degradation. She hears the voices: "Five shekels," "Eight shekels," and suddenly she begins to realize one of the voices is her husband.

She's thinking, "What is he doing here? After all I've done, what is he doing here?" Hosea pipes up, "Ten ... Twelve ... Thirteen ... Fifteen. Fifteen and a lethech." Fifteen shekels and a homer or lethech of barley, which is the equivalent total of about thirty shekels of silver, about the average price for a slave. "Sold!" to the undistinguished prophet.

Hosea would have come up and he would have covered her nakedness with a cloak and led her away. She must have been saying, "Why would he still want me?" Probably her first response was, "Oh, I get it. Revenge. Now you can do what you want with me." But verse 3 shows Hosea has no bitterness. He speaks tenderly to her.[23]

The Price of Your Redemption

Christ was sold for 30 pieces of silver, but what he gave in exchange for your freedom is breathtaking. What is the price of your redemption? Jesus paid it all! What radical comfort. He paid it all for you. Your sins are washed away. Your guilt is gone. He came after you. He "humbled himself by becoming obedient to the point of death, even death on a cross" (Phil 2:8). The price he paid was "his own blood on the tree" (Heb 10:10).

> You were ransomed from the futile ways inherited from your forefathers, not with perishable things such as silver or gold, [19] but with the precious blood of Christ, like that of a lamb without blemish or spot (1 Pet 1:18-19).

What a price that was paid for your salvation. That's why at this moment, there is now "no condemnation" for those who simply believe and trust in Christ's sacrifice (Rom 8:1).

---

[23] Ibid.

THE POWER OF REDEMPTION: TRANSFORMATION (3:3)

Hosea is told to take Gomer back. What glorious hope we have in this picture of Hosea and Gomer. The love of Hosea is so powerful, it transforms Gomer. Surely the love of God is infinitely more glorious and powerful.

The Power of Love

> **Hosea 3:3a |** And I said to her, 'You must dwell as mine for many days. You shall not play the whore, or belong to another man.

Hosea purchases his wife from the slave market. What does Hosea do? It looks like he wants revenge. We can tell from the text. He must've walked up, and instead of treating her as a slave, he covers her nakedness. He veils her head and covers her shame. He gives her back her dignity as a woman, takes her by the hand, and leads her away. Imagine what she's thinking. Imagine how she looks at him as he approaches her. Imagine her saying, "How could he love me? He couldn't love me. He has bought me as a slave. He's now going to tyrannize me. He's going to get revenge!"

Hosea 3:3 indicates that the prophet Hosea leads Gomer to a place of privacy, and he turns to her and he says, in effect, "I didn't purchase you to humiliate you as my slave." Do you see what he says? "I don't even want you back in the house just to be back in the house. If you come back, I want you to be my wife. I don't want you to sleep with other men. I want you to be faithful to me, and I will be faithful to you. We are married, and we belong to each other exclusively. I want you to be my wife."[24] Hosea, like God, keeps his end of the covenant of marriage, even when Gomer did not keep hers. Hosea does whatever it takes to redeem his wife. This is the power of love! It's a pursuit to unthinkable proportions. Christ's love for us is unrelenting. Even when we didn't pursue him, he pursued us. Look at the unrelenting love of Christ. "God shows his love for us in that while we were still sinners, Christ died for us" (Rom 5:8).

Here is this holy, dignified prophet pursing his wife to the very slave market. And look at God how he sends his Son to pursue us, even if it means a violent death on the cross. What love is this that does not

---

[24] Ibid

redeem us merely to be servants, but to be sons and daughters of the living God. This is exactly what happened when Jesus Christ came into the world. He's the Lamb sacrificed to bring us back into relationship with God. He's the "Lamb of God who takes away the sin of the world" (Jn 1:29). It required total commitment from Hosea. Even more, our Lord Jesus was totally committed to our redemption. He held nothing back. What love!

The Power of Renewal

Listen to Hosea's recommitment to his wayward wife:

Hosea 3:3b | ...so will I also be to you.

In other words, "I want to dwell with you. I will persevere with you. I will work hard to be an agent of healing." He says, "No, I don't want you as a slave. I want you as my wife. I want to build a home again. I want to have a life together with you." Hosea says: "I will indeed be yours." Do you know what he's saying? He says, "I want to rebuild our lives together. Of course, there's going to have to be a period here in which we do all the hard work of rebuilding. I will indeed be yours."

How amazing that Hosea, by loving Gomer as a husband when she doesn't deserve it, brings renewal to her life. That's what God's love does for us. Like it says in the Song of Solomon, "I am my beloved's and he is mine" (Song 2:16). That amazing love fills us. It transforms us. It cleanses us. Just to know that I belong to Jesus, and nothing can separate me from his love. That's powerful. Paul says,

> "I am sure that neither death nor life, nor angels nor rulers, nor things present nor things to come, nor powers, 39 nor height nor depth, nor anything else in all creation, will be able to separate us from the love of God in Christ Jesus our Lord" (Rom 8:38-39).

The love of Christ and his ownership of you is incredibly transforming. Listen to Puritan Thomas Brooks:

> I am Christ's by purchase, and I am His by conquest; I am His by donation and I am His by election; I am His by covenant and I am His by marriage; I am wholly His; I am peculiarly His; I am universally His; I am eternally His. Once I was a slave but now I am a son; once I was dead but now I am alive; once I was darkness but now I am light in the Lord; once I was a child of wrath, an heir of hell, but now I am an heir of heaven; once I was Satan's

bond-servant but now I am God's freeman; once I was under the spirit of bondage but now I am under the Spirit of adoption that seals up to me the forgiveness of my sins, the justification of my person and the salvation of my soul.

His love keeps transforming us on a daily basis. God promises to renew you and daily conform you into the image of Christ. "I am sure of this, that he who began a good work in you will bring it to completion at the day of Jesus Christ" (Phil 1:6)

What was Hosea doing? He's painstakingly showing Gomer the love of God, daily through love, rebuilding their covenant relationship. What love! Derek Kidner says in his commentary: There "were the disloyal habits of years to be broken, and the realities of personal relationship, which had hitherto stopped at the physical level, to be unhurriedly explored together."[25]

Hosea doesn't have any of this naïve, sentimental, "Oh, God will just make everything okay." No, he's paying a price. He's doing the hard work of renewal. That's what God does with us. Christ says: "You're my bride, and I'm not going to leave you. I'm not going to forsake you. You belong to me!" But you have to do something to receive his love on a daily basis. You have to open your arms to Christ. You have to welcome him in when he is "standing at the door" of your heart knocking (Rev 3:20).

MONERGISM AND SYNERGISM

Can I make an application here? Our regeneration is monergistic. God has to raise you from the dead. You are passive. God is active. Our sanctification (the growth of our love relationship with God through Christ), on the other hand, is synergistic. You have to cooperate with the Spirit of God and surrender, moment by moment, applying the Word. You obey the Spirit. You do not trust your own feelings or understanding (Prov 3:5-6).

Daily we need to "put off your old self, which belongs to your former manner of life and is corrupt through deceitful desires, 23 and to be renewed in the spirit of your minds, 24 and to put on the new self, created after the likeness of God in true righteousness and holiness" (Eph 4:22-24).

---

[25] Derek Kidner, *The Message of Hosea: Love to the Loveless*, ed. J. Alec Motyer and Derek Tidball, The Bible Speaks Today (England: Inter-Varsity Press, 1976), 42.

The great breakthrough that we all need is not to just know the Word of God and think that is enough. We have to surrender to the Word as the voice of God. We have to surrender to God in his Word. It's our only hope. We have to work hard at mind renewal. That's the only way to change. We need to take the time to renew our mind and be empowered by the Word of God and the Spirit.

THE PERSON OF REDEMPTION: JESUS (3:4-5)

Now we come to some verses that are clear only if you understand that the whole Bible is a love story, where God pays a price in his pursuit of a Bride for his Son. To the one who does not know the story line of the Bible the story of Hosea is just a shocking story. But we know there's more to the story than Hosea and Gomer. The whole idea is that Hosea is an image, an illustration, of God's love for his people: for you and me.

Messiah's Preparation

We come to the prophecy of what historians call the captivity. It starts with Northern Israel being taken off by the Assyrians in 722 B.C., and then in 539 B.C., the Southern kingdom (Judah) is taken by the Babylonians. It's the time when the children of Israel are stripped from their idols as well as their homeland, the sacrificial system, their annual feasts, and most importantly, their king. No one's going to sit on the throne of Israel during this time. Hosea talks about it in Hosea 3:4.

> **Hosea 3:4** | For the children of Israel shall dwell many days without king or prince, without sacrifice or pillar, without ephod or household gods.

We see clearly that Hosea first refers to the timing of Jesus coming into the world. This is clearly the time of Israel's captivity. It climaxes in the Judean captivity for 70 years. God sends his people into exile. First, he sends the people of Northern Israel to Judah, then ultimately, he sends the Southern Kingdom of Judah into a 70-year captivity. And they come out of their captivity without their idols. They also don't have a king. They come out and wait in the land for like 400 years after the last prophet Malachi. And Hosea says, basically, there's coming someone who's going to pay the price, rule on the throne, and bring you to God.

Even though this is the Hebrew Scriptures, the book is just crying out with the question: Where does God come into the marketplace? Where does God pay the price to get his people back? The answer is in verse 5. It's a bit hidden, because it's a prophecy. He pays it by coming personally for his Bride. It's ultimately a verse that points to the incarnation of Jesus Christ.

Messiah's Incarnation

There is coming a time when David, Israel's most famous king, shall return with Israel and point them to God. King David is the one who will one day heal Israel's relationship with God, just like Hosea paid a price to heal his relationship with Gomer. King David is coming!

> **Hosea 3:5** | Afterward the children of Israel shall return and seek the LORD their God, and David their king, and they shall come in fear to the LORD and to his goodness in the latter days.

Wait a minute. David is dead. This must be a descendant of David, and it is. The prophecy is unveiled a few pages over in Matthew 1. Verse 1 reads, "The book of the genealogy of Jesus Christ, the son of David, the son of Abraham." Aha! Here is our king. We've got to go to the incarnation. We've got to go to the genealogy in Matthew to find out who the true King David is. King David is dead, but the true David: Jesus Christ is very much alive. He's our king. Now the prophecy makes sense. He's the King David that Israel will see "in the latter days". After the captivity, the Messiah's coming.

The name King David refers directly to Christ, who, as Paul says, "was born according to the flesh of the offspring of David" (Rom 1:3).[26] In Jesus Christ, God entered the world. He entered the marketplace. He humbled himself. He paid the daunting, infinite, impossible price. He clothed us and covered our nakedness with his righteousness. On the cross of Calvary, Jesus Christ died and paid the price to buy us away from any competing enslavements, away from any other lover.

---

[26] Augustine of Hippo, "The City of God," in *St. Augustin's City of God and Christian Doctrine*, ed. Philip Schaff, trans. Marcus Dods, vol. 2, A Select Library of the Nicene and Post-Nicene Fathers of the Christian Church, First Series (Buffalo, NY: Christian Literature Company, 1887), 375.

The word "afterward" in 3:5, introduces a great turning point, for here is the longed-for climax. That climax centers on three actions that indicate a radical conversion: "return," "seek," "come in fear."[27]

God works with us the way he worked with Israel. He may bring discipline and difficulty into your life. But while that discipline is taking place, he "stands at the door and knocks" (Rev 3:20). He calls with the voice of the divine Lover of his church. Our Lord Jesus is the Husband and lover of his Bride and he will never leave nor forsake her. He will never stop pursuing, edifying and building his church. And he promises, "the gates of hell shall not prevail against it" (Mt 16:18). Sin and Satan and this world cannot prevail against you. God has lavished his love upon you and made you alive in Christ (Eph 2:1-10).

Can you say in your heart of hearts that you have sought Jesus Christ as your King? Knowing you are truly born again and belong to him is amazing. He's King of kings and Lord of lords. But he's even more than that. He's the Bridegroom and you are his bride. He loves you are cares for you like a husband. He will never cast aside his responsibilities and vows to you to care for you and to bring you into his eternal kingdom. What amazing love is this!

Conclusion

You and I were bought out of the slave market of sin by the precious blood of Christ. We are Gomer. We are the slave sold on the auction block of sin. The world bids for us. The world bids fame, wealth, prestige, influence, power—all those things that are the world's currency. But when all seemed lost, God sent the Lord Jesus Christ, his Son, into the marketplace to buy us at the cost of his life. If you can understand it as an illustration, God was the auctioneer. He said, "What am I bid for these poor, hopeless, enslaved sinners?"

Jesus said, "I bid the price of my blood."

The Father said, "Sold to the Lord Jesus Christ for the price of his blood." There was no greater bid than that.[28]

Remember that it was not we who sought him. It was he who sought us and who joined us to himself through spiritual marriage. He courted us. He won our love. Had he not sought us, we'd still be living

---

[27] H. D. Beeby, *Grace Abounding: A Commentary on the Book of Hosea*, International Theological Commentary (Grand Rapids; Edinburgh: Eerdmans; Handsel Press, 1989), 40.

[28] Boice, 36.

in the slave market of sin. "We love him because he first loved us" (1 Jn 4:19).

4 | HOSEA 4
DIVORCE COURT

Hear the word of the Lord, O children of Israel, for the Lord has a controversy [court case] with the inhabitants of the land... My people are destroyed for lack of knowledge because you have rejected knowledge.
HOSEA 4:1, 6

Divorce is always a last resort. Yet God goes there. Israel has violated their covenant with God. This section of the prophecy is like a prosecutor making a case in court, detailing specific charges and the corresponding penalties that await. All Israel is addressed, but the priests are called out specifically for their failure. The primary charge is turning from God to idols, specifically Baal.[29]

The Lord wants his people to come back to him. Though his people have broken the covenant, there is always hope because of the unrelenting love of God. These proceedings are Israel's wakeup call. Come back! You child of God, if you've been straying. He says to us: come back! God wants you to wake up to his love. "Morning by morning the LORD God awakens; he awakens my ear to hear as those who are

---

[29] Lydia Brownback, *Hosea, A 12-Week Study*, ed. J. I. Packer, Dane C. Ortlund, and Lane T. Dennis, Knowing the Bible (Wheaton, IL: Crossway, 2016), 19.

taught" (Isa 50:4). "You know the time, that the hour has come for you to wake from sleep. For salvation is nearer to us now than when we first believed" (Rom 13:11, quoting from Isa 52:1). We need to see an awakening in God's church. The world is on its way to hell, and we have this temptation to cozy up to a world at war with God.

Hosea 4 is the prophet Hosea's first recorded sermon. It takes place after Hosea buys his wife back from the slave market. She had become a prostitute. He had every right to abandon her, but he pursued her no matter what. It was not just a Hallmark movie love story. It was a divine love story. What incredible love must have Hosea had to track down Gomer and take her back and love her. But what incredible love God must have for us to pursue us unrelentingly in our sin and love us!

Hosea says in chapter 4, "Look you've got prophets like Amos and Isaiah and Hosea. You've got the Word of God crammed into your brain, but it means nothing." He says:

Hosea 4:6a | My people are destroyed for lack of knowledge...

The word *knowledge* (דַּעַת, *da'ath*) is like the most intimate personal, firsthand form of knowledge. My people are perishing, languishing because they have information about God, but lack intimacy with God. It is knowledge this is possessed by God and taught by God.[30]

Here we are in North America. Never in the history of the world have we had so much Bible teaching, with so many Bible study tools, and never has it made so little difference in the way people live. Listening, listening. Bible teaching can become a form of entertainment. We have so much information about God in our heads, but it's made so little difference in our lives. That's the message Hosea preaches to Israel, and it's a message we need to hear today.

Did you wake up to an alarm this morning? Some of you heard the alarm and wanted to chuck it as far as it could go out the window. The alarm could mean many things. It could mean get ready. Something important is about to happen. It could mean something's wrong, like a fire alarm or a check engine light. Have you ever ignored the "check engine light" in your car? If you have, you probably are not driving that

---

[30] Richard Whitaker et al., *The Abridged Brown-Driver-Briggs Hebrew-English Lexicon of the Old Testament: From A Hebrew and English Lexicon of the Old Testament by Francis Brown, S.R. Driver and Charles Briggs, Based on the Lexicon of Wilhelm Gesenius* (Boston; New York: Houghton, Mifflin and Company, 1906). From דַּעַת

car anymore. It's not in the parking lot, it's in the *junk heap*. Now alarm clocks or check engine lights aren't that important, but your soul is.

Hosea preaches his first recorded sermon in chapter 4, and it's an intense wake up call. We've heard the beautiful story of redemption in Hosea 1-3. Israel has broken God's heart like Hosea's unfaithful wife, Gomer. The great love story of Hosea and Gomer is concluded. He takes her back. He never leaves or forsakes her. It was a powerful illustration for what God is going to do for Israel and us. Can you imagine? After the fight to get his wife back, he now gets the heart of God. His message: Come back to God, like I've come back to my wife.

This is a message for the churches of today. It's for those who call themselves the people of God, the church, the Body of Christ. Come back! Come back to Christ! Hosea begins with a great shock: a summons for divorce.

THE SUMMONS FOR DIVORCE (4:1)

> **Hosea 4:1** | Hear the word of the LORD, O children of Israel, for the LORD has a controversy [*Heb "rib" – court case*] with the inhabitants of the land. There is no faithfulness or steadfast love, and no knowledge of God in the land.

Hosea 4 begins with divorce court. God has a controversy, literally, a legal case against Israel. From the context of Israel's spiritual adultery, we can see this is a divorce case. Any Jewish person reading this in Hebrew knows this is common wording for a divorce.

God basically says, "I have every reason to leave you. You are not acting like my people. You've forgotten my love and my covenant." Obviously from the story of Hosea in the first three chapters, God has no intention of divorcing his people.

The court case begins. The controversy, or charges, against Israel are presented. God's heart is expressed, "You say you love me. You say you know me. You say you worship and serve me. But your heart is far away from me. You don't know me. There's no love, no intimate knowledge of me. There's no faithfulness. You say you love me but you are committing spiritual adultery on me."

Here are the charges God is filing against Israel: No faithfulness, no steadfast love, and ultimately this is due to no knowledge in the land. They aren't faithful to God. They don't love God. All this is because they don't know God.

We were at one time a nation of people, many of whom loved and served God in this country. Something has happened. Erwin Lutzer, former pastor of the Moody Church in Chicago said:

> Despite its foundational Christian heritage, America is rapidly degenerating into a godless society. The church in America, although highly visible and active, appears powerless to redirect the rushing secular currents. Mired in a moral and spiritual crisis, America's only hope is a national revival, like God has graciously bestowed in the past.[31]

So God summons Israel for divorce to get their attention. "You deserve divorce!" but from the story of Hosea 1-3 where God illustrates his love for Israel through Hosea and Gomer, we see God has no intention at all of divorcing Israel.

Child of God, are you straying? It's awful that the world sins. But listen the world in moral darkness and chaos. But Christian, you are in the light. Do you realize what a heinous crime it is for Christians to sin? When we sin, oh how we deserve to be cut off from God. But God says no! "I will never leave you nor forsake you." "You are written on the palm of my hand." "Shall a mother forsake her child: indeed on earth there are mothers who forsake even their own children, but I will never forsake you." Wow. This is God's Word to us today saints. God will never leave us, but we deserve it. But listen closer to God's charges in divorce court:

Hosea 4:1b | There is no faithfulness or steadfast love, and no knowledge of God in the land.

As the Lord lays out his case against Israel, he accuses the people of having no faithfulness, steadfast love, or knowledge of him (4:1). Failure to be faithful and to love fit well with the marriage metaphor in Hosea.[32]

You say you have a relationship with me, but either you are severely backslidden, or you never were really a child of God in the first place. There is "no knowledge of God" – again, no intimate, personal, face to face knowledge of God. That's a problem. God has legitimate

---

[31] Erwin W. Lutzer. "America's Spiritual Crisis." *Will America Be Given Another Chance?* 1993. Accessed February 05, 2019. http://articles.ochristian.com/article3157.shtml.

[32] Brownback. *Hosea*, 20.

grounds for divorcing Israel, though he's going to pursue her and bring her back if she will repent.

The problem in Israel was not mainly about the people. We are going to find out it was about the leaders. This is a difficult message for me to preach. God in verses 2-14 singles out the leaders. He says, "You need to be like Hosea, and love these people. But you don't love these people. You love yourselves."

THE SINGLING OUT OF LEADERS (4:2-14)

Israel is falling away from God, and God lays the blame on the leaders. People and churches make a slow fade into unbelief. They know all the doctrine, but they stop walking with the Lord. It's just like Hosea says in verse 6.

Hosea 4:6a | My people are destroyed for lack of knowledge…

In most of the chapter, God sets down his criticism of the leaders of Israel. I'm so thankful for the leaders at Living Hope will let their hearts break today as we feel God's burden for his wayward people, not just in Hosea's day, but in the churches here and around the world today. It's got to begin with us. Where does it begin? We have to know God intimately. We need to be talking about our walk with God with one another. That's the measure of the health of the church. What is God saying to you *today*? How is he speaking to you right now? Or is he speaking to you? Are you backslidden? Are you far away from God right now, even though you know so much about him?

You see, Satan doesn't mind if you have sound doctrine, good church services, and a large congregation, as long as he can gut your spiritual life. Keep talking about the Lord, as long as you neglect your walk with him. Destruction comes when we neglect to know Christ. "That I may know him" Paul said (Phil 3:10). Neglect that, and your life and society will unravel. Your church will cease to be the salt and light in the culture. We need to have that intimate walk with God. We will perish from lack of truly knowing God intimately. God's people are destroyed for mere superficial knowledge of him. It starts in you and I. We have to lead! What do real leaders do?

Godly Leaders Expose Sin (4:2)

We've seen a massive moral free fall in our country in the last ten years, but what has the church done? We've built bigger churches. We turned up the music. We've gotten fancier. But we've lacked the courage to really shine a light into the darkness. The church is sleeping. The only way to wake her up is to sound the alarm of repentance. The only way repentance comes is to expose sin. You have to call sin what it is. That's what Hosea did.

> **Hosea 4:2** | There is swearing, lying, murder, stealing, and committing adultery; they break all bounds, and bloodshed follows bloodshed.

Hosea is so courageous. He's won his wife back, and he's God's instrument to win Israel back. Hosea is willing to call sin what it is: sin. In place of faithfulness, love, and knowledge are all manner of sins (4:2). God's commandments have been willfully broken, and the whole creation suffers as a result (vs 3)—as it has ever since the fall (*cf* Gen 3:17–18; Rom 8:22). This shows us that the nature of sin is more than my own personal sin. It always affects others. Indeed it infects the whole creation, so that it groans. [33]

Until we are willing to call sin what it is, there can be no true intimacy with God. We must own it as our own. Without sincere, personal repentance there can be no remedy. How can a person with cancer get treatment if they won't admit they have cancer? We must deal with sin as it is: personal rebellion against a holy God of glory. We must not excuse it by renaming it. Sin is moral evil. There is evil in the world. It starts in you. Until you come to that place, you cannot say that you have known God.

Hosea wasn't afraid to confront the culture of his day. He squares up and declares that it's the culture of this fallen world that has infiltrated God's people. David Jeremiah writes in his book *I Never Thought I'd See the Day*:

> Toto, I've a feeling we're not in Kansas anymore." With that famous line from the movie ... the Wizard of Oz, Dorothy and her dog, Toto, find themselves in the strange and wonderful land of Oz—quite different from the Kansas of her childhood. As I wake up and scan today's headlines, I am often tempted to think, Toto,

---

[33] Ibid.

we're not in America anymore. I'm exaggerating, of course, but only a little. When I look at the changes that have occurred in the land I love—and in the Church I love even more—just in my lifetime, I have to pinch myself to see if it's a dream gone bad. Sadly, what I see is all too real. I do a double take several times a week—sometimes several times a day—as I witness more and more changes I never thought I would see.[34]

I feel that way; don't you? But let's not fool ourselves. The world lies in darkness because of a church that is asleep. If we are going to see change in our culture, the church has to wake up. Listen to Evangelist Leonard Ravenhill. Twenty-five years ago, the year he died, he said:

> With index finger extended, Napoleon Bonaparte outlined a great stretch of country on a map of the world. "There is a sleeping giant. Let him sleep! If he wakes, he will shake the world." That sleeping giant was China. Today, Bonaparte's prophecy... makes sense.
>
> Today Lucifer is probably surveying the church just as Bonaparte did China. One can almost behold the fear in his eyes as he thinks of the Church's unmeasured potential and growls, "Let the Church sleep! If she wakes, she will shake the world." Is not the Church the sleeping giant of today?[35]

No one disagrees. The Church of Jesus Christ is asleep in the Western countries for the most part. How do we wake her up? The Gospel of Jesus Christ begins with the word repent! The first recorded words out of Jesus mouth in his public ministry were: "repent and believe in the gospel" (Mk 1:15). Until we see the sinfulness of sin, we cannot see the beauty of Christ. Until we as leaders begin to repent of our own sins, our own worldliness, our own lack of knowing God, we cannot begin to see the Lord's church change.

I'm calling the leaders of our church to a unity of repentance. Let's unite in this. Let's be done with mere superficial knowledge of God, no matter how pristine it is. It's wonderful, the Christian faith. I'm eternally grateful for the careful theology we preach in this church. But this is our sin: we don't know our God as we ought.

---

[34] David Jeremiah. *I Never Thought I'd See the Day!* (New York: FaithWords, 2011), xiii.

[35] Leonard Ravenhill. "Today's Sleeping Giant." *O Christian*, 1994. http://articles.ochristian.com/article6912.shtml.

All the sins listed by Hosea in 4:2 come down to this: we don't know God rightly. We are content to talk about our grasp on theology instead of our grasp on God. We need theology. But you can know theology without knowing God. Oh the sin we excuse when we don't know God. What sins are you excusing today?

> Search me, O God, and know my heart! Try me and know my thoughts! 24 And see if there be any grievous way in me, and lead me in the way everlasting! (Psa 139:23-24).

Leaders call sin what it is: sin. Hosea was not afraid to confront the world, but really, he was confronting God's people who adopted the world and became powerless. Hosea's indictment is not primarily an indictment against the world, but the church of Hosea's day. The people of God were following after the world in every way. When the world influences the church, we are in trouble.

The church today is sick and dying. Thankfully Christ will build his church, and the gates of hell will not prevail against it. But God is beginning to remove the power of the Western churches and put their candles of influence out. We need to repent. We need to know God personally. Gross sin is happening today, not only in the world but also in the church. All of these kinds of things are taking place among God's people. Where is the holiness that the people of God had of old?

Godly Leaders Recognize Signs of Judgment (4:3)

Not only did God warn the people of the rapid moral decline in Israel's culture, he sent drought and barrenness during the time of Hosea in northern Israel in order to turn their hearts back toward him.

> **Hosea 4:3 |** Therefore the land mourns, and all who dwell in it languish, and also the beasts of the field and the birds of the heavens, and even the fish of the sea are taken away.

Certainly, natural disasters do not always mean God's judgment, but they are always an alarm to get our attention, and to point to the brevity and frailty of life. Every natural disaster is God's dress rehearsal for judgment day. There is coming when the earth will quake and not stop quaking until Jesus is done judging it. Every time we see a natural disaster, we ought to realize that this is the mercy of God, giving us a dress rehearsal before the actual day of judgment.

C.S. Lewis said, "Pain is God's megaphone" to get our attention.[36] Creation groans to see sin dealt with. Sometimes creation itself trembles with earthquakes and hurricanes and tornadoes because the creation is groaning for Christ to return and wipe out sin.

According to the National Weather Service and the Insurance Information Institute, "The top 10 costliest U.S. natural disasters between 1980 and 2010 caused more than $501.1 billion in damage and up to 22,240 deaths."[37] They include hurricanes, floods, earthquakes and droughts. God used natural disasters in Hosea's day and he's using them today. He wants our attention. He's mercifully making us become aware of our own mortality. The truth is, it doesn't matter how much we put in the bank or build on the earth. A natural disaster reminds us that God can take it all away in an instant. We take nothing with us anyway. You don't see U-Hauls behind hearses.

Natural disasters were God's warning of mercy for Israel. It will be the same at the end of the age for the whole world. Natural disasters will increase as the end of the age winds down. According to Jesus: "There will be famines and earthquakes in various places... all these are but the beginning of the birth pains" (Mt 24:7-8). Jesus describes the events preceding his Second Coming as birth pains. Just as a woman has horrible labor pains before delivering the beautiful child, so Jesus says there are horrible labor pains that come before him making the earth new again in his Second Coming. Wake up and see creation groaning.

Godly Leaders Accept Accountability (4:4-9)

God's biggest contention is with the leaders. The leaders of a nation or a country or a church can turn things around if they will be courageous. Sadly, the leaders in Israel were laying down on the job. The priests were to take spiritual care to teach and instruct God's Word to the people. The prophets were to be careful to hear from God. They were never to sugar coat or edit God's message.

---

[36] C.S. Lewis. *The Problem of Pain* (New York: HarperCollins, 1996), 93.

[37] Kim Fulscher. "Natural Disasters Are Costing More Money." Bankrate. September 03, 2017. Accessed March 15, 2019. https://www.bankrate.com/finance/insurance/natural-disasters-are-costing-more-money.aspx.

ACCOUNTABLE FOR SPIRITUAL EDUCATION (4:4)

God speaks first to the priests since they were the ones who should have been caring for the souls of the people, instructing them in his holy Scriptures. They should have been the counselors among the congregation, pointing them to God's grace and willingness to forgive. Instead, it seems they were simply blaming and accusing the common people.

> **Hosea 4:4** | Yet let no one contend, and let none accuse, for with you is my contention (*Heb "rib" – case, same as verse 1, controversy*], O priest.

The priests were contending or making excuses for themselves. The responsibility of the nation's decline falls directly upon God's leaders. God's chief target for this verse is—in modern terms—pastors, elders, and teachers. "We can use that rough equivalent because it is the priests in their neglected capacity as teachers, not as sacrificers, who are now under fire. The prophets are no better, but here they are not the main concern." [38]

The priests the nation's spiritual educators. Unlike most religions, where priests were mere sacrificers, the OT priests were to bring God's revelation to bear upon every mind and conscience, 'making wise the simple'. The priests' duty was both profound and crucial: a matter of life and death. Learn of Christ and live. Don't learn of Christ and die. So a spiritually sightless priest is a mortal danger to himself and a disaster to others. Hosea spells out in detail what Christ would one day sum up unforgettably in his saying on the "blind who lead the blind" (Mt 15:14).[39]

ACCOUNTABLE FOR SPIRITUAL INTIMACY (4:5-6)

God moves from the priest on to the prophet and their system of teaching people, which he calls a "mother" metaphorically. The culture and institutions of Israel are the greatest impediment to spiritual integrity in the people.[40]

---

[38] Kidner, 49.
[39] Ibid..
[40] Garrett, 116–117.

Hosea 4:5-6 | You shall stumble by day; the prophet also shall stumble with you by night; and I will destroy your mother. **⁶** My people are destroyed for lack of knowledge; because you have rejected knowledge, I reject you from being a priest to me. And since you have forgotten the law of your God, I also will forget your children.

The Bible and teaching of the Word were a mother to Israel, as the next verse (4:6) reveals. The prophet and the people live in the night of their sin, stumbling along. Since they won't feed the people with the love and nourishment of a mother, he will remove the system of priests and prophets from Northern Israel. Though there were other prophets in the south, after the Assyrian invasion, there were no prophets in the north until the time of Jesus and John the Baptist.

The ultimate sign of a failure in leadership is the failure to teach, live, and apply the Word of God. God pinpoints the reason for a nation's decline: lack of knowledge. There is a neglect of preaching and teaching of the Word of God. The priests and prophets of Israel were guilty for not instructing the people in the Scriptures. The people's destruction comes because they do not know the Bible well. They came to a place where the leaders and the people rejected biblical knowledge and had forgotten the law of their God. Truth is preached but ignored.

The coming of Jesus Christ illustrates the knowledge of God to the fullest degree. Jesus died for the sins of all people, offering every person the opportunity to come to faith in him (Jn 3:16; Eph 2:8-9). To those who do believe, Jesus is "wisdom from God" (1 Cor 1:30). Because of Christ, there is no need for anyone ever again to be "destroyed from a lack of knowledge." Many pastors are responsible for the lack of sound Bible teaching in the churches today. How might pastors neglect the Word?

1. We are more concerned about "tickling the ears" of people than cutting their heart with the Word.

2. We entertain the goats instead of feeding the sheep.

3. We do not teach through the Bible systematically or expositorily so that we end up only preaching on our favorite passages of the Bible.

4. We preach and teach morals or purpose without preaching Christ.

5. We might place a theological system above a personal relationship with Christ.

6. We turn the Bible into a law to obey instead of pointing people to the grace and love of God in Christ, which gives us power to obey.

7. We water down the hard doctrines of the Bible and try to reinterpret it to say that the Bible really doesn't say what it obviously says.

8. We fail to preach the majesty and greatness of the triune God.

9. We do not apply the Word practically to everyday situations in life.

10. We confuse preaching long with preaching to feed the people.

11. We have the right teaching and position on Scripture without having the right disposition and attitude of love and gentleness.

12. We are imbalanced in our emphasis in Scripture. We often over focus on a pet doctrine or pet passage of Scripture to the neglect of the full counsel of God's Word.

13. We do not emphasize the need for conversion (a new heart with a Spirit-filled life) in order to live out the Scriptures.

14. We fail to preach Jesus Christ and him crucified and risen from every text of Scripture.

ACCOUNTABLE FOR PERSONAL INTEGRITY (4:7)

The priests thought the increase of prosperity meant they were right with God.

> **Hosea 4:7** | The more they increased [*in prosperity*], the more they sinned against me; I will change their glory into shame.

Prosperity has fostered a spirit of independence from the Lord, which has made the people callous to sin, and it will cost them their glorious heritage (4:7).[41] The priests increased in prosperity and number. There was complete compromise. Northern Israel accepted anyone as a priest. There were virtually no qualifications. That's why they grew so quickly in number. They saw that as success. God saw it as great sin because they were changing "their glory into shame." Our glory as Christ's church is not "numbers, nickels, noses and nonsense". We can be rich and increased with good, but spiritually be "poor, miserable, blind and naked" (Rev 3:17). Our glory is the living and eternal God and our relationship with him.

---

[41] Brownback. *Hosea*, 21.

The answer is not more self-glorifying and self-serving preachers. The more leaders lift themselves up, the more they sin against God. "God resists the proud but gives grace to the humble" (1 Pet 5:5). For the proud preacher, God can turn all his glory into shame.

I've seen this happen in multiple ministries. God blesses a ministry. It expands. It grows. It is blessed. The preacher or the church gets proud. The church and pastor may become worldly. Before long, God puts out the candlestick (Rev 2:5). How we need to be humble when God blesses us!

ACCOUNTABLE FOR SHEPHERDING (4:8-9)

God says he has nothing for proud priests and proud people but judgment. The priests excused the sin they were supposed to expose. Instead of exposing it, they actually feed on the sin of God's people as part of their ministry.

> **Hosea 4:8-9** | They feed on the sin of my people; they are greedy for their iniquity. And it shall be like people, like priest; I will punish them for their ways and repay them for their deeds.

It was so bad, that God was going to bring the nation to nothing. James Montgomery Boice puts it this way:

> The period of moral and spiritual decline about which the book is written was not a period of the withering up of "religion." Religion actually increased! Here was a period characterized by cursing, lying, murder, stealing, and adultery; but during this period the priesthood grew in numbers as those who were professional religionists moved in to capitalize on the debauchery.[42]

For these religionists, God is for sale. I've seen it with my own eyes. I've heard Joel Osteen answer Larry King when he asked if he would go to hell if he didn't believe that Jesus is the "way, the truth, and the life" (Jn 14:6). Osteen responded, "I don't want to judge anyone Larry, I'll let God do that." That might seem shocking, but that is exactly what is happening today. You can go on CNN or NBC NEWS, and they all have what they call their "God Squad" of religious leaders who have either fallen away from the true faith or serve a false religion. It may be a priest or a rabbi, or a popular evangelical teacher. It's often what people refer to as a "rock star" preacher who everyone loves, and who is

---

[42] Boice, 45.

willing to say or do just about anything to fill a church, sell a few books, fill a stadium, or get on TV.

We see pastors today not only water down the offense of the Gospel but also water down the ugliness of sin. Today we hear of "gay Christians" and "alcoholic believers". That's the same as saying "murderous Christians" or "drunk believers". Pastors need to be sure that Christians are calling sin what it is: sin. When we start remaking sin so it sounds acceptable, you can be sure the nation is spiraling downward.

Godly Leaders Unplug from the World (4:10-12)

Since the people lacked a full and satisfying relationship with God, they pursued gods of food, sex, wealth, and religion.

Unplug from that which Can't Satisfy You

> **Hosea 4:10-11a** | They shall eat, but not be satisfied; they shall play the whore, but not multiply, because they have forsaken the Lord to cherish [11] whoredom, wine, and new wine...

Israel was playing the whore like Gomer. They went after everything but could not be satisfied. They left their God to play the whore, but God goes after his people. Hosea the prophet was living this out with his wife Gomer. She kept going back to the whore house. And Hosea kept going back after her. Hosea had nothing to gain from loving Gomer. She didn't even seem to love him back! But Hosea's love did not depend on what Gomer did or did not do. In this way, Hosea is a picture of God, while Gomer represents you and me. God continues to love us regardless of where we run. He comes to the darkest, messiest places to find us and rescue us, again and again, because he loves us. God loves us even if we run and even if we choose not to love him back. God chases after us because he hurts when we hurt.

In this passage, four things are named that Israel pursued to fill their empty souls: food, sex, wealth, and religion. The world might look to such things and wonder what more one could want. But God tells us that he has arranged life in such a way that if these things are pursued apart from holiness, the result will be frustration rather than satisfaction. Nothing satisfies. God knows that even the best the world can offer us will not satisfy the longing in our souls. We try to fill our hearts, minds, and bodies with new things and new relationships, but the emptiness always catches up.

Unplug from That Which Can't Sophisticate You

Hosea 4:11b | ...they have forsaken the Lord to cherish [11] whoredom, wine, and new wine, which take away the understanding.

It's interesting that Hosea reminds us the more we give ourselves to idols like food, sex, wealth, and self-righteous religion, they will take away our understanding (4:11b). The self-centeredness of sin makes people stupid. Puritan Thomas Watson said it in a gentler way: "Sin brings a man low in his intellectual parts. Sin has ruined the rational part."[43]

Unplug from That Which Can't Give Solutions

Hosea 4:12 | My people inquire of a piece of wood, and their walking staff gives them oracles. For a spirit of whoredom has led them astray, and they have left their God to play the whore.

We may not talk to idols, but there's a problem if we talk to our "smart phone" more than we talk to God. God alone has the solution for what you face.

People go after the strangest things for answers. In Israel, they went after an idol made from a piece of wood or a walking staff that gives them oracles and messages from a god. The story of Israel involves seeking help in all the wrong places. It's our story as well. Rather than dealing with the root of the issue – our spiritual waywardness – we keep trying temporary solutions. We change locations, jobs, friends, relationships. We read the next book, go to a new conference, or talk about the accountability that we need. But the problem is our fundamental waywardness that we keep bringing to every so-called solution.

Godly Leaders Lead Others (4:13-14)

Look at the boldness of Hosea. He confronts the church of his day. In verses Hosea 4:13-14, Hosea goes on to show how and why the entire nation got to be so lost and backslidden. It's not the fault mainly of the women, but of the men.

Hosea 4:13 | They sacrifice on the tops of the mountains and burn offerings on the hills, under oak, poplar, and terebinth, because

---

[43] Thomas Watson. *The Mischief of Sin* (Grand Rapids, MI: Soli Deo Gloria Publications, 1994), 36.

> their shade is good. Therefore your daughters play the whore,
> and your brides commit adultery.

The trees described on the hilltops are still there today: oak, poplar, and terebinth. One of the most delightful places to go in Israel is the city of Tel Dan in the very north of Israel, where the Baal altar to the golden calf is sadly still there. Of course, the idolatry is no longer happening. Tel Dan is now a nature reserve where thousands visit each year. The shade is good there, and the trees still provide a desirable environment. The remnants of the idol altar is in surprisingly superb condition. God has allowed it to remain as a testimony to the authenticity of the Scriptures as well as a warning to all true believers to flee from idols.

In these verses (4:13-14), the men are charged, but the women are let off the hook. Why? The Lord is holding the men of Israel accountable for the lust and sexual license of the women in the Baal worship cult. Sadly, the daughters (a term used for married women in Israel) are out at the Baal temples in Dan and Bethel fornicating and committing adultery. Where are the men? They are supposed to lead and protect. The problem goes back to Adam who should have been protecting and leading Eve, but instead allowed the serpent access to his wife and left her vulnerable to the devil's beguiling. If the men of the churches of Jesus would just begin to lead, we could have a great revival.

Hosea 4:14 | I will not punish your daughters when they play the whore, nor your brides when they commit adultery; for the men themselves go aside with prostitutes and sacrifice with cult prostitutes, and a people without understanding shall come to ruin.

Passive men are the problem in Israel as they are today. Men do not want to stand up for their women. Like Adam in the garden, we stand by while the serpent harasses and overcomes Eve. We let it happen just like Adam did, plunging the human race into oblivion. Because the women are victims of passive men, God rightly says, "I will not punish your daughters when they play the whore, nor your brides when they commit adultery" (4:14a).

When a nation leaves God, God gives them the leaders they deserve and the sin they crave, and that is punishment enough for anyone. The culture begins to live for these idols which make a culture tolerate of everything except intolerance. This will be a culture that accepts everything, but vehemently rejects the true and living God.

The guilt is laid here in Hosea 4, and in our society today, at the feet of passive men. Oh, that godly men would rise up and repent and lead in the right direction. That men would again be courageous and stop blaming others and take responsibility for their own sin. Then the idols of society would be destroyed and rooted out. If a nation is given to idolatry, it is because of passive, immature, entitled, childish men. God have mercy.

THE STEPS BACK TO GOD (4:15-19)

The only way back to God for Israel is for God to strip them of everything. That's Jesus' call. "If anyone would come after me, let him deny himself and take up his cross and follow me" (Mt 16:24). Spurgeon said,

> If you will not have death unto sin, you shall have sin unto death. There is no alternative. If you do not die to sin, you shall die for sin. If you do not slay sin, sin will slay you.[44]

God will do whatever it takes to strip you of your sin.

The men have to lead. Israel is radioactive. They can't go down to Judah. They need to repent. They don't need to swear and say "the Lord lives" and jump through hoops. They need to repent right where they are. They need to stay away from Gilgal and Bethel which were places of idolatry at the time.

Though a nation does indeed decline, God's people are to remain faithful and separate from false teachers. The church is to rise up with intentional men who are willing to lead.

Boice says, "Israel was not the whole of the Jewish homeland at this stage in history. She was the larger nation, the northern one. But further south there was still the half of the nation known as Judah, and Judah (thanks to the greater faithfulness of her kings) had not slipped so far on the moral scale as Israel. For her there was still hope."[45] God addresses the unfaithful first.

---

[44] Charles Haddon Spurgeon. "The Dual Nature and the Duel Within" from *Metropolitan Tabernacle Pulpit, Volume 25* (London: Passmore & Alabaster, 1879), Sermon 1495b.

[45] Ibid, 47.

The Warning: Repent

Though northern Israel played the whore, God was looking out for Judah (southern Israel) who had a number of godly kings leading them in the right direction.

> **Hosea 4:15** | Though you play the whore, O Israel, let not Judah become guilty. Enter not into Gilgal, nor go up to Beth-aven, and swear not, 'As the LORD lives.'

The exhortation to Judah not to visit Israel's favorite Baal temples is meant for the ears of those who did worship in them. It was a startling, infuriating thing for Israelites to hear—far more effective than a straight onslaught.[46]

In order to appreciate fully what Hosea is saying, you have to know a bit of Bible geography. **Gilgal** was the place where King Saul lost the kingdom because of his] disobedience in not utterly destroying the Amalekites. **Beth-aven** (house of wickedness) is a nickname for Bethel (house of God). It is one of two sites that hosted the golden calf Baal worship in a replica of Solomon's temple. Both places are near Jerusalem, the place of God's presence and Temple.

God says "Don't go near **Judah**. Don't bring them into your idolatry. Repent right where you are. Don' t jump through hoops and use "Christianeese": "As the Lord lives" as if you know the Lord. Repent. Admit you don't know him.

Jesus told his disciples, "If anyone would come after me, let him deny himself and take up his cross and follow me. 25 For whoever would save his life will lose it, but whoever loses his life for my sake will find it. 26 For what will it profit a man if he gains the whole world and forfeits his soul? Or what shall a man give in return for his soul? (Mt 16:24-26). We've got to be willing to die right where we are to all other ambitions but knowing God. We perish because we lack God's revealing himself to us!

The Wandering: Examples

God now describes Israel with three pictures of things that wander to wake them up: a stuck cow, a lost lamb, and a desperate prostitute.

---

[46] Kidner, 55.

Hosea 4:16-18 | Like a stubborn heifer, Israel is stubborn; can the LORD now feed them like a lamb in a broad pasture? ¹⁷ Ephraim is joined to idols; leave him alone. ¹⁸ When their drink is gone, they give themselves to whoring; their rulers dearly love shame.

The Stubborn Cow: Stuck

First, he says Israel is like a backslidden heifer and a lost lamb to illustrate how idolatry makes us wander. The stubborn, or literally "backslidden" cow is stuck. Addiction and idolatry will bring a marriage into a place that seems impossible. It will bring a person's life into something that seems impossible.

The Wandering Lamb: Lost, Away from the Shepherd

He also compares Israel to a wandering lamb who is lost and wandering in a large and broad pasture. Though there seems to be plenty of good grass, it is mixed with poisonous herbs that will hurt and possibly kill the lamb. Without the good shepherd there to guide the sheep to good pasture, the lambs are in trouble. The question is asked, "Can the LORD now feed them?" It brings to mind our Lord's lament, "How often would I ... and you would not!" (Mt 23:37). It is God's desire to feed us, but we must stop going astray as sheep (Isa 53:6) and return back to Jesus.

The Desperate Prostitute: Curing the Pain

Going back to the theme of the first several chapters, God then describes them as a whoring, desperate prostitute who goes back to walking the street, giving sexual favors for money whenever she runs out of drink and food. That brings us as Christians back to the foundational truth about idolatry: anything we are willing to sin in order to get, or sin if we don't get, is an idol.

God's verdict: "Ephraim is joined to idols; leave him alone" (4:17). Sometimes the most humbling thing God can do is leave us to the consequences of our sins. We often can't hear God's merciful voice until he shows us that the "way of the transgressor is hard" (Pro 13:15).

Sometimes the most severe thing God can do to chasten and humble us is allow us to harvest what we planted with our idols. I've seen successful businessmen and women lose it all through drug and alcohol abuse. Families have been torn in pieces over and over again due to adultery and abandonment. As bad as those situations are, God can finally work in hearts that are torn up due to the devastating consequences. God's desire is not to punish, but to correct and heal.

The Wind

Hosea closes by reviewing the problem and giving the ultimate solution. The problem is their unfaithfulness and whoredom (4:19a). The solution is repentance and shame for their sinful sacrifices (4:19b). The Hebrew word for "wind" can also mean "spirit" as in Hosea 4:12 where "a spirit of whoredom" has engulfed Israel like a whirlwind. This wind is so powerful, it will carry the children of Israel into exile, where they will be ashamed because of their sacrifices.

> **Hosea 4:19a** | A wind has wrapped them in its wings...

The spirit and wind of whoredom is so powerful. We must never trust ourselves to defeat temptation on our own. Like Jesus, we need the Word of God, and because we are not Jesus, we need the accountability of other Christians. Starting with faithful attendance on Sundays is a good beginning, but if you want to grow, you need a couple other people in your life. Paul had a Barnabas who he could pull up and he had a Timothy who he could encourage. You need that person who will hold you accountable and you need another person who you can pour into. The more you teach what you know, you will cement your godly character. You need to make disciples now, and not wait until you are completely mature. If you wait till you are fully perfect, you will never make disciples. Discipleship is a wonderful way of staying away from the whoredom of this world.

Today as then, God's people need to stay separate from this unfaithful culture, and the false teachers and the worldly churches. Let us stay faithful to Christ. Don't be wrapped up like a whirlwind in their idolatries.

In 1844, a Philadelphia school wanted to teach morals without using the Bible at the Supreme Court in Vidal vs. Girard. The Court said "Why may not the Bible, and especially the New Testament, be read and taught as a divine revelation in the schools? Where can the purest principals of morality be learned so clearly or perfectly as from the New Testament?" Consider our nation today. Since 1963 violent crime has increased 544%. The nation has been deprived of an estimated 50 million citizens through legal abortions just since 1973. We are now bringing down the institution of marriage as well as the idea of biological gender. Our debt is so high in the USA that recently at the G20 summit our creditor nations told us we need to restructure our economy so we can repay them. Can God have mercy? Yes!

The Awakening

Hosea 4:19b | ... and they shall be ashamed because of their sacrifices.

The people of Israel had offered sacrifices to the golden calf in the name of Jehovah. God says, there will come a day when they will repent and be ashamed because of their sacrifices, which included human sacrifices of their infant children. God is essentially saying, "As wicked as you are, I will save a remnant. I will cut your heart and cause you to feel shame again." What's it going to take for Israel to awaken to their shame and repent? It takes "a wind" that carries northern Israel into exile for 70 years, where they are cleansed from their idols and return to their land. The believing remnant in the north had to flee around 722BC when the Assyrians invaded. The northern remnant runs to Jerusalem, and Hezekiah has to enlarge the walls of the holy city (2 Chron 32:5).

God wants us as men and families to take responsibility for our sin. The most important commodities we have are not our job or our country. The souls of ourselves and our families and our nation are what matters. What shall we as Christians do when the world (and even the church) around us goes mad? We have to keep doing what Jesus commanded: make disciples of all nations (Mt 28:18-20). Stay holy so life and character and fruitfulness stays healthy and powerful. Flee idols! Pray for and promote a true revival among the lost: believe God's reach is long!

Conclusion

The lemming is found in Norway and is a short-tailed animal that looks like a miniature rabbit. Through the sub-Arctic Norwegian winter it lives completely buried under snow through which it burrows in search of food. Females can conceive and produce offspring within four weeks of their birth. Talk about reproduction, these things make rabbits look infertile. Mass reproduction! Eventually they outgrow the tunnel system, and the lemmings fill the tunnels, and there's not enough food and not enough space.

God has put a little alarm inside the lemmings to give us a picture. A warning for us. What these lemmings do is about every two years, when the population is too high, most of them will crawl out of the ground and start a march. They come out of the ground in Norway.

This is so bizarre that the people come outside and watch this happen. First 10 and then 100 and then thousands and then hundreds of thousands join this massive march across the landscape so that you can't even see the ground. They get to the sea, and they go right over the cliff, and right over into the ocean and *drown*. This is silly. It's stupid of these animals to do that. That animal has a brain as small as your fingernail, yet some of you are on the same path. You are about to make some decisions that are going to harm your future. Others of you need to be bold and trust God and go forward with God's revealed will.

We have been given a great warning in Hosea 4. We need to listen to it! We need to speak more about our walk with God than all the mechanics of Christianity. Systematic theology is good and necessary. Christian music is amazing and good. But what about your walk with God? Do you know him? Do you walk with him? What's he saying to you? We can go down a long hard road if we don't know him. We can be supremely interested in the things of God without actually knowing God. God must not be a mere curiosity. He must be your all in all, your heavenly Father, your everything.

5 | HOSEA 5
COME BACK AND SEEK ME

*I will return again to my place, until they acknowledge
their guilt and seek my face, and in their
distress earnestly seek me.*
HOSEA 5:15

God is far more compassionate than we are. Often, I hear people say, why does God have a hell? Their questions assume that God lacks compassion. Let me say that God is infinitely compassionate, but he is also infinitely just. He must have both. So when we read of God's compassion for the apostate priests and leaders in Israel, we are a bit shocked by God's heart to call them back to repentance.

Hosea felt the culture of Israel crumbling around him. The people of God are to hold the culture accountable. The leaders in the church are to lead the effort. That was not happening in Israel. Remember God told the prophet Hosea to marry a prostitute as a picture of God's love for Israel. Hosea went after Gomer, and in Hosea 5, God is going after Israel. Specifically, God is going after the leaders of the congregations.

In Hosea 4, Hosea's first recorded sermon, Hosea informs Israel that God is seeking a divorce from Israel. Israel has broken the marriage covenant. God laid out his case and showed how he had every legal reason to divorce Israel and depart from her. Yet, like Hosea's love for Gomer, God loves Israel and has no intention of leaving or forsaking her even though she deserves it. Learn this lesson of grace: God loves undeserving sinners. God gives second and third and fiftieth chances. What a God of great love and mercy.

In Hosea 5, God gives the pathway back to relationship with him. The Lord has a message for Israel through the prophet Hosea: the leaders need to listen to God and repent so that he can bless Israel. Hosea's main point is clear: Leaders can turn the tide of a corrupt culture if they will be bold and repent. There is a way to turn around a morally corrupt culture. Though we are completely unable to do it, God is willing to change the hearts of those in a culture, but it's going to take some bold leaders to stand up and repent. Repentance is not about making multiple changes in our lives and jumping through hoops and making rules. We've all done that, and that is exhausting. That is not repentance, but penance. That's law keeping, and that never sanctified a Christian or changed a culture. Repentance is about a change of mind, a radical new perspective; repentance is about seeing God in his glory and beauty and turning from all idols to worship him alone as truly and fully satisfying. God is still willing to love Israel if they will repent and turn back to seek him. This is the message of Hosea 5.

This leads us to a question so vital for today. What should be our attitude toward unfaithful churches, who, like Israel of old, have leaders who are lost and have apostatized from the living God? Jesus calls out two of his own beloved churches for this kind of unfaithfulness. One group harassing the church, Jesus calls a "synagogue of Satan" (Rev 2:9) and another he says has "Jezebel as a prophetess" (Rev 2:20). There are so-called churches that are more at home with Satan than they are with the Spirit of truth. There are those churches who ordain Jezebels and Ahabs (who taught Israel to fornicate in the prosperity cults of Baal and Asherah) as leaders.

We need to stand up to the false leaders in the churches today and call them to repentance. This is the message we need today. Calling out false teachers begins with understanding God's omniscience. He knows us to our core. He measures our thoughts and our motives. There are "hired hands" who are not true shepherds in our churches. They do ministry to make a name for themselves, or to fleece the sheep of finances, or to exercise their authority and "lord" it over the flock. But never forget this: God knows your motives. We will all give an account to him.

GOD'S KNOWLEDGE (5:1-7)

Hosea 5:3 | I know Ephraim, and Israel is not hidden from me.

God knows us through and through. He knows the depths of our hearts. Hosea 5 is directed to shepherds and priests of God's people. Leaders need to know God and walk with him in sincerity truly experiencing God. If they are faking it, God knows. There are marks of leaders who are faking it. They existed in Israel, and they exist today. God knows and will hold pastors and leaders in the church today accountable, just like he held Israel accountable.

God Knows Their Neglect (5:1)

God tells the leaders of Israel: pay attention to my people. False teachers don't care about the flock of God. The downfall of a society always begins with self-serving leaders. Leaders first and foremost must listen to God. The leaders in Hosea's day didn't know God so they were listening and taking cues from their culture.

Hosea 5:1 | Hear this, O priests! Pay attention, O house of Israel! Give ear, O house of the king! For the judgment is for you; for you have been a snare at Mizpah and a net spread upon Tabor.

The priests of Israel were distracted with their own comfort, and they needed to start "paying attention" to the care of God's people. By addressing the "house of Israel" he's referring to the king and his court. All in the royal court are to "give ear." Why? Because "the judgment is for you." The leaders of Israel will be held responsible for their neglect of the souls of God's people. Instead of helping people to God, they tend to their own needs and forget about God's little lambs. Remember what Jesus said about neglectful shepherds.

> He who is a hired hand and not a shepherd, who does not own the sheep, sees the wolf coming and leaves the sheep and flees, and the wolf snatches them and scatters them. —*John 10:12*

Mizpah and Tabor are mentioned because they were once bastions of faithfulness. Mizpah was the place the prophet Samuel cleansed Israel from idolatry and put up an Ebenezer stone, a sign of spiritual victory, since the Lord "helped" Israel be done with idols of Baal and Ashtaroth (1 Sam 7:21). It was a turning point from the apostate time of the

Judges. Tabor was the place of the victories of Deborah and Barak. Instead of leading Israel to victory in the Lord, the priests and kings of Israel laid a snare and spread a net upon the people of God by serving themselves. Kidner says:

> If many an ordinary hilltop had its Baal shrine, wooing dozens of frequenters away from the true faith, the shrines on high places as famous as Mizpah and Mount Tabor would seduce their hundreds.[47]

Standards had shaken. Leaders had fallen. Holiness was gone from the culture, and now the people were filled with lust and idolatry. The Spirit of the Lord was removed for the most part.

Here is a powerful principle we can learn from this. Even in judgment God wants to show mercy. He upbraids them to bless them. If they will turn back, he will receive them.

God Knows Their Exploitation (5:2)

Those priests in Hosea's day are not only lazy shepherds – they are rebelling against God—willing to neglect the sheep and even lead them to slaughter where other nations will take them as slaves, which would actually happen not long from Hosea's day in the Assyrian captivity of Israel.

Hosea 5:2a | And the revolters have gone deep into slaughter...

God calls these lazy leaders revolters, or insurrectionists against God as King and Lord. The power of the term revolters is very strong. It means "those who willfully turn aside" from their own conscience against God's marriage covenant with his people. These leaders are traitors to the heavenly kingdom. They lead God's people away from divine Husband, leading them to perish for lack of knowing the Lord (4;6; 5:4). It's like these lazy leaders are allowing kidnappers to come into God's house and rip his beloved wife (Israel) out of his arms, to sell her into slavery. We have a name for these kinds of leaders: sociopaths or narcissists. It would be like a fireman who sees a burning building filled with people, and turns his back on it, refusing to go in and rescue anyone. He takes no hoses out or ladders to rescue people, but instead, ignores his training and puts on his headphones, turning his music up

---

[47] Derek Kidner, *The Message of Hosea: Love to the Loveless*, ed. J. Alec Motyer and Derek Tidball, The Bible Speaks Today (England: Inter-Varsity Press, 1976), 57.

louder to deafen his ears from the cries of the perishing. These kinds of leaders are hard hearted, looking out of a lens of self-idolatry, idolizing personal comfort and pleasure. Sadly, they are more and more in leadership both in the pulpits of the church and in the governments of the world.

We must open our eyes and see that God gave these self-serving priests to Israel as a judgment. What does that mean? It means they are going to sell everyone out for their own comfort until they are wiped out of the land, and God is going to replace them with something else. God is going to take these people out of the land in order to prepare for something far better, something far greater.

Eventually, he whittles Israel down to a mere 120 faithful, believing people in an upper room and then through these Spirit filled people, he turns the world upside down. Imagine what the Lord could do with us if we remain faithful.

Instead of standing against the culture, the leaders of Israel were leading the people deep into the slaughter. The people of God did not stand up against their corrupt leaders, so they instead paid a high price.

We have a similar slaughter today. God's judgment is already upon our culture. Romans 1 says that when God judges a culture there is a handing over to a depraved mind. And what we have is such a slaughter in our country and in our world today all over the civilized West is like a death cult. We are literally killing ourselves where you abort the young, you destroy marriage, you kill off the elderly, and the sick and the infirm. What kind of future does a culture like ours have that does these things? God has handed us over to judgment. But let's remember the optimism of Hosea. He's going to judge Israel in order to clear the way for something better: for Christ. He's judging our country, and it can only lead to destruction, but God has something better for us. There will be revival. There will be awakening. There will a desperation that leads us to Christ. God promises that he will have his heaven full.

I believe a similar judgment of God, such as in Romans 1, is upon our nation. God has given our nation which was once broadly Christian influenced but is now headed to the slaughter. We are well on our way to destruction. We must be like those 120 in the upper room. God always uses a faithful remnant that refuses to bow the knee to Baal. He will use us if we are faithful to turn the world upside down for Christ. There is a darkness that envelopes the earth in the last days, but there is at the same time great revival and awakening. Our cry and prayer ought to be awaken us Lord. Keep us faithful in the midst of the slaughter.

God Can Use Even the Worst Evil for Good

Hosea 5:2b | ... but I will discipline all of them.

God says, "I will discipline all of them" (5:2b). The idea of this word "discipline" is to fetter in order to correct all Israel. It indicates God's compassion even in the midst of horrible judgment. The word for discipline in Hebrew (*musar*) often refers to "instruction designed to correct bad behavior, using painful means" (*cf* Isa 26:16; Jer 5:3; Job 5:17; Pro 3:11).[48] The word though very strong is one of fatherly correction and instruction.[49] It is clear from this language that the Lord is referring to the soon captivity of Israel. God is merciful and will redeem them, but not without much pain. The glory must depart first. God's people will lose their freedom. They will be placed in captivity, far from the glory of God's presence, far from their homeland of Israel. Yet this too is a mercy. "It's going to hurt, but you will learn of me. You will know me intimately as a result." What a merciful God we serve! The people will be taken off to captivity, but it will prepare the way for Christ. God can take the worst evil (like crucifying the Son of God) and turn it into the greatest act of redemption.

Don't be frightened or shaken by the judgment against our country. God is clearing the way for revival. The church of Jesus Christ cannot be defeated. The gates of hell will not prevail. God may discipline his church, but it will never be destroyed. He disciplines it to preserve it.

God Knows Their Unfaithfulness (5:3)

Hosea 5:3a | I know Ephraim, and Israel is not hidden from me.

God knows our hearts. If we are sinning, we are not hiding it from God. The Psalmist tells us that wherever we go, whatever we do, God is there. Where can I go from your Spirit? Where can I flee from your

---

[48] George M. Schwab Sr., "Hosea," in *Daniel–Malachi*, ed. Iain M. Duguid, James M. Hamilton Jr., and Jay Sklar, vol. VII, ESV Expository Commentary (Wheaton, IL: Crossway, 2018), 204.

[49] Mackay, 160.

presence? **⁸** If I go up to the heavens, you are there; if I make my bed in the depths, you are there (Psa 139:7-8).

One of the things we tell ourselves when we attempt to run away from God is that if we forget him he will forget us. He won't leave you in your sin. When you sin, he is there. God does not forget us. On the contrary, he knows all things, including all we are and do, and this is frightening[50] and comforting. God sees you. You cannot hide from him. He is shining a light on you. He is after you.

Don't run from God! Don't cover and hide your sin. Bring it out into the light. Christians are those who walk in the light! Who knows about your sins? Of course, God knows, but if you really are a godly leader you will not hide your sin. The Apostle John warns us: "If we say we have fellowship with him while we walk in darkness, we lie and do not practice the truth. **⁷** But if we walk in the light, as he is in the light, we have fellowship with one another, and the blood of Jesus his Son cleanses us from all sin (1 Jn 1:6-7).

We can't conceal our sins! We need to bring them to God and to a brother or sister that is close to us. It's as the book of Proverbs warns us: "Whoever conceals his transgressions will not prosper, but he who confesses and forsakes them will obtain mercy" (Pro 28:13).

Hosea 5:3b | I know Ephraim, and Israel is not hidden from me; for now, O Ephraim, you have played the whore; Israel is defiled.

Here God calls out the leaders for playing "the whore" and committing spiritual adultery against God. There are leaders today committing literal fornication, using sexual activity outside of marriage as an idol. This was a major part of the Baal worship of the Old Testament, and it is a major part of false teachers who "play the whore" today. There are pastors of church and officers in the church who not only view porn but also cheat on their marriages. There are those who call themselves Christians who uphold and approve of unlawful and lascivious relationships. When leaders legalize sinful activity, God gives that society over to that sin as a judgment against them. That's what's happening today. This is why popular culture and the media are constantly promoting sin as normal; they are trying to normalize it. God says when

---

[50] James Montgomery Boice, *The Minor Prophets: An Expositional Commentary* (Grand Rapids, MI: Baker Books, 2002), 48.

this happens this is a sign of his judgment in the first chapter of Romans.

> For this reason God gave them up to dishonorable passions. For their women exchanged natural relations for those that are contrary to nature; 27 and the men likewise gave up natural relations with women and were consumed with passion for one another, men committing shameless acts with men and receiving in themselves the due penalty for their error. —*Romans 1:26-27*

No one claiming to be a leader of God's church can hide from God. They can pass resolutions that approve of sin, but God sees it. These leaders will be held accountable in the most shocking way, not just in the coming captivity of Israel, but ultimately on Judgment Day. Remember the warning of Jesus in the book of Matthew.

> Not everyone who says to me, 'Lord, Lord,' will enter the kingdom of heaven, but the one who does the will of my Father who is in heaven. 22 On that day many will say to me, 'Lord, Lord, did we not prophesy in your name, and cast out demons in your name, and do many mighty works in your name?' 23 And then will I declare to them, 'I never knew you; depart from me, you workers of lawlessness.' —*Matthew 7:21-23*

God Knows Their Enslavement (5:4)

Hosea 5:4 | Their deeds do not permit them to return to their God. For the spirit of whoredom is within them, and they know not the LORD.

There are leaders that are enslaved, and their addiction to power, or pleasure, or comfort, or esteem is keeping them from repenting and turning to God. Leaders need the Lord to turn people from their sins. Only God can change the heart. Here we have a picture of total depravity. God stretches out his hands all day long (*cf* Isa 65:2; Rom 10:21), but people do not want to repent because their deeds do not permit them to return to God. By nature, we are all as Ephesians says, "children of wrath" enslaved to Satan, the world, and the passions of our flesh. Truly God alone can deliver us from such epic bondage (Eph 2:1-4).

Worldliness is compared in Hosea to spiritual prostitution. Truly "Ephraim played the whore" (5:3). Jeroboam I set up an alternative altar at Bethel and Dan that was an architectural replica of Solomon's

Temple at Jerusalem. Upon the altar was a golden calf that was set up in defiance of God's decree that his name would be in Jerusalem. They are trying to serve the Lord and the pagan prosperity gods. Of course, Jesus tells us serving two masters is impossible (Mt 6:24).

Worldly people think they can repent anytime, but God warns Israel that this is not the case.

> **Hosea 5:4a** | Their deeds do not permit them to return to their God.

They think they can return to God whenever they want, not realizing that sin hardens the heart. The more we indulge with sin, the more impossible it is to return to God.

How do you turn a people to God whose deeds do not permit them to turn to God? You have to introduce them to the Lord. You need to pray for them, teach them, and weep for them. George Whitefield used to stand in the Boston marketplace in Massachusetts and weep for people. He would say, "I weep for you because you cannot weep for yourselves."

Are you that kind of leader that weeps for souls? Do you "stand in the gap" when no one else is there? Leaders are bold to point those around them to Christ. Open your eyes to the harvest!

God Knows Their Delusion (5:4b-7)

What is the result of bad leadership? If we decide to go along with the culture, what happens? It's clear that the current generation will not know or care about Lord. They will likely say they know God because they go to church, but they will not have an intimate walk with him.

A People who don't know the Lord (5:4b)

> **Hosea 5:4b** | They know not the LORD...

Israel is cut off from knowing the Lord not because God had neglected to show them mercy. It was not that God had refused to help them. It's because they loved the idols of this world more than the satisfying walk with the one true God. Whoredom blinds people. Worldliness is a killer more dangerous than Hitler or Stalin. The blindness of worldliness destroys our only hope: knowing the Lord. When we choose the world, we reject the Light of the world. We choose blindness.

The great scandal for those who know the truth but do not obey it is that they will stumble.

A PEOPLE ENSLAVED TO SIN (5:5)

Hosea 5:5 | The Pride of Israel testifies to his face; Israel and Ephraim shall stumble in his guilt; Judah also shall stumble with them.

The "Pride" of Israel "testifies" against it—yet another witness to the guilt of the accused. The sentencing portion of the trial is stated here in part: Israel will fall and will take Judah with it.[51] Gomer was brought to the slave market as a slave, probably with her hands tied. She's being led by an owner who is selling her. So God, the Glory and Pride of Israel uses a slavery analogy. Both northern and southern kingdoms will stumble in their guilt. They'll be led about as slaves because of their guilt and sin. They could be free in the Lord, but here's a powerful truth: choose sin, choose slavery. Sin is a miserable slavery isn't it?

Historically, the Lord is referring to their utter downfall. Ephraim (northern Israel) in 722BC will be destroyed forever by the Assyrians. Because of this stumbling, multitudes of Jewish people from the northern tribes will swell the borders of Jerusalem. King Hezekiah will have to massively expand the walls of Jerusalem. Yet even Judah will eventually fall to the Babylonians and be hauled away from God's land as slaves to Babylon beginning in 605 BC.

If you don't hold leaders accountable, and you decide to follow them into sin, it will lead to enslavement. The cost of idols is infinitely higher than the cost of serving God. "The way of the transgressor is hard" (Prov 13:15), much harder than obedience to God. God allows his children to stumble in order to humble them so that they might seek him again.

A PEOPLE WITHOUT FELLOWSHIP WITH GOD (5:6)

The people of Israel will not let go of their idols. They think God is with them, but he has withdrawn his presence from them. Israel's sins are so serious that the Lord refuses to commune with them.

---

[51] Schwab, "Hosea," in *Daniel–Malachi*, 205.

Hosea 5:6 | With their flocks and herds they shall go to seek the LORD, but they will not find him; he has withdrawn from them.

In Bethel and Dan, the people would seek the Lord with their flocks and herds. They were worshipping the golden calf in honor of Yahweh. We might say in our day, "How absurd." Yet, there are people in churches all over the world who love the world in their heart but have a religious spirit that is antichristian. God is not impressed with religious worship. We can teach the Bible faithfully, raise our hands in worship and still not find the Lord.

How fearful to be living the Christian life and not even realize he has withdrawn his presence from you. One day we go to seek the LORD, but we will not find him (5:6a). Those who will not serve God with their whole heart may look for the Lord. They may seek him half-heartedly, but they will never ever find the Lord in that condition. Why? He has withdrawn from them (5:6b) because God always hides himself from half-hearted people.

What is the requirement for finding God? The requirement for finding God is *whole-hearted seeking*: "You will seek me and find me, when you seek me with all your heart" (Jer 29:13; *cf* 5:15).

They could not find God because God will not be found by a person with a divided heart. If we want to find the Lord, there has to be a complete forsaking of idols. If you forsake the world and walk with the Lord, he tells us that you will "receive a hundredfold now in this time, houses and brothers and sisters and mothers and children and lands, with persecutions, and in the age to come eternal life" (Mk 10:30). You will be able to say: "I found him whom my soul loves. I held him, and would not let him go..." (Song 3:4).

A People without Faith in God (5:7a)

The great loss in spiritual adultery is a great hardness of heart. If we give up the Lord of angel armies, what do we have left? Idols that cannot satisfy is all we have. These idols are not passive but bring a hardness to the heart. Those who have a hard heart lose their ability to discern the Lord's presence. They try to return to the Lord without forsaking their idols, and he withdraws from them (5:6). What's the verdict?

Hosea 5:7a | They have dealt faithlessly with the Lord.

The Israelites knew of the Lord, but they would not return to him in the way he has designed, by grace through faith. They dealt faithlessly with the Lord. They were so caught up with themselves and the world, they could not discern the Lord's presence anymore, so they wanted something tangible to worship. They would not forsake their golden calves and serve the Lord exclusively. They constantly heard the prophets but would not tear down the high places where the idol groves were. Now that the Israelites' sin and their unbelief were such a fixed habit of mind and heart, they lost their tenderness and discernment. They had become hard-hearted.

Origen of Alexandria, Egypt first said, "The same sun softens the wax and hardens the clay."[52] The same word of God that can set you free forever, can also be your prison if you neglect it and ignore it. Remember what we hear in the book of Hebrews: "How shall we escape if we neglect such a great salvation?" (Heb 2:3). John Owen that such people become "sermon proof and sickness proof." They don't feel the sickness of their sin as much.

God's people had become calloused. In spite of the convicting preaching of Hosea and Amos, and in spite of the fact that they saw the judgment of God already beginning to occur, yet they were passed being affected by the Word of God. They could not repent. They could not leave their sins, nor did they want to. Are you growing in your faith? Peter shows us how we grow.

> Add to your faith virtue, to virtue knowledge, **6** to knowledge self-control, to self-control perseverance, to perseverance godliness, **7** to godliness brotherly kindness, and to brotherly kindness love. — *2 Peter 1:5-7*

You are either growing in your faith as a leader or backsliding. Don't become faithless!

A People without a Future in God (5:7b)

The people of Israel had started families with pagan women. This was a common problem for God's people in the Old Testament. They would not turn back to God because of family pressure. They had foreign wives with whom they have borne alien children. They thought they were too far in to turn back to God.

---

[52] Origen of Alexandria. trans. by G.W. Butterworth. *On First Principles* or *De Principiis* (Eugene, OR: Wipf and Stock, 1936), 175.

Hosea 5:7b | For they have borne alien children. Now the new moon shall devour them with their fields.

They don't want to lead their families in the worship of Yahweh. Further, they don't want to give up their new moon pagan festivals. Because they hang on to their pagan practices, the fields will be devoured by the Assyrians in 722BC. The image is that the new moon devours the fields. Hang on to idols, and you will be devoured by them. Idols don't satisfy. In fact, in the end, they leave you impoverished.

For leaders who follow God and are willing to stand alone and be separated unto God, he gives a promise: "For I know the plans I have for you, declares the LORD, plans to prosper you and not to harm you, plans to give you hope and a future" (Jer 29:11).

GOD'S MERCY (5:8-11)

Hosea 5:8a | Blow the horn in Gibeah, the trumpet in Ramah. Sound the alarm at Beth-aven...

What are we to do as leaders? Godly leaders sound the warning, no matter what the cost. The horn is an instrument of mercy. It warns beforehand of danger. Israel needed to repent or God would send the Assyrians to judge them and hall them away in slavery or slaughter, and in 722 B.C. that actually happened. Northern Israel is judged in 722 B.C. and never comes back to the land. They become the mix breed Samaritans. Yet there is still mercy here. Jesus goes through Samaria in his earthly ministry and saves a woman at the well, who evangelizes her whole town. Hosea's generation never recovered. They were hardened. They were sermon proof and sickness proof. Let us hear the word Hosea has for us.

We need to be leaders that are merciful toward God's people. Sometimes people will say, "That preacher is so unkind to preach about hell." Or, "How can that pastor preach so boldly, it seems rude!" Is it rude for a doctor to tell his patient he has cancer? Is it unkind for an architect to tell his client there's a swamp on the land, and it's unbuildable? Leaders need to give a clear message of warning. To warn God's people is merciful and kind. That's what we see here in Hosea 5:8, the mercy of warning someone about the dangers of continuing in sin.

The Mercy of Courage (5:8)

Leaders are called to be bold in preaching the Word of God. Paul wrote to Timothy: "Preach the word; be ready in season and out of season; reprove, rebuke, and exhort, with complete patience and teaching" (2 Tim 4:2). When leaders have the courage to blow the trumpet of warning, it is such a mercy.

> **Hosea 5:8** | Blow the horn in Gibeah, the trumpet in Ramah. Sound the alarm at Beth-aven; we follow you, O Benjamin!"

God is so merciful to give the church leaders that will "blow the trumpet". He called on Hosea to "blow the trumpet". As leaders we can't be uninvolved. We can't pretend like our culture is ok. It's not ok. And we have to speak up. We are all called to "blow the trumpet." Benjamin is named because that is the tribe where Jerusalem is. Leaders are to follow Benjamin – in other words, they are to follow the true worship of God at his temple in Jerusalem, in the tribe of Benjamin.

A call is issued for the leaders to blow the trumpet and shout, citing specific military installations and strongholds (5:8). This rhetoric invokes the panic of an invasion, the anticipation of imminent battle.[53] In the role of watchman (*cf* 9:8; 8:1), the prophet shouts the battle alarm, calls for both kinds of trumpets to sound the danger signal, summoning all sentinels to lift the cry of warning (*cf* Josh 6:5).[54] The ram's horn shofar and the silver bugle trumpet were to be blown in Gibeah, Ramah and Beth-aven. These cities all straddle the border of the two kingdoms and were the "axis of evil" in Hosea's time. The three cities were once bastions of faithfulness but are now ground zero for Baal worship.

Gibeah was the place where a prophets' school was located, and where Saul began to prophesy and reside after that. It was such a holy place, Samuel refers to it as "Gibeah of God (Elohim, 1 Sam 10:5). *Ramah* is the place of Rachel's burial. *Beth-aven* (house of wickedness) is a nickname for Bethel (house of God). It's no longer the house of God, but the house of wickedness because it is the city of golden calf worship that replaced the worship of God at Jerusalem, where God placed his name. The three cities form a triangle in the tribe of Benjamin, near

---

[53] Schwab, 208.

[54] David A. Hubbard, *Hosea: An Introduction and Commentary*, vol. 24, Tyndale Old Testament Commentaries (Downers Grove, IL: InterVarsity Press, 1989), 131.

Jerusalem. These three towns were leading and complicit in the golden calf worship.

Leaders must be bold and call sin what it is: it is moral evil and rebellion against a holy God. Sin always leads to misery. It is unkind not to warn people that sin leads to a life of chaos and fear and anger. The only remedy is to repent and turn to Christ.

The Mercy of Correction (5:9-10)

God is so merciful to give the church leaders that will warn the church of correction and chastening. Leaders and pastors who say "peace, peace" all the time are lying to you. Those who say, "God wants you to be rich and prosperous" are wrong. They don't read the Bible carefully. God is going to correct his children. He'll bring them to desolation on this earth if that's what it takes to bring them to holiness. We can't back down as leaders from bringing correction. Leaders are responsible to do a number of things for the sheep.

> We urge you, brothers, admonish the idle, encourage the fainthearted, help the weak, be patient with them all.
> —*1 Thessalonians 5:14*

CORRECTION OF FALSE PEACE (5:9)

Hosea 5:9 | Ephraim shall become a desolation in the day of punishment; among the tribes of Israel I make known what is sure.

The people are not worried about God's correction. God says to the people he loves: "I'm going to cut you down." They are prosperous, and they equate success and prosperity with God's blessing. Ephraim (Samaria) is so prosperous right now in Hosea's day, more than in the days of David and Solomon. This is the richest times in Israel's history. But God mercifully tells them that he's going to strip them of everything. They can't imagine being cut down and brought to desolation.

Don't confuse success and prosperity with God's blessing. Wake up and repent and live for Christ. You may be thinking, as a Christian, "God's not going to chasten me." Listen, just because God is patient, doesn't mean his correction won't arrive. "Whom the LORD loves he chastens" (Heb 12:6, NKJV). If you have your days of sinning, you will have your days of correcting, even if God has to bring you so low, to an utter desolation. If you've committed your life to Christ, he'll have you, body and soul.

Correction of False Worship (5:10)

Hosea 5:10 | The princes of Judah have become like those who move the landmark; upon them I will pour out my wrath like water.

Why is the Lord condemning the princes of Judah? Haven't they been faithful? Actually, they have not. King Ahaz of Judah is has followed after those who moved the ancient landmark of God's Temple to Bethel and Dan and erected golden calves.

Ahaz was overcome with the glory of his monarchy and in 732 he went to Damascus to swear homage to Tiglath-Pileser and his gods. While Ahaz was in Assyria, he took an interest to an altar which he saw there, he had one like it made in Jerusalem, which, with a corresponding change in ritual, he made a permanent feature of the Temple worship. Changes were also made in the arrangements and furniture of the Temple, "because of the king of Assyria" (2 Kgs 16:18). Furthermore, Ahaz built an astrological observatory with accompanying sacrifices, after the fashion of the pagan kings of his day. In other ways Ahaz lowered the character of the national worship. Ahaz offered his son as a human sacrifice by fire to Moloch (2 Kgs 16:3), a practice condemned by God's law (Lev 18:21).

Idolatry is a worship problem. King Ahaz was willing to "move the ancient landmark" of worship in the Jerusalem Temple. He wasn't exactly like the northern tribes (Ephraim) who moved the worship of God to Dan and Bethel, but he still changed the worship of God to be like the pagans, offering his sons in human sacrifice (2 Chron 28:3). How do we move the ancient landmark of true worship to the living God?

There is a great cost when we twist the worship of God. For this reason, God's judgment is coming. He says to the princes of Judah, "I will pour out my wrath like water" (5:10). Even some of the leaders in the faithful southern kingdom will be affected. We don't want to get too close to idolatry. The Assyrians will utterly destroy northern Israel. Thousands of refugees from the north will enter into Jerusalem, and later Hezekiah will have to enlarge the walls of the holy city. Yet most will be lost – either killed or enslaved – forever blended into another land and culture, never to return. Judah is warned that God's wrath against idolatry can pour on them too. Wise and godly people will not play with sin, or temptation, or the world, or unbelief.

The Mercy of God's Crushing (5:11)

Sometimes God shows his mercy by crushing us to bring us back to himself. If we see a brother or sister pursuing sin, and God brings crushing trials into their life, we need to see what a mercy this is. When things get difficult and hard and crushing, it often keeps us from pursuing sin and filth.

> **Hosea 5:11** | Ephraim is oppressed, crushed in judgment, because he was determined to go after filth.

In the days of Hosea, northern Israel delayed in repenting, and was "crushed in judgment" under the foot of Assyria. She did everything she could to compromise, being oppressed (*lit* "exploited") as a vassal state, a slave of Assyria.

Israel didn't realize she was enslaved to Assyria and under God's judgment. Israel was immensely prosperous at this time. This is why the kings of northern Israel as well as King Ahaz of Judah would literally travel to Assyria and pay homage to their pagan gods. It seemed like the more they went after filth, the easier life was, for a while.

Israel didn't feel "crushed in judgment", but the fact is she eventually became a slave of Assyria. The kings of Israel went to Assyria in 732 B.C. to pay homage the Assyrian gods. Little did they know that a mere 10 years later, northern Israel would be utterly sacked by the Assyrians, crushed by the judgment of God.

Sin will take you farther than you want to go. We must be swift to repent, or we will be "crushed in judgment", that is, disciplined by God. The crushing God describes for northern Israel is not one of condemnation, but of correction (*cf* 5:15). God crushes to correct. He tears us that he might heal us (6:1).

As a leader, we must not put band-aids on God's crushing. We need to let God have his full work of humbling that sinner or saint. We also need to be of a blameless character. We must not go after filth but set the example for the believer. "Let no one despise you for your youth, but set the believers an example in speech, in conduct, in love, in faith, in purity" (1 Tim 4:12).

GOD'S INVITATION (5:12-15)

A godly leader will recognize certain moments and use them for the kingdom. That's what Hosea is doing.

An Invitation to Reflect (5:12, 14)

Reflect on the great love of God, who will first send you the moth of his chastisement before he sends the lion to take you out.

> **Hosea 5:12** | But I am like a moth to Ephraim, and like dry rot to the house of Judah.... **14** For I will be like a lion to Ephraim, and like a young lion to the house of Judah. I, even I, will tear and go away; I will carry off, and no one shall rescue.

God here is said to be one who sends hardship both like a lion and a moth. Donald Grey Barnhouse commented on this unusual way of God's love.

> This is the progress of God's love. He will not let us lose ourselves without exhausting all of the resources of his love. The moth may have eaten valuable possessions, but we can turn the rug around, we can put the couch against a wall where the ravages cannot be seen, we can move a lamp so that the light will not shine upon the destruction. Then he is forced to send the lion. With no warning at all, great trouble springs upon us like a beast of prey. Fear grips us. Our blood runs cold. Happy are we, if we realize that this is the Lord of love, who calls us to turn from the path where lions lurk and to run to the path of his will where no enemy can assail us.[55]

The unraveling of the northern kingdom of Israel is coming "like a moth" who eats holes in clothing. Like a moth, God will eat away at the things we treasure on earth because he wants us to seek him. Even evil, lost, unregenerate leaders can repent and find mercy in the Lord.

If leaders don't respond, he will send in lion like things that will utterly tear the society apart. When a person or a society is falling apart, or if there is some sort of life crisis or difficulty, as leaders, we need to help people see God's activity as a moth. He's bringing pain so that we will deal with our sin before it gets worse. If leaders don't lead people to repentance, God will take that society of people out. He'll let their hearts, their families, and their peace of mind be torn to pieces like a prey being attacked by a lion.

Let me say practically, that God is merciful to his people. He first sends discipline and chastening, for "the Lord disciplines the one he loves," (Heb 12:6). But if his child refuses to respond to chastening, he

---

[55] Donald Grey Barnhouse, *Let Me Illustrate: Stories, Anecdotes, Illustrations* (Westwood, N.J.: Fleming H. Revell, 1967), 20.

will bring them home. Remember Paul's warning, how if the Corinthians persisted in sin, God would take them home early from this earth. "That is why many of you are weak and ill, and some have died" (1 Cor 11:30). Reflect on God's mercy before it's too late!

An Invitation to Rest (5:13)

Godly leaders don't panic and go to the world for answers. We rest in the Lord's sovereign control of all things, and we are at peace no matter what the circumstances may be. We set a blameless example and take responsibility. We take time to seek after God so we won't be tempted to seek after the world. Israel did not turn to God, but instead turned to the nations to take care of them.

> **Hosea 5:13** | When Ephraim saw his sickness, and Judah his wound, then Ephraim went to Assyria, and sent to the great king. But he is not able to cure you or heal your wound.

What a mercy that "Ephraim saw his sickness and Judah his wound" (5:13). But Ephraim and Judah are like the man in the letter of James who "is like a man who looks intently at his natural face in a mirror. For he looks at himself and goes away and at once forgets what he was like" (Jas 1:23-24). Instead of seeking the Lord, Israel "went to Assyria and sent to the great king" for this spiritual disease. Who is this "great king"? One cannot be certain, but there were two great kings who ruled in Hosea's day: Tiglath-Pilezer III and his son, Shamaneser V. Hosea is saying, you should have gone to see the doctor, but instead you went to the circus. Will you be distracted at the circus from your pain? Yes. But you will eventually die. You need help that the world cannot give. The world cannot help you. You must seek the Lord. Isaiah cried out— "Seek the LORD while he may be found; call upon him while he is near" (Isa 55:6).

Many people attend a church for some time but still delay to answer the Lord, still delay to come. All day long he stretches out his hands and says: "Come unto me, and I will give you rest" (Mt 11:28). "Learn of me," he says. "Look unto me and be saved all the ends of the earth" he says (Isa 45:22). Yet there are so many who hear these beautiful words and will not seek the Lord for help. Many in the church today would rather seek relief in the world: entertainment, worldly pleasure, even alcohol and substance abuse. True believers seek the Lord. Those pretenders among God's people who insist on seeking relief in the world will ultimately be torn up and carried off in their own misery. The longer you continue to delay in accepting the mercy and salvation which he has offered you, the longer God will hide his face.

An Invitation to Repent (5:15)

God is merciful. If you seek him, he will return. But you have to humble yourself. He says:

> **Hosea 5:15** | I will return again to my place, until they acknowledge their guilt and seek my face, and in their distress earnestly seek me.

God's visible presence, the glory cloud, was so great that in the days of Solomon, at the building of the Temple, it is said that "the priests could not stand to minister because of the cloud, for the glory of the LORD filled the house of God" (2 Chron 5:14). But now, in the days of Hosea, God determines it is time to remove his presence from earth and return again to his place in the heaven of heavens. Earth was originally designed to be a Temple for God with Eden as his garden Temple. But since that time, beginning with Adam and Eve, God removed himself from his garden Temple. After the flood of Noah, Yahweh intended on dwelling with Abraham's family in the city where his name would be written (Jerusalem), and promised Solomon at the inauguration of the Temple: "I have consecrated this house that you have built, by putting my name there forever. My eyes and my heart will be there for all time" (1 Kgs 9:3).

Augustine said, "Do you wish to rise? Begin by descending. You plan a tower that will pierce the clouds? Lay first the foundation of humility."[56]

Certainly, if the Lord abandoned his own city for a time in order to chasten his people, he will chasten those who truly know him (Heb 12:6). God may hide himself from you in response to your stubbornness and pride. As Robert Murray McCheyne once put it: "God has last knocks."[57] Oh, how do you know, my friend, that this is not his very last knock on the door of your heart and that failing to get you to open the

---

[56] David Walls and Max Anders, *I & II Peter, I, II & III John, Jude*, vol. 11, Holman New Testament Commentary (Nashville, TN: Broadman & Holman Publishers, 1999), 86.

[57] Robert Murray McCheyne. "Christ a Merciful High Priest" in Works, vol 2 (New York: Robert Carter, 1847), 56.

door today, he may never come to knock again? Seek him now. "You will seek me and find me when you seek me with all your heart" (Jer 29:13).

You need to acknowledge your guilt and seek his face. It is when you seek him earnestly in your distress that you will find him! If you don't seek him now, the reality is, you may never find him. To be fully committed to seek the Lord earnestly with "all our hearts" means 100 per cent commitment. It means seeking his face and what gives him glory. It means rooting out anything that is bad – ruthlessly tearing down the high places and getting rid of the other gods in the midst of our own lives.

Conclusion

We as leaders need to lead the way. This passage is addressed to priests, and in the New Testament, we are all priests of the living God. We all have the ministry of reconciliation. Are you living a blameless life? Are you qualified to be a leader in this church? The qualifications for a Christian leader is merely to be living a consistent Christian life for the Lord.

The first time I visited my present church's meeting place at night, I couldn't see the sign. The lights were out. I passed the place up. When we designed a new sign, I made sure it was all lit up so people could see. Are you light for this world so that people can see Jesus? Turn to him now anew and afresh and surrender and let his light shine through you. As a leader, be a light that leads people to God and broken light that leads to compromise or confusion.

6 | HOSEA 6

RESURRECTED ON THE THIRD DAY

After two days he will revive us; on the third day he will raise us up, that we may live before him. Let us know; let us press on to know the Lord.
HOSEA 6:2-3

This sixth chapter is a message from the heart of Hosea. Remember, he has now seen the recovery of his own wife from harlot to faithful spouse. Hosea has witnessed the grace of God transforming her from her idolatry, and he has come to the conclusion that if Gomer can do it, then so can Israel. We are all Gomer in this story. We once were enslaved to sin and completely unfaithful to our Creator. But now we are redeemed from the slave market of sin. Hosea 6 is a call to celebrate that redemption with a particular focus on what Hosea did for Gomer and what God can do for Israel.

Hosea went to that slave market and purchased Gomer back and gave her a new life. Hosea's main point to Israel and to anyone who wants to know him is: Return and live. God says in Hosea 6:1a,

Hosea 6:1a | Come, let us return to the Lord...

Hosea's message is a call to faith in the Lord. There were so many unconverted in Israel. He calls Israel, who knows about the Lord, but does not know him tenderly and personally, to return. This is a call to repentance. Repentance is more than an act for a Christian. It is a posture.

Gomer in the slave market represents our lives before Christ. Gomer coming back home to Hosea in marital faithfulness represents true Christians.

THE PATHWAY TO RESURRECTION (6:1-3)

Hosea wanted his wife free from prostitution, dedicated and restored to himself. So God is calling out a people from this world to come to him. "He is not wanting that any should perish, but that all come to repentance" (2 Pet 3:9). Come! On this pathway to resurrection we *hear the invitation* to live and return to the Lord.

Hear the Invitation to Live (6:1)

Hosea 6:1a | Come, let us return to the Lord...

Hosea's first word in this message is a cry to "Come!" The idea is to come together with God. He's inviting you to a face-to-face meeting of mercy. There is good news beyond what you can imagine!

Jesus invites all who are burdened to come.

> Come to me, all you who labor and are heavy laden, and I will give you rest (Mt 11:28).

Jesus invited the children to come.

> Let the little children come to me, and do not forbid them; for of such is the kingdom of heaven (Mt 19:14).

Jesus invited his disciples to commune and dine with him after the resurrection.

> Come and dine (Jn 21:12).

The prophet Isaiah often invites Israel to come to the Lord.

Come now, let us reason together, says the Lord: though your sins are like scarlet, they shall be as white as snow; though they are red like crimson, they shall become like wool (Isa 1:18).

Come, everyone who thirsts, come to the waters; and he who has no money, come, buy and eat! Come, buy wine and milk without money and without price (Isa 55:1).

God's call to all of us is to "come!" Come to Christ and find full forgiveness, communion, and joy.

This Invitation is a Word of Return

Hosea 6:1a | Come, let us return to the Lord...

Returning to Yahweh implies a new posture of repentance and is a major theme of the book.[58] It's not only referring to unbelieving Israel coming back to the Lord in faith, but once they come, they have a posture of repentance due to their new life.

There's coming a time for Israel, when they will return to the Lord. He's going to have to take them into captivity for 70 years, and later Jesus comes to the earth, and he's stripped believing Israel down to basically 120 people in an upper room and gives them his Holy Spirit. And with the Spirit comes a great posture of hatred toward sin and a great love for the Lord.

All the grace of God flows through this return and repentance. For those who have repented and put their faith in Christ, we are told, "There is therefore now no condemnation for those who are in Christ Jesus" (Rom 8:1). That means "there is no sin so great, that it can bring damnation upon those, who truly repent" (WCF 15.4).

Simply put, God says, "Come" and you will be welcomed to him upon your return. This is Jesus' invitation: Come! He always delivers! Can I get a witness?

This Invitation is a Word of Healing

Hosea 6:1b | Come, let us return to the Lord; for he has torn us, that he may heal us...

---

[58] Garrett. 158.

God is like a doctor that wants to heal us, yet he must cut and tear into the flesh in order to cut out the tumor. He says God has torn us: literally "torn us to pieces." There's so much disease to cut into, God has to tear us to pieces. This is how the sinner feels when he comes to God: torn apart. The word for "tear" is fierce. It pictures a deep tear into the flesh with the sharpness of lion's teeth. [59] We see the image of a surgeon removing a tumor. There is a deep spiritual cutting to remove the spiritual cancer of sin in the soul. The picture of the Lord tearing us that he may heal us is one of a doctor opening up a wound to drain the puss and ugliness from the wound. In coming to Christ, we tear sin out of our lives, like the surgeon opening a wound and letting all the junk come out. Even after coming to Christ, we have dead branches that need to be cut and pruned from us (Jn 15:2).

It's like Pentecost, after Peter preached to the crowd, the Bible says the people were "cut to heart" by the Spirit. They were torn to pieces and said, "What shall we do?" (Acts 2:37). And Peter tells them, "Repent... receive the gift of the Holy Spirit" (vs 38). Inwardly and outwardly, they return to the Lord.

When we come to know Christ, we have a posture of hostility toward sin. This is the essence of repentance. We see sin as odious and filthy and contrary to the glory and majesty and holiness of God. When we heed his invitation, we receive real healing. God has torn us that he may heal us. This is certainly true in the medical profession. From our modern frame of reference, we can easily relate to this necessity. Sometimes a body part has to be taken off to save the entire body. Sometimes a bone must be broken in order to set it correctly. Everything outside of Christ is chaos and disease, but in Christ we are healed. We are whole in Jesus. What is the extent of this healing? It's a complete healing, a complete reconstitution. Look at how Hosea puts it.

This Invitation is a Word of Reconstitution

Hosea 6:1c | ...he has struck us down, and he will bind us up.

---

[59] Francis Brown, Samuel Rolles Driver, and Charles Augustus Briggs, *Enhanced Brown-Driver-Briggs Hebrew and English Lexicon* (Oxford: Clarendon Press, 1977), 382.

Here we have another illustration of repentance. It's like a death. God strikes us down in death to put us back together again and "bind us up". The idea is like a person be struck so hard, they die, and their body is mangled. God says, "I'll strike down your old life in death, and I will bind you up and put you back together so that you live." This is resurrection language.

We all know the mother goose rhyme:

Humpty Dumpty sat on a wall,
Humpty Dumpty had a great fall;
All the king's horses and all the king's men
Couldn't put Humpty together again.

But that's the thing. God can put you back together again. Remember when Jesus came to earth, all the hurting and outcasts fled to him. He came to "heal the brokenhearted and bind up their wounds" (Psa 147:3).

God loves you. This is his nature. He strikes you down only in order to bind you up. He may inflict pain upon you in arresting you, but he promises to care for your wounds. Listen to this amazing invitation to be brought back to life and healed. Now Hosea says it plainly in verse 2.

Meet the Author of Life (6:2)

On this pathway to resurrection, we *hear the invitation to life*, and then we *meet the Author of life*!

> **Hosea 6:2** | After two days he will revive us; on the third day he will raise us up, that we may live before him.

A Promise to Israel

It is clear that in its original context this passage describes the captivity and restoration of Israel, the people of God. Ezekiel develops this concept in his dry bones vision (Eze 37:1–14). The people of Israel would be cut down through the captivity, but they would be brought back and fully revived after the third day.

This is a word to Israel. God says, "I'll bring you out of your physical captivity." When they were taken to Assyria and later to Babylon, it was like the nation of Israel was dead. But remember in the days of Ezra and Nehemiah, God brought them back into the land.

While the mention of *the third day* would sound to Hosea's hearers as the mere equivalent of 'very soon', the prophet spoke more significantly than perhaps even he knew; for it is only in Christ's resurrection that his people are effectively raised up, as all the apostles teach us.[60] It is in Christ's resurrection that believing Israel and the church, grafted together into one people of God, find the ultimate restoration out of captivity. In Christ you have the true resurrection of the people of God.

A Promise to the Church

So this is not just a word to Israel, it's a word to the church. Augustine says:

> Hosea foretold the resurrection of Christ on the third day, but in the mysterious way that is proper to prophecy.[61]

It is impossible for the Christian to read this text and not see that it foreshadows Christ's resurrection on the third day. 1 Corinthians 15:4 asserts that Christ arose on the third day "in accordance with the Scriptures," and no other text speaks of the third day in the fashion that Hosea 6:2 does.[62]

This is a Messianic prophecy. The pronouns in Hosea's prophecy become vitally important and teach us about Christ's union with his people. It's not just about "them" but about "us". "Revive **us**...raise **us** up, that **we** may live..." Wait. I thought this was about Christ. It is. It's also about his people, his body. All God's people are united to Christ in his resurrection.

> WCF 26.1, "All saints are united to Jesus Christ their Head by His Spirit and by faith, and have fellowship with Him in His grace, sufferings, death, resurrection, and glory".

This is the prophecy of the resurrection of Jesus as the true Israel of God, that brings all God's people out of their captivity. On the third day when Christ was risen, sin's hold was broken and death was put to death for all of God's people.

---

[60] Kidner, 66.
[61] FC 24:123, Augustine, *The City of God*.
[62] Garrett, 158.

Let me just shout it out: Jesus Christ is risen from the dead, just as the Scriptures in Hosea prophesied. It happened. The tomb is empty. Death is defeated. He has overcome sin, death and hell. Death has no victory. The sting of death is gone. Death is now the entrance to life. He is risen! He is risen indeed!

Experience Life with the Lord (6:3)

Hosea 6:3a | Let us know; let us press on to know the Lord...

In Hosea 6:3, we get the reason we were invited and raised from the dead: to know the Lord. This resurrection is given to us that we might press on to know the Lord. What does this mean to press on?

Meaning of "Press on"

The word for press on has the idea of this zeal to pursue and overtake, like hunting an animal,[63] or like Paul persecuting Christians,[64] or like Jacob wrestling with God (Gen 32:22-32). Paul explains this verse in what is likely an allusion to Hosea in Philippians 3. Paul, what does Hosea mean to "press on"?

> That I may know Him and the power of His resurrection and the fellowship of His sufferings, being conformed to His death; [11] in order that I may attain to the resurrection from the dead. [12] Not that I have already obtained it or have already become perfect, but I press on so that I may lay hold of that for which also I was laid hold of by Christ Jesus. [13] Brethren, I do not regard myself as having laid hold of it yet; but one thing I do: forgetting what lies behind and reaching forward to what lies ahead, [14] I press on toward the goal for the prize of the upward call of God in Christ Jesus (Phil 3:10-14, NASB).

Hosea says: Press on to know Yahweh. Paul says: Press on to know Jesus. That's the goal for the prize of the upward call. This is what spiritual resurrection does. Christ lays hold on us to give us a knowledge of him. Let's press into what Christ obtained for us: a knowledge, a relationship with him.

---

[63] Keil and Delitzsch. *Hosea*, OT vol. 10, 64.
[64] Jeremiah Burroughs, "An Exposition of the Prophecy of Hosea," in *An Exposition of the Prophecy of Hosea*, ed. James Sherman (Edinburgh; London: James Nichol; James Nisbet & Co., 1863), 315.

Let's press on to know the Lord. We press on to know him more and more, from one degree of glory to a higher level, and then a higher level (2 Cor 3:18). We turn to what we know about God. We press on to know him more and more, even though right now even the best that we see is "in a mirror dimly" (1 Cor 13:12), knowing that one day very soon, when Jesus comes, and that perfect One arrives, we shall see him "face to face." The more you sincerely press on and pursue God, the more you will know of him, for "the pure in heart shall see God" (Mt 5:8).[65] What does it look like to press on to know the Lord? We can press on to know him more and more because he is as sure and steady as the dawn each morning. He is as sweet as the spring rains.

LIKE THE DAWN & GLORY CLOUD

> **Hosea 6:3a** | Let us know; let us press on to know the Lord; his going out is sure as the dawn...

You can press on and pursue Yahweh as your highest ambition, because his going out is as sure as the dawn (6:3b). The going out of the Lord was first understood as his glory cloud, the manifest presence of Yahweh among the people. Whenever the pillar of glory would move, the people would move and follow God wherever he took them.

Today, God's manifest presence is his indwelling Spirit. His going out with you in fellowship is as dependable as the rising sun. Actually, it's more dependable. The Lord is always there for you. He never leaves you. You may leave him, but he will never leave you. There is no one like him. Everyone and everything else changes. The Lord remains the same, like the sun that comes up every day. "Jesus Christ, the same yesterday, today, and forever" (Heb 13:8). His going out with you in fellowship is predictable and dependable.

LIKE THE RAIN

> **Hosea 6:3b** | ...he will come to us as the showers, as the spring rains that water the earth.

---

[65] Ibid.

Knowing God is a rain shower in a place it rarely rains, like the Middle East. The Lord's fellowship is like a river that never runs dry. Hosea says knowing God is like the showers that come after a long dry season, like spring rains that water the earth.

> There is a river whose streams make glad the city of God, the holy habitation of the Most High (Psa 46:4).

Never forget that you are the holy habitation of God by his Spirit.

THE INSTRUMENTS OF RESURRECTION (6:4-6)

Hosea 6:4a | What shall I do with you, O Ephraim? What shall I do with you, O Judah?...

Now God gives three instruments he uses for resurrection: his kind dealings with Israel, his Word through the prophets, and his unrelenting love. He also gives proofs of Israel's spiritual deadness: self-serving love, hardness to God's Word, and self-righteousness. These proofs are listed as a mercy to us. God's heart is never to shame a lost person. God didn't send his Son into the world not to condemn the world but to save it (Jn 3:16-18).

God gives the law to condemn us but to show us that we are dead and need Christ. The law is like an autopsy report. You shall not lie. You shall not lust. You shall not steal. You shall honor God above all else, and so on. Love God. Love neighbor. We don't have the ability to do these things. The Bible gives us the autopsy report: we are dead in trespasses and sins (Eph 2:1-3). One of the purposes of God's law is to give us the knowledge of sin, pointing us to our need for Christ as a school master (*cf* Rom 3:20; Gal 3:24). God gives us his law not to condemn us but to show that we are already condemned. Lost people are dead in their sins, in a spiritual morgue. The motive of God's heart in showing us this is not to rub our nose in our filth and sin. It is to show us the reality of the wretchedness we are experiencing so that we might put our hope in Christ and experience God's everlasting love.

We Need Awakening (6:4)

Hosea 6:4b | ... Your love is like a morning cloud, like the dew that goes early away.

Oh how we need awakening. The sinner outside of Jesus is cold and hard and dead. Often there is initially a tenderness, but if a sinner walks away from that, they get hardened.

Ephraim (the northern kingdom) and Judah (the southern kingdom) are both named. At one time they were united and were inhabited by the Lord of hosts, filled with his love. Now their love was cold. They had a form of love (Heb, *hesed*) to God, but it was fleeting, like clouds and dew. Like the morning fog, it vanished quickly. Like the dew on a sunny day, it disappeared suddenly.

God has been so kind to Israel but has received a very tepid response. "What shall I do with you?" obviously is a cry of frustrated love, borne of their refusal to "return" to God and pursue the knowledge of him. It's like Paul's exasperation to those at Rome:

> "Don't you see how wonderfully kind, tolerant, and patient God is with you? Does this mean nothing to you? Can't you see that his kindness is intended to turn you from your sin?" (Rom 2:4, NLT).

God wants to bless us, but he cannot until we return to him. Here, for the first time, we see Yahweh taking on role of the wounded husband whose love has been rejected after he has given all his love to his wayward spouse. This is the constant cry of God in the Scriptures:

> All day long I opened my arms to a rebellious people (Isa 65:2, NLT).

If you see God's mercy, you need to humble your pride and embrace his kindness.

God's Word Awakens Us (6:5)

There is a call here in Israel for a spiritual resurrection, and we find a powerful tool that God uses to wake us up is his Word. The people of Israel were spiritually dying and dead, and they need to be awakened. God sends out his messengers the prophets with his Word to cut open their hard hearts. God's Word is here likened to a sword in the hands of the prophets. God's Word is powerful to awaken you if you are without a true relationship with Christ.

God's Word Cuts

The prophets of Israel are described as hewning the people – literally *cutting the people to pieces* with God's Word.

> **Hosea 6:5a** | Therefore I have hewn them by the prophets; I have slain them by the words of my mouth…

Israel is said to be "slain" by God's Word. In response to Peter's Pentecost sermon, the people responded and "they were cut to the heart, and said to Peter and the rest of the apostles, 'Brothers, what shall we do?'" (Acts 2:37). God's Word cuts to the heart and touches our innermost being.

God's agents, the prophets, in Hosea are said to have faithfully and forcefully conveyed the cutting words of Yahweh's mouth. Their preaching are described as acts of 'hewing' or 'hacking' and 'slaying' the very souls of God's people, tearing them up.[66] We ought to rejoice that God's Word cuts us deep! *The Scripture is described as a sword that can cut us to pieces.*

"For the Word of God is living and active, sharper than any two-edged sword, piercing to the division of soul and of spirit, of joints and of marrow, and discerning the thoughts and intentions of the heart" (Heb 4:12).

God's Word Enlightens

> **Hosea 6:5b** | …my judgment goes forth as the light.

God's Word is also said to "go forth as the light…" (6:5). It shows the way. "Thy Word is a lamp unto my feet and a light unto my path" (Psa 119:105). If there is no response, there is a hardening. This is a true warning for the sinner! Spurgeon said,

---

[66] Hubbard. *Hosea*, 136.

The same sun which melts wax hardens clay. And the same Gospel which melts some persons to repentance hardens others in their sins.

Sadly, the people in Hosea's day were "hewn" by God's Word in a negative way. The Lord wanted to give them life through his Word. He offered them abundant life, but they dodged the sword of his Word. They therefore had to undergo the discipline of his Word. If our hearts remain unchanged by God's Word, like Israel we will have to experience the discipline of the curses of God's Word (Deut 30:1-10). Essentially if God's people do not respond in tenderness to God's Word they lose every earthly blessing so their soul can be saved for heaven.

Since God's Word is so powerful to enlighten us and awaken us, we should meditate, memorize, and hold on tightly to it.

> My son, be attentive to my words; incline your ear to my sayings. Let them not escape from your sight; keep them within your heart (Prov 4:20-21).

God's Love Awakens Us (6:6)

God lays down the bottom line – *"I want you to know my love. I don't need your sacrifices."* Those who think God needs religious ritual is for God are mistaken. God desires a heart of steadfast love and worship. Outward worship is great, but it can be faked. God wants you to worship him in steadfast, covenant love. The Lord, through Hosea, says:

> **Hosea 6:6** | For I desire steadfast love and not sacrifice, the knowledge of God rather than burnt offerings.

The northern kingdom is mainly unbelievers. The true believers have the responsibility to take back the true worship of God. John Calvin comments on this verse:

God desires to be worshipped differently than lost people imagine; the lost only display their outward ceremonies, and neglect the spiritual worship of God, which stands in faith and love.[67]

---

[67] John Calvin and John Owen, *Commentaries on the Twelve Minor Prophets*, vol. 1 (Bellingham, WA: Logos Bible Software, 2010), 231.

It is easy for us to criticize the false worship of other religions but much harder for us to recognize where our praise has degenerated into mere formalism. Let us regularly examine our worship to make sure it is in spirit and truth.

More than anything, God desires to demonstrate his steadfast love. The word "desire" denotes the very highest pleasure possible.[68] The thing God delights in most is expressing his unconditional, unrelenting, steadfast love (Heb, *hesed*) to sinners, and he wants that love returned rather than the outward activities of sacrifices.

If you have faith in the Lord, you will have a deep love for him. That's what he wants. He wants you to return his love for him. As Paul says in Philippians 3:

> I press on so that I may lay hold of that for which also I was laid hold of by Christ Jesus (Phil 3:12).

Christ laid hold of me that I may know him, so I'm going to lay hold of him for that purpose. In the same

OUR HOPE FOR RESURRECTION (6:7-11)

No one can raise themselves from the dead. Just like Gomer couldn't redeem herself from the slave market, God makes it very clear that those who are still in their sins cannot come to him on their own. It's very clear that all mankind can do well is break God's covenant. This is the emphasis of the last five verses.

Applied to the picture of resurrection at the beginning of Hosea 6, we might say that Israel's love for God is dead. The marriage is dead. Their only hope is resurrection. They are lost, and they can't reach God through rituals or mere intellectual knowledge. They need surrender.

So first we have an autopsy report on the marriage by looking at three covenants in the Bible that illustrated Israel's spiritual marriage covenant with God.

---

[68] W. E. Staples. "The Meaning of Hēpeṣ in Ecclesiastes," JNES 24:110–12. THAT, I, pp. 621–22.

We Need Hope, like Adam in Eden (6:7)

> **Hosea 6:7** | But like Adam they transgressed the covenant; there they dealt faithlessly with me.

Adam is the first man, the original sinner, and thus the model for Israel's unfaithfulness. Like Adam, we've committed spiritual adultery. We've put ourselves in a place where only God in mercy can help us. We need God to resurrect our spiritual marriage covenant with God. He still loves us.

We all know the story of Adam and Eve in the garden. Adam was given a covenant with God to enjoy everything in the garden, worshipping God in his garden temple. Adam had every sign of God's love there. He was told simply not to touch the tree of the knowledge of good and evil (Gen 2:15-17). It was what we might call the "God" tree. It symbolized that God alone is God and Adam had freedom to do all things except be his own god. We all know what happened. Adam crossed the line that day. He transgressed the covenant he had with God and faithlessly hid himself from God, running from accountability. If this were a marriage covenant, we would say that Adam and Eve were unfaithful. They committed spiritual adultery on God.

Since Hosea's hearers are extremely familiar with this story, the prophet says: "You're just like Adam. You are running from God: lost and hiding in your sins."

We Need Hope, like Jacob's in Gilead (6:8)

> **Hosea 6:8** | Gilead is a city of evildoers, tracked with blood.

Gilead is a mountain region with a very famous town: Peniel (Heb— "face of God"). Instead of Gilead being praised for her city that shines with God's face, it is here called the city of evildoers. God is saying to the northern kingdom: you've changed. You've gone back to being Jacob. You've taken on his worst characteristics—selfishness and cunning—without having his redeeming experiences—encounters with God.[69] Instead of faithfulness there is adultery, the spiritual marriage covenant is dead. Resurrection

---

[69] Garrett, 163.

needed. This is a message for the younger generation. You need a Gilead experience. You need to see the face of God.

We Need Hope, like Abraham at Shechem (6:9)

If Adam in Eden and Jacob in Gilead are not two of the most famous places of covenants in the Bible, then Hosea gives the third and most important place of covenant: Shechem, where God sealed his covenant with Abraham. It was that covenant place where God blesses Abraham's Seed, for through that Seed, our Lord Jesus Christ, "all the families of the earth shall be blessed" (Gen 12:3; *cf* Gal 3:7-9, 16). This should be the most celebrated and joyous mention of all the places of covenant, for it is here in Shechem that God "announced the gospel in advance to Abraham" (Gal 3:8, NIV), but God, through Hosea, says no! Those who govern Shechem today are not in any way faithful to the Gospel covenant of Abraham. Instead of giving out God's grace, they are thieves and robbers.

> **Hosea 6:9** | As robbers lie in wait for a man, so the priests band together; they murder on the way to Shechem; they commit villainy.

Instead of shepherding the people, the band together to hurt the people of God, hence the priests commit "murder on the way to Shechem." The word for "murder" means a premeditated, cold blooded, calculated taking of life. They may literally be taking the lives of God's people, but this is likely metaphorical. If it is metaphorical, it is not watering down the meaning but making it stronger. They are not merely taking away temporal physical life but everlasting life from the people.

Either way, the priests are certainly like bands of robbers who are taking advantage of their position to get something for nothing. The priests of Israel are completely out of control, using their position to commit villainy (every kind of sin imaginable). Instead of loving and teaching and caring for the spiritual needs of God's people, Hosea rightly compares them to *serial killers*. They should be dispensing mercy and grace to Israel, but instead they rob them of God's comfort, his promise, and of life itself.

Instead of celebrating God's covenant of grace with Abraham at Shechem, the priests make a compact with the devil to prepare the people of Israel for hell. Again, the current state of the priests in Israel gives us the same conclusion: Israel is in dire need of God's mercy. They have done everything to break his covenant of undying love. The marriage is over. It's nothing to celebrate but only lament.

Jesus: Our Only Hope for Resurrection (6:10-11)

God makes his final review of his marriage with Israel: they are spiritual whores. The marriage is over. The covenant is broken. The marriage bed is defiled.

It can't be us (6:10)

> **Hosea 6:10** | In the house of Israel I have seen a horrible thing; Ephraim's whoredom is there; Israel is defiled.

God's conclusion is that the spiritual adultery ("whoredom") of Israel is a disgusting atrocity that is in full view of God's eyes. God has examined his bride, the house of Israel, and concluded that his marriage to her is truly a horrible thing. This describes something that is inedible or unpalatable. It is something like a refrigerator surprise. "I wonder what is in this Tupperware—*Blecch!*" But here it is more. It is something so gross that you do not even desire to look at it. It is truly horrid.

The priests are guilty of causing Israel to be defiled, i.e. violated over and over again, like pimps in the sex trade. The reason for their defilement is spiritual prostitution—not fornication among men, but spiritual adultery against God in the form of idolatry. The priests have led the way to religious syncretism. With the golden calf worship, they have led the people to whoredom by moving the central place of worship in Jerusalem to Dan and Bethel. The altar in Dan is still standing to this very day.

The point is, Israel has made choices that have destroyed their marriage to God. God sees his marriage to the house of Israel and says, *I can't continue in covenant with you as you are. The marriage is dead, but I have a plan to resurrect it.*

It must be Jesus (6:11)

> **Hosea 6:11** | For you also, O Judah, a harvest is appointed, when I restore the fortunes of my people.

Our only hope is in the mercy of God. The Lord gives polar opposites as options: For Judah, a harvest of judgment is appointed that will actually lead to a restoration of the fortunes of Israel. Judah has a choice – to go down with northern Israel, or to be restored. In Christ, of course, there is no condemnation to anyone with genuine repentance and faith (Rom 8:1). The restoration of the fortunes of Israel are found in Christ. In him we have all spiritual blessings. Outside of Christ, there is only the harvest of God's judgment.

Judah is about to watch as the northern kingdom is slaughtered by the Assyrians but must not be too proud. Why? A harvest is appointed. Judgment is coming for all unbelievers. But for those who trust Yahweh an amazing restoration is coming. God will restore the fortunes of his people. God will have Israel ready for that time when the restoration begins: Messiah's coming.

Conclusion

What is the point? Spiritual resurrection cannot be manufactured in ourselves. "Can an Ethiopian change his skin or a leopard its spots? Neither can you do good who are accustomed to doing evil" (Jer 13:23). We are beyond self-help. We need a spiritual resurrection (6:2). We need a new nature. Our own attempts at real change and transformation will come to nothing. The ultimate restoration for Israel and for us is on the third day with Christ in his resurrection. Without this regeneration, we can only look forward to the harvest of God's judgment. In Christ, God restores the fortunes of his people. Our only hope is resurrection with the one who was raised on the third day.

Sam and Mr. Frodo

In the books and film series, Lord of the Rings, there is a scene with Samwise and Frodo Baggins. Frodo is hanging off a precipice of Mount Doom in Mordor, barely hanging on, dangling over the Crack of Doom, lava belching and splashing in the abyss below his exhausted body. Samwise is the humble savior figure, leaning over the cliff holding on to Frodo with all his might, keeping him from plunging into the abyss. The ring has been destroyed, but Frodo is hanging on for dear life. Frodo looks down, and you can see the utter despair on his face. He just wants it to end. He's tired of fighting. He's so exhausted, scarred by the ring's evil. He's set free, but he also wants it all to end. Sam almost reads his mind. He sees the despair in Frodo's eyes. He says, "Don't you let go Mr. Frodo!" And Sam and Mr. Frodo tighten their grip on each other. Sam thwarts death for Mr. Frodo and drags him off the precipice. What happens to Frodo? Frodo is saved. He's redeemed. He's free from the ring.

Jesus is the one who has broken the power of the ring over you. The deadly ring of sin's reign is destroyed. Jesus is like Sam: he's got his grip on you. He's looking at you saying, "Don't you let go! Don't you dare let go." The beautiful thing about our precious Jesus is that even if we do let go, he still carries us. He's got you! You may be exhausted by sin's effect on you from your former life. Its lingering effects are discouraging, making you long for heaven. But don't lose heart. Don't let go. You are dead to the ring's power. You are alive in Christ. You are raised from the dead with Christ.

You are tired, but you are safe. You are alive! You are not completely healed yet, but Jesus has you, and he will never let go of you. By his death, death and sin are defeated. And in the power of his resurrection, we walk in the power of his life far from that crack of Doom in Mordor. Jesus carries us to higher places.

7 | HOSEA 7
THE NET OF GOD'S LOVE

God As they go, I will spread over them my net;
I will bring them down like birds of the heavens.
HOSEA 7:12

Somtimes we humans have such vengeful spirits, that when we say, "God's gonna get you" we mean, "God's gonna judge you." "Look out: God is dangerous." And God is dangerous. And God judges the wicked. That's all true. But this passage is a bit different than that. I want to lift up a word to you today: "God's gonna get you." That's what Hosea says in chapter 7 of his prophecy. What he means is not: God's going to condemn you, but instead: God's going to get you with his net of love. That's what the prophet presents to us this morning.

Christ calls out, "Come to me and I will give you rest." He wants you. And he's going to get you. He's going to show you a beauty and a love so powerful that it can truly be called "irresistible grace". God loves to "get" dying sinners and *save* them! That's the theme of Hosea 7. Hosea is a holy prophet giving a message to people who are familiar with the Word, but have not sought God in faith, but remain in idolatry. People love sin instead of loving God, and they want to stay there.

Before we look at God's net of love in verses 11 and following, let's take a look at the broken down house of sin. Sin breaks everything. Paul Tripp noted:

> "Sin has ravaged the house that God created. Our world sits slumped, groaning for the restoration that can only be accomplished by the hands of the Builder. The bad news is that we're living in the midst of the restoration process. But the good news is that the divine Builder will not relent until his house is made new again. Someday we'll live forever in a fully restored house. In the meantime, Emmanuel resides with us today, returning his house to its former beauty."[70]

Yet in Hosea's day, Israel was kicking Emmanuel out and asking pagan gods like Baal to move in. And there was great destruction. In fact, the first ten verses of Hosea give us four pictures of sin's misery.

PICTURES OF SIN'S MISERY (7:1-10)

Sin is miserable! It leaves you stupid and blind. Look at the prophet Hosea's visual illustrations of sin in verses 1-10. In the first ten verses of Hosea 7, God gives four pictures of the brokenness of sin.

- Dying in the Hospital (7:1-2)
- Mocked at a Party (7:3)
- Burned in the Bakery (7:4-9)
- Forgetful in Old Age (7:9-10)

These pictures illustrate a very important fact: Sin makes you stupid. Idolatry impairs you. Addiction scars you. First, we go to a hospital. Those who choose to remain in their sin are like those dying in a hospital, refusing the cure.

Dying in the Hospital (7:1-2)

Hosea 7:1a | When I would heal Israel, the iniquity of Ephraim is revealed, and the evil deeds of Samaria; for they deal falsely...

---

[70] Paul David Tripp. *Broken-Down House* (Wapwallopen, PA: Shepherd Press, 2009), 9.

The scene is clear: the damage of sin is revealed, and God says: I will heal you. Isn't that amazing? We serve a merciful God. But Israel doesn't want healing.

Hosea 7:1b | ... the thief breaks in, and the bandits raid outside.

The cause of the beating is revealed for Israel: the neighbors that she trusted have been like thugs and thieves and have left her for dead. Egypt and Assyria have mugged her. That's what sin does. It promises friendship and relief. That's why God says,

> Do not love the world or the things in the world. If anyone loves the world, the love of the Father is not in him (1 Jn 2:15).

Sin will leave you stripped of joy, sad with suffering, and groaning for help. And God is ready to help. God is ready to any one of us. He is a God who is merciful and gracious in spite of our guilt and constant transgressions of his law. Though God would fully heal and restore Israel, they can't see it. Israel is like a patient in the hospital who doesn't want to hear the bad news.

Hosea 7:2 | But they do not consider that I remember all their evil. Now their deeds surround them; they are before my face.

God is here like a doctor who informs and educates the uninformed patient. Israel was sick unto death, but they didn't want to consider it or hear it. When we sin, it is right in front of God's face.

> There is no creature hidden from his sight, but all things and naked and open to the eyes of him to whom we must give account (Heb 4:13).

Have you been living like God doesn't see, hear or know? Are we successful at hiding anything from God? Shockingly, we unconsciously convince ourselves that if we excuse our sin, God must not see it. No! Never! Like Israel, we too can sometimes forget the Lord. We live as practical atheists, as if we can pull the wool over God's eyes. The Bible is clear that God searches our hearts at all times.

> The LORD looks from heaven; he sees all the sons of men. From the place of his dwelling he looks on all the inhabitants of the earth; he fashions their hearts individually; he considers all their works (Psa 33:13-15).

> God would surely have known it, for he knows the secrets of every heart (Psa 44:21).

So God sees it all, and actually, we know he's dealt with it all at the Cross. Look at the work of Christ.

> Look to Me, and be saved, All you ends of the earth! For I am God, and there is no other (Isa 45:22, NKJV).

Our brokenness is so great, we are like the dying person as the hospital. Don't run from your diagnosis. The Word of God reveals the sin in your heart so that God might heal you.

Mocked at a Party (7:3)

We go from the hospital to a party. It's a circus atmosphere. The leaders of northern Israel in Hosea's day are entertained by the people's sin. They mock them and laugh because they are merely using the people.

> **Hosea 7:3** | By their evil they make the king glad, and the princes by their treachery.

The king and princes are glad, literally entertained, by Israel's sin.[71] If the church is going to thrive again, godly leaders need to kick the circus out of the church. What is the answer for Israel and for us? We should be a people who take sin seriously. We should blush at sin. Sin is no laughing matter. John Bunyan, writer of the Pilgrim's Progress book said:

> Sin is the dare of God's justice, the rape of His mercy, the jeer of His patience, the slight of His power, and the contempt of His love.

Sadly, sometimes the church can be turned into the circus. Ministers who do not have their hearts for the sheep will always fleece the sheep. They may turn church into a circus. Charles Spurgeon said,

> A time will come when instead of shepherds feeding the sheep, the church will have clowns entertaining the goats...Unless our faith makes us pine after holiness and pant after conformity to

---

[71] The history of Israel at this time is important. There was a succession of four kings in northern Israel during the time of Hosea (Zechariah, Shallum, Menahem, and Pekahiah). One of them reigned as short as one month. They all did "did what was evil in the sight of the LORD" (2 Kgs 15:24). Each king dedicates himself more fully to Baal worship. One after another of the kings had short reigns because God was not at all entertained by the sin these leaders allowed in Israel.

God, it is no better than the faith of devils, and perhaps it is not even so good as that. [72]

You know as well as I do, that sin mocks us. It mocked Israel. As God's people we cannot be entertained by sin. We cannot be amused by what Christ died for. If you are without Christ today, come out of the circus. Leave the world behind. Don't be entertained by the sin Christ died for. Let him take your sin. He was nailed to the cross for it. He's rich in mercy. He'll bury your sin in the depths of the sea (Mic 7:19)!

Burning in the Bakery (7:4-8)

We go from the hospital to the circus, and now to the bakery. Hosea says people's hearts are sinful in two ways: like leaven sinful desires spread, and like a hot oven sinful desires burn. Sin cannot satisfy the heart of man. Only the Lord can. The heart of man burns but cannot be satisfied without the Lord. Sin promises everything, but it leaves you unsatisfied.

BURNING HEARTS DESCRIBED

In Hosea's day, the people's hearts were compared to hot ovens. They wanted to be satisfied. They turned to the world, but nothing could tame the fire in their hearts.

> **Hosea 7:4** | They are all adulterers; they are like a heated oven whose baker ceases to stir the fire, from the kneading of the dough until it is leavened.

Here is a baker who does nothing while leaven spreads through the dough. This illustrates the kings of Israel who do nothing while evil (leaven) spreads through society and the court.[73]

The entire society, from the kings to the people, are aflame with lust, like a heated oven that is so hot, the baker doesn't need to stir the fire. The picture is of how sin just burns through families and societies, while the leaders do nothing.

BURNING HEARTS DEBASED

The leaders of Israel didn't have a solution. They looked at sin like a big joke.

---

[72] C.H. Spurgeon. *A Golden Prayer*, Sermon 1391, December 30, 1877.
[73] Garrett, 169.

> **Hosea 7:5** | On the day of our king, the princes became sick with the heat of wine; he stretched out his hand with mockers.

On the royal holiday (on the day of our king), perhaps one of the three annual pilgrimage feasts in Israel (Exo 23:14-17), the leaders of Israel get drunk – to the point of sickness. They were definitely sick with the heat of wine. The king and leaders of Israel are made fun of by those around them but end up laughing with them. They stretch out their hand, laughing hysterically with the mockers (7:5).

Burning Hearts Destroy

The king and princes are laughing, but it's no laughing matter. One after another all the kings of Israel will fall because they never seek divine help. The people have hearts like an oven, ready to dethrone the king if they don't get what they want.

> **Hosea 7:6-7** | For with hearts like an oven they [the people of Israel] approach their intrigue [plot to overthrow the kings]; all night their anger smolders; in the morning it blazes like a flaming fire.
> ⁷ All of them are hot as an oven, and they devour their rulers. All their kings have fallen, and none of them calls upon me.

Hosea 7:5-7 is talking about a 20-year period when four Israelite kings were assassinated (2 Kgs 15). From Shallum to Pekah, they were all kings who burned like with lust for the world and her pleasures and treasures. They were all quickly assassinated. God says, "All their kings have fallen, and none of them calls upon me" (7:7b).

This is what sin does. Sin is like a raging, flaming fire burning down a house. Sinful desire burns within them like a hot oven. If a leader can't give them what they want, they take him down and put up another king. It's like that game Whack-A-Mole, but it's Whack-A-King. The end result is that all Israel's kings will be dethroned and fall. Why such short reigns? Because none of them walk with the Lord in faith, calling upon him. Instead they all call upon God's enemies, the nations that surround them. Sin always ends up in destruction.

Burning Hearts Distracted

The baking metaphor continues, and we find out that Israel is not baking with the wrong ingredients, mixing with those who have no desire to serve the true and living God.

Hosea 7:8a | Ephraim mixes himself with the peoples...

Hosea 7:8a references the mixing or intermarriage of the people of Israel (Ephraim) with pagan peoples. Israel should have been a light to the nations. Instead, Israel was influenced by their evil practices.

It should be noted that the forbidden mixing has nothing to do with ethnicity. This text forbids the marrying of unbelievers and is in no way a pretext for racism. Instead, this is a text that is reflected in the theology of the New Testament.

> Do not be unequally yoked with unbelievers. For what partnership has righteousness with lawlessness? Or what fellowship has light with darkness? [15] What accord has Christ with Belial? Or what portion does a believer share with an unbeliever? [16] What agreement has the temple of God with idols? For we are the temple of the living God (2 Cor 6:14-16).

I've encouraged my children that the most important thing about marriage is that the potential mate has a rich relationship with Jesus. Don't let sin distract you from what is most important. A person can be talented, beautiful, winsome, but if they don't know Jesus they are not for the child of God.

Burning Hearts Placated

The baking metaphor continues, and we find out that Israel is not only baking with the wrong ingredients, in addition he's only half-baked. The sinner must never be placated by half-hearted faith.

Hosea 7:8b | ... Ephraim is a cake not turned.

What effect did Ephraim's mixing with the world produce (7:9)? Ephraim is like a cake not turned – "half-baked." Not fully there. How sad is it to have the truth and still not be saved? To know the Gospel but not be born again? That's not only sad, it's scary. Going to church does not make you a Christian any more than going to McDonald's makes you a hamburger. Don't be half-baked. Embrace Christ completely. There is no half-way salvation. Christianity is not about mere superficial knowledge, but it's about knowing Christ and walking with him. If you don't have some kind of walk with Christ, you are not a Christian.

Now let me make an application, because there are some who are truly born again, but you are not growing as you ought to. Sin will keep a true Christian stunted in growth. Listen, if you are not yet in Christ, come. Sin can't satisfy, but Christ can.

> Come, everyone who thirsts, come to the waters; and he who has no money, come, buy and eat! Come, buy wine and milk without money and without price (Isa 55:1).

The baker is ready to satisfy you. Christ alone can satisfy the desires of your burning heart.

Forgetful in Old Age (7:9-10)

Israel had come to time in their history as a nation that they are compared to an old person getting taken advantage of.

> **7:9** | Strangers devour his strength, and he knows it not; gray hairs are sprinkled upon him, and he knows it not.

Old age is really hard. Everything wears out. Everything is deteriorating. Your hair either turns gray or turns lose. Teeth fall out. Your joints get replaced. Your eyes get dim. And your memory gets weak. How sad it is if you are young and this happens to you.

> It's like we go into a retirement home, and we suddenly realize that the nurses and doctors who are charged with caring for you are actually robbing you. They sell most of your clothes, they raid your bank account, and they cut you off from family and friends. The Assyrians had been like strangers who had taken advantage of "old" Israel. G. Campbell Morgan wrote of this blindness,

> Sin is like signs of old age, which are obvious to others, yet undiscovered by ourselves; and we go on, and on, and on, the victims of ebbing strength, becoming degenerate, without knowing it! We are blind to the signs which are self-evident to onlookers. There is no condition more perilous to our highest well-being than this of unconscious spiritual atrophy.[74]

---

[74] G. Campbell Morgan, *Hosea: The Heart and Holiness of God* (1948; reprint, Grand Rapids: Baker, 1974), 57.

Israel wasn't that old as a nation, but suddenly, they are in hospice care. One of the worst things about getting old is losing your memory. It was of Israel as it had been of Samson so many years before:

> He did not know that the Lord had left him (Jdg 16:20).

Sin makes God's people forgetful. The apostles saw it as part of their responsibility to remind the disciples of Christ of things that they already know. Peter often wrote the same things, because we are so forgetful:

> For this reason I will not be negligent to remind you always of these things, though you know and are established in the present truth (2 Pet 1:12).

We need reminders because we are so quick to forget.

Hosea 7:10 | The pride of Israel testifies to his face; yet they do not return to the Lord their God, nor seek him, for all this.

Sin can make you so deaf that you can't hear God anymore. God is always talking to people through their conscience according to Romans 1. But people "suppress the truth" because they love their unrighteousness. God is talking, but sin has deafened people. God testifies to Israel's face, but they are so deafened by sin they can't hear.

God is called the Pride, or Glory, of Israel. As an act of mercy, God testifies to the face of northern Israel. He's revealing their sin to them. He speaks to them in compassion and love. They need to return to the Lord and seek him or they will perish.

Wow, isn't God so loving and amazing? Remember when he spoke to you in your sin and drew you to Christ? What amazing love! Yet Israel won't listen even though God has laid out his argument so clearly through his prophets. This is really addressed to the dear people who have not yet fully surrendered in faith to the Lord. Don't ignore God. He's talking directly, facing you. Hear him. Listen to him. Don't wait. Don't waste your life. God is ready to receive you: open arms. He testifies of your need. He shows you that you've forgotten what you know. Come back to him. He's ready to receive you.

God is the doctor is ready to heal you.

He's ready to take you out of the circus and give you dignity.

He's the baker who is ready to satisfy you.

He's your glorious Creator who is ready to rescue you from spiritual dementia.

PROMISES OF GOD'S LOVE (7:11-16)

We don't have much time, but I want to take the last few verses together and describe Gods net of love. God loves you. Maybe you are lost, like most of Israel. Maybe you are a child of God who has wandered into the world. The net of God's love will catch you. Look at the picture of the net of God's love in verses 11-12.

A Promise of Capture (7:11-12)

> **Hosea 7:11-12** | Ephraim is like a dove, silly and without sense, calling to Egypt, going to Assyria. **12** As they go, I will spread over them my net; I will bring them down like birds of the heavens; I will discipline them according to the report made to their congregation.

The first thing we see is the people described. They are described as birds (doves) who are silly and senseless.[75] Birds are generally stupid. They may be pretty, and sound pretty, but they are not bright creatures. The term "birdbrain" is not used in flattery. God is describing a group of people who were familiar with God and his Word through his prophets, but the sin that we just described has made them stupid. Can we all agree, that sin hardens us so that we don't come to God when he is the divine Doctor who can heal us? He's offering salvation, but we've passed him by. The people of Israel were birdbrained for going to Egypt and Assyria for help.

There have been dozens if not hundreds of dear people young I have known who heard the Gospel but went away unchanged. Instead of seeking Christ, they sought the world. It's birdbrained to do that. Sin makes a person hard hearted and spiritually silly and

---

[75] In the same way as the dove, Israel makes pretty sounds to the Egyptians and the Assyrians—predator nations. And these nations are completely aware of Israel's weakness. But there is God, looking down on this silly dove, flitting this way and that looking for strength in other nations. And being above, he is ready to drop the net on their flight at any time. A net on a dove during flight adds up to an imminent and destructive crash.

senseless. To be blunt: sin makes a person stupid. Don't be hardened by sin. Surrender to Christ.

The key to these verses is the word "discipline" in 7:12. The Hebrew word (יָסַר – *yacar*) is used for the instruction and training of children. God calls sinners as a father calls his children. He's calling them because he loves them. This is a very tender word.

> **Hosea 7:12** | As they go, I will spread over them my net; I will bring them down like birds of the heavens; I will discipline them according to the report made to their congregation.

Instead of rejecting Israel, he is embracing her. God is treating the country as a dear but disobedient little one. We know there was a remnant there mostly because God is addressing them as children. He rejects those who are not his children, but to those who would respond, God is calling out a people who he is drawing to himself. God has a net of love he has cast out to catch you.

The point of 7:11 is that we are weak for a reason. We are like a weak dove, and this is a good thing. When we are at our weakest, it is then that we see God's love in the details. We often think God is punishing us, but Hosea's message here is that God refuses to punish us, but he does want to train and instruct us. When we are crushed, we distinctly feel our need for Christ. Here is something for which we ought to rejoice: it is in our weakness that we fall into God's **net** of love. We are so weak that we cannot escape it. God says that he will now pull northern Israel down, and he will capture them with great ease:

> **Hosea 7:12a** | As they go, I will spread over them my net; I will bring them down like birds of the heavens.

God says: "When I hear them flocking together, God says, I will catch them."[76] We ought to all know by now that we cannot outrun God. He will throw the net of his love over us and catch us. I'm so glad he will. God will easily catch us, like frail birds of the heavens. God easily captures us. The motive of God's discipline is to draw us near to himself. Sometimes God's capture of us is sudden, like a frantic bird captured in a net.

---

[76] Boice, Ibid.

> **Hosea 7:12b** | I will discipline them according to the report made to their congregation.

The report, or news that reached their assembly was that Egypt would protect Israel. How absurd! The world cannot help you. Don't trust in the world. So God brings his net of love to capture us. He takes us down.

Perhaps right now you are caught in the net of trials, difficulties, discouragement and even perhaps danger. This is not a net of confusion or malice. This is God's net of love. If you are lost, he wants to bring you to Christ. If you are a believer, he wants to draw you closer to him. If God brings you down and crashes you with his net of love in order to save you, don't think he'll withhold trials once you are a child of God.

> God has no pleasure in afflicting us, but he will not keep back even the most painful chastisement if he can but thereby guide his beloved child to come home and abide in the beloved Son. – Andrew Murray

A Promise of Compassion (7:13-15)

In verses 13-16, we see what happens if you don't turn to God when he gets you with his net.

The Lost's Misery (7:13)

When God calls you, you need to respond. If not, there is no hope for you.

> **Hosea 7:13** | Woe to them, for they have strayed from me! Destruction to them, for they have rebelled against me! I would redeem them, but they speak lies against me.

God always sends his net of love into your life and you feel like it's the end. You feel like a trapped bird. But God has caught you in order to perform heart surgery. If you are lost, he wants to save you, like he wanted to save Israel. Some came responded to that net of love in faith. But for those who don't: **Woe to them**. There is no hope outside of a loving God. Don't look elsewhere.

> ...whoever comes to me I will never cast out (Jn 6:37b)

God's Mercy (7:14)

When shattering circumstances come into our lives, we get disoriented, like a trapped bird. We sometimes get the disposition of a beggar, envisioning God as a stingy, selfish version of ourselves. Let me say God is not like us! He is generous and gracious. He's ready pour out oceans of blessings upon you out of his free mercy and grace. Israel didn't understand God's goodness but envisioned him through the lens of a Baal worshipper. Look at their worship practice.

> **Hosea 7:14** | They do not cry to me from the heart, but they wail upon their beds; for grain and wine they gash themselves; they rebel against me.

When northern Israel did cry to God what was wrong? They saw God with the heart of a Baal-worshipper. We don't need to beat and gash ourselves for God to answer our prayers. God's people in northern Israel wailed to God on their beds, begging God as if the Almighty had more important things to do than answer their prayers. Come to Christ dear sinner. Forsake your Baal-worshipping heart.

God's people of old were trying to convince God to be good to them. Dear saints, we know we don't need to convince God to be good. God is already infinitely good. God sent the Assyrians to northern Israel in order to free them from their slavish hearts. They were lost and had hearts enslaved to idols.

Listen to the language God uses to describe their approach to God: "for grain and wine they gash themselves; they rebel against me" (7:14b). Those who worshipped Baal were taught a very wrong view of God. One commentator, Derek Kidner, explains:

> Approach to God was made with self-pity and piling on the pressure by self-mutilation, more like the blackmail of a child's tantrum than a genuine heart-cry. That was how one prayed to Baal.[77]

In order to get Baal's attention, you could bang your head against a tree or gash your body in self-mutilation. God's not like

---

[77] Derek Kidner, *The Message of Hosea: Love to the Loveless*, ed. J. Alec Motyer and Derek Tidball, The Bible Speaks Today (England: Inter-Varsity Press, 1976), 74.

stingy Baal. God's not like you or me. He is generous. Dear sinner, you already have his attention. Come to Christ, and you'll have all things.

> He who did not spare his own Son but gave him up for us all, how will he not also with him graciously give us all things? (Rom 8:31).

And if you are in Christ, you have his attention already. He's never once taken his eye off of you. Listen to the words of one of the Psalms and then to Isaiah:

> He will tend his flock like a shepherd; he will gather the lambs in his arms; he will carry them in his bosom (Isa 40:11a).

God is eager to care for us. We don't have to act like Baal worshippers to get his attention. Yet it seems we are really good at acting like Baal worshippers, screaming and doing crazy things when we don't get what we think we need.

THE WORLD'S INSANITY (7:15)

Isn't it silly to use the strength God gave you to serve the world?

> **Hosea 7:15** | Although I trained and strengthened their arms, yet they devise evil against me.

Look at the love and gifts God poured out to Israel, and what does he get in return? Rebellion. Northern Israel uses the strength God gave them: all their armies and people, to rebel and devise evil against God. God's many blessings to his people in northern Israel actually served to forget God and become self-reliant, taking God's many gifts to them for granted. Don't let that happen to you. If you are without Christ, turn to him now.

A Promise of Change (7:16)

> **Hosea 7:16a** | They return, but not upward [to the Most High]...

God's net of love catches us to change us. You must surrender totally to him for God to change you. Israel didn't want to surrender. They didn't want to repent. They were plenty religious but not to God, the Most High. "They return but not upward..." Outwardly we might have said Israel repented. They seemed sorry. They cried.

They lamented. But they weren't repentant. Their heart was still hard. They did not return upward, to the Most High God.

The kind of repentance that is marked by the true and living God results in a transformed heart that lives out a transformed life. Any other repentance is not from the Most High. It's so easy to settle for sorrow that doesn't change us and doesn't last. Hosea illustrates false repentance with two pictures: a crooked bow and a wagging tongue.

False Repentance is like a Crooked Bow

> **Hosea 7:16b** | ...they are like a treacherous bow...

A treacherous or crooked bow is unreliable, never hitting the intended mark. Don't be like that. Don't shoot arrows aiming at the wrong target. Our Aim to surrender all to Christ. If you are aiming for anything else: personal peace, pleasing parents (or people of any sort), then you are aiming with a crooked bow. Aim to surrender all for Christ because he is worthy.

False Repentance is like a Wagging Tongue

> **Hosea 7:16c** | ... their princes shall fall by the sword because of the insolence of their tongue. This shall be their derision in the land of Egypt.

The princes and leaders of Israel talked a lot about repentance, but never surrendered to God. They were all talk, no action. The person who merely talks about how sorry he or she is and makes a huge show of repentance is missing the point. Certainly, there is an outward repentance, but long prayers or great tears do not equal real repentance. Those things surely accompany godly sorry, but the most important part of repentance is that it is God-centered. God requires a change of the heart, not a wagging of the tongue.

Let me illustrate it. The prodigal son awoke and didn't just tell others around him how sorry he was. He got up and went to his father and confessed to God and his father that he was a great sinner and didn't deserve to be a son, but only a servant. Real repentance gets up, and by faith, goes home. Look how the father responded.

> While he was still a long way off, his father saw him and felt compassion, and ran and embraced him and kissed him. [21] And the

son said to him, 'Father, I have sinned against heaven and before you. I am no longer worthy to be called your son.' ²² But the father said to his servants, 'Bring quickly the best robe, and put it on him, and put a ring on his hand, and shoes on his feet. ²³ And bring the fattened calf and kill it, and let us eat and celebrate. ²⁴ For this my son was dead, and is alive again; he was lost, and is found.' And they began to celebrate (Lk 15:20-24).

Come to Christ! What happens when God captures you with his net of love? He will save you to the uttermost. He'll give you his Spirit. And you'll never be separated from the love of God in Christ.

> Who shall separate us from the love of Christ? Shall tribulation, or distress, or persecution, or famine, or nakedness, or danger, or sword?... ³⁷ No, in all these things we are more than conquerors through him who loved us. ³⁸ For I am sure that neither death nor life, nor angels nor rulers, nor things present nor things to come, nor powers, ³⁹ nor height nor depth, nor anything else in all creation, will be able to separate us from the love of God in Christ Jesus our Lord (Rom 8:36-39).

Conclusion

Sinner come home! Praise God for Hosea 7. In this chapter God reiterates the entire theme of the prophecy: his unstoppable, amazing, relentless love is like a net that God is throwing at you. He captures you in order to bring you home. Come home sinner, come home! And you know if you've come home, God's got you. He will capture you with his net of love. He's gonna get you, that he might save you. He will hold you fast.

8 | HOSEA 8-9

THE SINFULNESS OF SIN

For they sow the wind, and they shall reap the whirlwind
HOSEA 8:7

Sin is so incredibly destructive, but it often presents itself as a delightful surprise, full of wonder and happiness. In C.S. Lewis' series on the *Chronicles of Narnia*, in his book *The Magician's Nephew*, Digory and Polly find some cryptic words written in stone:

Make your choice, adventurous Stranger,
Strike the bell and bide the danger,
Or wonder, till it drives you mad,
What would have followed if you had!

Do you remember what happened when the young boy named Digory did "strike the bell?" Later he regrets having done so because it results in Jadis being freed. You remember her, don't you? She's better known as the evil White Witch in *The Lion, the Witch and the Wardrobe*! I don't believe the characters in that story were too fond of it being "always winter and never Christmas."

We all remember before we knew Christ when it was "always winter and never Christmas". Oh, how painful and ugly that life of sin was. We were bribed by Satan. We were enslaved. But we came out of Egypt! We left our slavery behind.

Saint, don't ever forget the deception you were under when you were lost. Sin is the great deception. By eating the forbidden fruit, Adam and Eve thought they would gain everything but instead they lost everything. They were deceived. What is deception?

Deception – concealment or distortion of the truth for the purpose of misleading; the act of representing as true what is known to be false; a stratagem; a trick; something that is done to mislead.

The message in Hosea 8 is all about sin's deceit. It just tells you lies. It promises life but gives you death. Beware! Stay far away.

I remember a anchor lady on television who was doing a morning show on dogs. She loved dogs. Most dogs are amazing. She was comfortable with her dogs, but this dog was a pit bull. She treated that Pitbull like she would her Labrador at home and touched her nose to the dog's nose. That lady trusted the dog, but didn't realize you can't do that with a Pitbull. And that dog attacked her. She had to have reconstructive surgery.

That's how sin is. You think it's fine until it ruins your life. Sin is more dangerous than any animal, even the most vicious animal. Don't go near it. That's why the Prophet Hosea says: Blow a trumpet of warning.

SIN'S DECEIT (8:1-14)

Blow the Trumpet (8:1)

Sin is so deceptive and blinding that we need to warn against it. It doesn't advertise its danger. God tells Hosea to lift up a trumpet and warn Israel to turn from their sin to the Lord, but they won't listen.

> **Hosea 8:1** | Set the trumpet to your lips! One like a vulture is over the house of the Lord, because they have transgressed my covenant and rebelled against my law.

God blasts trumpets and sends vultures as a harbinger, a warning of what's coming if you choose sin. A vulture is a bird of prey. Sin, like a vulture wants to eat you for lunch. Sin sends people to hell every day. All who are without Christ are circled by the vultures of eternal destruction. "The wages of sin is death" (Rom 6:23).

The Assyrians were about to destroy Israel. God sends the prophet Hosea to blow a spiritual trumpet through his preaching. He wants Hosea, and us today, to blow a trumpet for the lost.

Blow the trumpet. Who are you praying for? Who are you speaking to? God's given you a mouth. Don't be silent.

The Spirit of God is God's trumpet to the soul. No one can be saved without an epiphany: the lost must wake up to faith in Christ. They must come to yield their life to the absolute Lordship of Christ.

How will they hear without a preacher? (Rom 10:14, KJV).

Sin Makes God's Enemies your Friends (8:2-4)

Israel thought they knew God, but they had no victory.

Hosea 8:2 | To me they cry, "My God, we—Israel—know you."

Israel things they can be friends with God and friends with the world. The greatest deception is for people to think they know God, yet they do not experience his presence and power. There are people who go to church, and yet are very acquainted with the enemy. They are satisfied with an outward commitment to the church but have little or not walk with God.

> You adulterous people! Do you not know that friendship with the world is enmity with God? Therefore whoever wishes to be a friend of the world makes himself an enemy of God (Jas 4:4).

SIN PROMOTES BAD CHOICES

Hosea 8:3 | Israel has spurned the good; the enemy shall pursue him.

The enemy was overtaking them. Assyria and Egypt had so much power that little Israel had to pay them taxes. Israel boasted of a great big God, but he seemed powerless. If God seems powerless to you, you may not know him.

Israel spurned what they knew was right. They thought it would really work out. They thought the pagan nations would take care of them. Nope. The enemy always brings hurt.

Israel's enemy was Assyria. Yours is the devil. He hates you. He loves blinding the lost. Sin will try to introduce you to God's enemies and try to have you call those enemies your friends. Listen the devil is not your friend.

> The thief comes only to steal and kill and destroy. I came that they may have life and have it abundantly (Jn 10:10).

If you are in Christ, the enemy has no victory over you.

> Greater is he that is in you, than he that is in the world (1 Jn 4:4).

Without Christ, the enemy will take you to hell with him. If you are lost, the vultures of sin are circling you. Don't let the devil win.

But woe to you, O earth and sea, for the devil has come down to you in great wrath, because he knows that his time is short!" (Rev 12:12).

Christ is our victory. Don't let the devil win. If you are lost, come to Christ. Yield to the voice of the Spirit and come! If you are saved, blow the trumpet. Mark the enemy. Raise a victory banner over the enemy. He is defeated!

> He [God] disarmed the demonic rulers and authorities and put them to open shame, by triumphing over them in him [Christ] (Col 2:15).

Don't spurn Christ, who is our ultimate Good. He is victory. He triumphs over all enemies. Sin will blind you so that you make good friends with the devil. Don't fall for that.

SIN PROMOTES BAD PEOPLE

Hosea 8:4a | They made kings, but not through me. They set up princes, but I knew it not.

Israel chose some really bad people to be their kings. As God's people we need to surround ourselves with godly leaders. We all need help. We can't live the Christian life alone. We need each other. That's how discipleship works. Submit yourself to godly people. Lost people don't want accountability. Christians beg for accountability. We are teachable. We want correction. We need godly leaders in our lives so that we can see where we need to grow and change.

Christians want godly leaders. You need the church. You need fellowship. If you despise the fellowship of the saints, something is seriously wrong. We cannot grow as lone rangers. We cannot afford to neglect the right kind of accountability in our lives. Two bad models Christians follow that gets them in the most trouble is (1) try to go it alone and live the Christian life in isolation, or (2) allow the wrong leaders or influences to guide your life.

Follow the example of Paul. He had a Barnabas in his life. He had someone above him who was stronger. He had someone to whom he was accountable. He also had someone below him who he was helping. He had a Timothy. Who is your Barnabas? Who is your Timothy?

Sin Gives False Peace (4b-6)

The pagan nations attributed their wealth to their gods of prosperity, the chief of which was their calf gods. Those idols were their saviors.

> **Hosea 8:4b-6** | With their silver and gold they made idols for their own destruction. ⁵ I have spurned your calf, O Samaria. My anger burns against them. How long will they be incapable of innocence? ⁶ For it is from Israel; a craftsman made it; it is not God. The calf of Samaria shall be broken to pieces.

God hates Samaria's golden calf. And he hates any idol you may have. The false gods of today are even more tantalizing than the golden calf, but they are just as empty. Sin is deceitful because it makes you think everything is ok. It gives you false peace. That's what the golden calves did.

There is a false peace attached to sin. It seems like everything is ok. Sin deceives us by convincing us that what happens to others will never happen to us. Let's say that we know that ten times out of ten, people get caught when they sin. Ten times out of ten, and yet sin convinces us that we are going to be the exception. We know that for the history of time people who have done this sin have suffered for it. But sin says "Wait a minute. Are you kidding me? You're going to be different. You're going to get away with this!" Just like the serpent said to Eve, "You shall not die."

The calf-gods promised health and wealth but had no power. Health and wealth were the whole point of the fertility cult.[78] They offer gratification, but they cannot deliver. This is clear to any modern thinker. This kind of worship seems absurd. Yet the lessons are ever relevant. Anything we love in place of God is an idol. You do

---

[78] Garrett, 183.

not have to say, "I am worshiping an idol," to be actually worshiping an idol. We can say that we are worshiping God but be worshiping an idol—our money, homes, cars, position, wife, husband, children—even when we associate those things with God or think of them as the gift of God.

Sin Promises Good, but Delivers Hurt (8:7-10)

Sin deceives us by creating in us a desire for that which we know can only hurt us. A little voice says, "Go ahead." And we stupidly go ahead even though we know we're going to suffer for it. When Eve looked at the fruit she saw that it was good to look at, good to touch and good to taste. So she took it and she ate it and we've been taking and eating ever since. We're no different even though we know that every time we take and eat it will hurt us. That's the deceitfulness of sin.

Regardless of the way we sow seeds of sin in our lives, Hosea gives us a warning: sin is like a hurricane. Sow to the wind and you will reap the whirlwind.

> **Hosea 8:7-10** | For they sow the wind, and they shall reap the whirlwind. The standing grain has no heads; it shall yield no flour; if it were to yield, strangers would devour it. ⁸ Israel is swallowed up; already they are among the nations as a useless vessel. ⁹ For they have gone up to Assyria, a wild donkey wandering alone; Ephraim has hired lovers. ¹⁰ Though they hire allies among the nations, I will soon gather them up. And the king and princes shall soon writhe because of the tribute.

Sometimes sin is like a hurricane in our lives. Only once in my life have I been close to the eye of a hurricane. It was August 29, 1985. Hurricane Elena. There were 14 fatalities and three billion dollars in damage.[79] I was a young boy at the time, and we lived in Louisiana, near the Gulf of Mexico and Lake Ponchatrain. While we were there a hurricane moved up the coast passing within ten or twenty miles of where we were living. As news of the approaching

---

[79] Thomas C. Frohlich. "From Elena to Katrina: These Are the Costliest Hurricanes to Ever Hit the US." USA Today. September 14, 2018. Accessed February 14, 2019. https://www.usatoday.com/story/money/2018/09/12/most-destructive-hurricanes-of-all-time/36697269/.

storm reached our community, many people evacuated and left the state. Our family stayed, and I will never forget the storm.

The wind began gently, then grew to a mammoth intensity; the rains were torrential. The streets surrounding our house in Ponchatoula, Louisiana were flooded. Trees snapped at the high winds. Rain was pouring sideways. As I stood watching the storm, I asked myself what could ever produce winds of such intensity and violence. Nearly one million people in low lying areas from New Orleans, Louisiana to Tampa, Florida were forced to flee.

I still do not know everything that goes into the making of a hurricane. But because of the book of Hosea I do know what produces similar scenes of spiritual force and destruction. It is not big things. It is "little" things, like forgetting God and then trusting in our own perception of things. This neglect seems small at the beginning, but it grows big and ends in destruction.[80] You might say it is the "respectable sins" that cause the hurricanes in our lives. I can tell you from personal experience and from observing some very sad situations that this is absolutely the case.

Hosea 8:7 tells us that sin is like a hurricane, "For they sow the wind, and they shall reap the whirlwind." Israel planted little sins like forgetting and neglecting God, and it resulted in the destruction of their nation. Since "wind" in Scripture often refers to what is empty or illusive, the proverb means that Israel has sown the seed of meaningless religion along with their little "respectable sins" and shall therefore reap a harvest of judgment at the hand of God.[81]

Sin Tries to Replace God (8:11-14)

Here's another lie of sin: You can be satisfied by the things of this world. Sin will make you think you can replace the great Almighty God with the little bitty things of this earth. What a lie.

> **Hosea 8:11-14** | Because Ephraim has multiplied altars for sinning, they have become to him altars for sinning. ¹² Were I to write for him my laws by the ten thousands, they would be regarded as a strange thing. ¹³ As for my sacrificial offerings, they sacrifice meat and eat it, but the Lord does not accept them. Now he will remember their iniquity and punish their sins; they

---

[80] Boice, 63-64.
[81] Ibid.

> shall return to Egypt. ¹⁴ For Israel has forgotten his Maker and built palaces, and Judah has multiplied fortified cities; so I will send a fire upon his cities, and it shall devour her strongholds.

Verse 14 says it all: "Israel has forgotten his Maker and built palaces." God burns down the cities. That's a mercy for God to take away from us whatever takes the place of God.

The lost sinner always has a substitute god. We are all worshippers. We have to give ourselves to serve something.

Nothing, absolutely nothing is glorious enough to replace the living God in your life? Everything else leads you back to slavery. God alone can set us free.

I like C.S. Lewis and what he said, our desires are too puny. We want little, tiny things when we can have the great big God.

> It would seem that our Lord finds our desires not too strong, but too weak. We are half-hearted creatures, fooling about with drink and sex and ambition when infinite joy is offered us, like an ignorant child who wants to go on making mud pies in a slum because he cannot imagine what is meant by the offer of a holiday at the sea. We are far too easily pleased. – C. S. Lewis

What deceit! You will never be satisfied by more of this world. Christ alone can satisfy.

SIN'S DESTRUCTION (9:1-17)

What sin takes from you. In chapter 9 of Hosea, we see a total decimation of the nation due to their sin. Here Israel loses everything: joy (9:1-2), protection (9:3-6), sight (9:7-9), livelihood (9:10-14), and God's Blessing (9:15-17).

Sin destroys. When God says "don't", he's saying don't hurt yourself. Choose to sin, choose to suffer. A common saying expresses it well: sin will take you farther than you want to go, keep you longer than you want to stay, and cost you more than you want to pay.

Hosea 9 is the prophecy of Israel's destruction. It's like reading the record beforehand. They didn't plan on forfeiting their lives and livelihood for sin, but it happened. It always happens. The devil seeks to kill and destroy. He was a murderer from the beginning. He wants to end you. Sin brings deep suffering. The devil wants to keep the lost from true joy. Look at what Israel loses.

A Loss of True Joy (9:1-2)

Hosea 9:1 | Rejoice not, O Israel! Exult not like the peoples; for you have played the whore, forsaking your God. You have loved a prostitute's wages on all threshing floors.

Israel was at one of the most prosperous times in their history, but God says, "Stop rejoicing! You are a harlot. There's nothing to rejoice about." Instead of sin benefitting them, they became slaves and "played the whore" and "forsook their God". Real joy comes from God.

It's like they're going back to Egypt. They are getting ready to go back into slavery, though this time it will be Assyria. God says: don't rejoice. The pleasure of sin is short lived. You can only "enjoy the pleasures of sin for a season" (Heb 11:25). Then sin brings rottenness to your bones. It will strip you of everything. God says, stop rejoicing at your sin and take it seriously. It may give you pleasure now, but it's setting you up for misery.

When Israel forsook their God, they settled for earthly things which cannot satisfy.

Hosea 9:2 | Threshing floor and wine vat shall not feed them, and the new wine shall fail them.

Without Christ there can be no lasting satisfaction. The lost will always be lacking because they don't have Christ. Christ alone satisfies. The most satisfying bread and finest wine cannot compare to the face of God. Bread and wine will not feed them – that is, it will never be enough. It will run out because of the coming famine. New wine shall fail them. God's pleasures, on the other hand, are inexhaustible. No earthly joy ought to occupy the place of God in our heart.

God doesn't just tell you to turn from sin, he offers you himself. He is like living, eternal water to satisfy your thirst (Isa 5:13, 41:17, 44:3, 49:10, 58:11; Psa 42:1-2, 63:1; Amos 8:11) and wine to make your heart glad (Psa 104:14-15). Listen to God's offer:

> On the last day, the climax of the festival, Jesus stood and shouted to the crowds, "Anyone who is thirsty may come to

me! **38** Anyone who believes in me may come and drink! For the Scriptures declare, 'Rivers of living water will flow from his heart.'" **39** When he said "living water," he was speaking of the Spirit, who would be given to everyone believing in him... (Jn 7:37-39a).

A Loss of God's Protection (9:3-6)

In Hosea 9:3-6, we have a picture of removal from the promised land and a prophecy of the coming Assyrian military invasion. The only way to cleanse the nation of its idols is through drastic measures, tearing down their divine hedge of protection.

REMOVED FROM THE LAND (9:3)

The immediate effect of God's withdrawal from Israel's affairs is to cede the land to their enemies. Not only famine, but military defeat is on the horizon. God is Israel's strength; if he is withdrawn, they will be taken from their land.

> **Hosea 9:3** | They shall not remain in the land of the Lord, but Ephraim shall return to Egypt, and they shall eat unclean food in Assyria.

Taken away from the land of the Lord, they'll get new homes as servants of other nations like Egypt and Assyria. It won't be like having momma's home cooked meals. They'll eat foreign food in a foreign land that is unclean, not conforming to the Levitical food laws.

REMOVED FROM THE TEMPLE (9:4)

No longer will they worship God in Jerusalem. Remember Jerusalem is the place where God manifested his presence in a fiery pillar of his glory. God says through Hosea:

> **Hosea 9:4** | They shall not pour drink offerings of wine to the Lord, and their sacrifices shall not please him. It shall be like mourners' bread to them; all who eat of it shall be defiled; for their bread shall be for their hunger only; it shall not come to the house of the Lord.

Sacrifices of wine and lambs will not please the Lord because they will be nonexistent in a foreign nation. It will be like a perpetual funeral with everyone eating mourners' bread. Mourners are not permitted to worship because in Israel you could not offer bread if you had touched a dead body (Lev 21:11). They are like those who are defiled and ceremonially unclean.

Their bread is for their hunger only since they will not be coming to worship at the Temple, the Lord's house in Jerusalem. They will be so far removed from their home place of worship, scattered among the pagan nations that surround them.

Removed from the Yearly Pilgrimage Feasts (9:5)

Not only are God's people removed from their land and the Temple worship in Jerusalem, but of course they can no longer attend the three nationwide festivals, especially the Feast of Tabernacles.

> **Hosea 9:5** | What will you do on the day of the appointed festival, and on the day of the feast of the LORD?

Though northern Israel had given themselves to the worship of the golden calves, they also thought themselves to be faithful to Yahweh. God says, "I'm taking you far away from your homeland, and you will not be able to celebrate you pilgrimages," specifically, the Feast of Tabernacles (*cf* Lev 23:39–43, where it is twice called a "feast of Yahweh").

Removed from their Homes

Israel would lose their land, their Temple, their festivals, and obviously, they would also lose their homes when the Assyrian military would decimate them.

> **Hosea 9:6** | For behold, they are going away from destruction; but Egypt shall gather them; Memphis shall bury them. Nettles shall possess their precious things of silver; thorns shall be in their tents.

The people of the northern kingdom are trying to get away from destruction, running away from the Assyrians, but they cannot ultimately escape.

The land of Egypt that God took them out of, many will now return to as refugees. The city of Memphis, the ancient capital of Lower Egypt[82] is said to bury them. Literally, some will die there instead of in Israel.

---

[82] Lange & Schaff, et. el, *Hosea*, 76

They will be taken captive, never again to return home. While they are gone, nettles and thorns will overtake their precious possessions. The land will overgrow their tents. Their homes and cities will become desolate habitations – ghost towns.

Isn't it amazing how people are willing to risk everything for their sin? Marriage, home, reputation, their relationship with God, their jobs – so much is at stake, yet they are willing to lose it all. This is why God brings discipline into our lives. It is so important that we respond to God's chastening love. God's motive is to give us a satisfied soul in him. Idols can never satisfy. If God sends pain through discipline, it is only for our good. He is merciful in taking away our idols in order to give us the very best of himself.

A Loss of Spiritual Sight (9:7-9)

Sin steals our joy and remove God's protection, but it also blinds us from seeing God and hearing his voice. He wants to reveal the beauty of his presence to us, but idols will steal our sight every time.

BLIND TO GOD'S WORD

> **Hosea 9:7-8** | The days of punishment have come; the days of recompense have come; Israel shall know it. The prophet is a fool; the man of the Spirit is mad, because of your great iniquity and great hatred. ⁸ The prophet is the watchman of Ephraim with my God; yet a fowler's snare is on all his ways, and hatred in the house of his God.

God's people are blind to his presence, his Word, his prophets, and their own sin. They are blind to God's Word as now, the prophet (the man of the Spirit) is a madman (9:7). God's prophets are men of the Spirit. They speak the message from the Yahweh's Spirit, the Holy Spirit. We must understand that the lost person has a sinful nature that is hostile and hateful to God.

> The natural person does not accept the things of the Spirit of God, for they are folly to him, and he is not able to understand them because they are spiritually discerned (1 Cor 2:14).

The lost person is blind to the Gospel. "The god of this world has blinded the minds of the unbelievers, to keep them from seeing the light of the gospel of the glory of Christ" (2 Cor 4:4).

BLIND TO THEIR OWN SIN

Now Hosea reveals how northern Israel was blinded by idols in the first place: they were introduced to idolatry way back during the book of Judges in Gibeah.

> **Hosea 9:9** | They have deeply corrupted themselves as in the days of Gibeah: he will remember their iniquity; he will punish their sins.

To say the "days of Gibeah" is to say "the days of the judges." This is referring to Judges 19-21, in which the most depraved act in Israel took place. This was the time when "everyone did that which was right in their own eyes." And truly it was the most depraved time. When you give yourself to sin, you lose your conscience. You lose your ability of spiritual sight. You can't hear God's voice!

A Loss of Your Livelihood (9:10-14)

We now turn again to a familiar theme: sin will take away all that makes life good: it steals our worship, our family, and our financial stability and so much more.

LOSS OF WORSHIP (9:10)

God calls us from our mother's womb. There is that general call of the Gospel that goes into all the world. God called Israel to come to him. But when they gave themselves to sin and rejected him, they lost the possibility of repenting and worshiping God. He gave them over to their idols.

> **Hosea 9:10a** | Like grapes in the wilderness, I found Israel. Like the first fruit on the fig tree in its first season, I saw your fathers....

God delighted in finding Israel in the time of the patriarchs: Abraham, Isaac, and Jacob. His love was so great, he describes himself as a desert person, like a nomadic shepherd, who delights in finding grapes in the wilderness. When God found Israel in his youth, he took special pride and joy in his people. God delighted the patriarchs (fathers): Abraham, Isaac and Jacob like a desert person delights in the first fruit on the fig tree in its first season. What a joy to know the delight of God over our souls (Zech 3:17). He loves us.

Yet Yahweh's delight turns to dismay and discipline at the apostasy of Israel.

Hosea 9:10b | ... But they came to Baal-peor and consecrated themselves to the thing of shame, and became detestable like the thing they loved.

They worshipped the Baal god at the city of Peor, renamed Baal-peor where 24,000 of God's people died of a plague that God sent as a result of their deviant worship. Baal-peor holds a prominent place in Israel's geography of shame (Num 25:1-5; Deut 4:4; Psa 106:28; cf Josh 22:17).[83] It was here that the people coming out of Egypt were introduced to the cultic rituals of fornication in Baal worship for the first time.

The prophet Balaam has been hired to curse Israel, but instead pronounces a blessing over them. According to the account in Numbers 25, the Israelites, begin to engage in Baal worship, a part of which was to fornicate with the Moabite women. A plague is sent from the Lord and 24,000 die.

Phinehas, grandson of Aaron, with a desire to stop this idolatry, rises up with a spear, follows a Baal-worshipping Israelite man into a tent and thrusts the spear through both the man and woman, who were evidently fornicating to the idol Baal. Finally, after 24,000 dead, the plague stops.

Why such destruction? The Israelites had become detestable like the thing they loved (Baal, the fertility god which included the worship of money and pornography). Now in their later history, they are losing everything because of it.

The saddest truth about idolatry, is that we can become detestable like the thing we love. You become what you worship. Whatever we esteem in our hearts, we begin to bear that image in our souls and in our lives. Greg Beale said his book *We Become What We Worship*:

> What people revere, they resemble, either for ruin or for restoration. — Greg Beale[84]

The is the paradigm of worship. We become what we worship. Baal and all idols are worthless. When you worship worthless

---

[83] Hubbard, 174-175.
[84] G. K. Beale. *We Become What We Worship: A Biblical Theology of Idolatry* (Downers Grove: IVP Academic, 2008), 16.

things, you become worthless. You lose everything. It's like Paul said in Romans 1:25,

> They exchanged the truth about God for a lie and worshiped and served the creature rather than the Creator, who is blessed forever! Amen (Rom 1:25).

Loss of Family (9:11-13)

The loss that sin brings will eventually extend to your family.

Hosea 9:11-13 | Ephraim's glory shall fly away like a bird— no birth, no pregnancy, no conception! **12** Even if they bring up children, I will bereave them till none is left. Woe to them when I depart from them! **13** Ephraim, as I have seen, was like a young palm planted in a meadow; but Ephraim must lead his children out to slaughter.

Israel's idolatry results in the loss of their children. Israel's glory is his children (9:12a). Children bring a special glory: respect, joy, financial prosperity if they are brought up to work hard. But all this glory will fly away like a bird with no birth, no pregnancy, and no conception (9:11b). In other words, the prophet is predicting a sudden end to the happy and prosperous life enjoyed by the people of the northern kingdom. Remember the book of Hosea is written during a time of great financial prosperity and material comfort. They were having families as large as they wanted. The warning God gives through Hosea seems so far from possible. God says the children brought up in northern Israel will be bereaved (taken away in death) from their parents in some cases till none is left. How might this happen? Primarily through war with Assyria. This sense of safety and prosperity can be taken away fairly quickly. The love and legacy they have in their families can be snatched away.

At one time Israel's youth had so much potential, like a young palm planted in a meadow. But now it is the citizens of northern Israel that are leading their children out to slaughter (9:13). How are they leading their children to slaughter?

(1) Through the Baal cult. The mothers and fathers are offering their sons and daughters as human sacrifices like the pagans. (2) Through war with Assyria.

Today the war is spiritual (Eph 6:11-12ff). Our children's souls are at stake. We must lead our kids in holiness, kindness, love, and conviction. We need to see our children truly follow Christ. Going to church is not enough.

LOSS OF FINANCIAL STABILITY (9:14)

Sin promises so much. It give a false sense of security, especially when it comes to finances. Northern Israel was experiencing unprecedented prosperity at the time of the prophet Hosea. But the prophet prays for God to take away this false security from them. What is Hosea's prayer? What Hosea prays for is not the march of ravaging armies or the swinging of their swords but the cessation of birth and infant nurture. Their financial prosperity was about to ripped away.

> **Hosea 9:14** | Give them, O Lord— what will you give? Give them a miscarrying womb and dry breasts.

Hosea's prayer was: Lord don't allow them to bare children. The very sign of prosperity was to have a big family. Now they would be left with barren mothers who could not nurse their babies. This was indicative of the horrible loss of their entire livelihood. Can you testify that sin will wipe you out emotionally, physically, and spiritually, and financially? It will strip you of your livelihood. Can anyone hear testify that if you are in Christ, that he can "restore the years that the locusts have eaten"? (Joel 2:25).

A Loss of God's Blessing (9:15-17)

The entire nation is being put into captivity. The curses of unbelief are being placed upon the people. From the very beginning of the founding of Israel as a nation, there were warnings that clearly outlined the blessings and cursings of God's covenant (Deut 28-29). Trust in Yahweh and be blessed. Forsake him, and you lose everything. That's essentially the summary.

THE BLESSING OF GOD'S LOVE REMOVED (9:15)

The people have rejected God, so he agrees to withdraw his divine and everlasting love with a divorce decree.

> **Hosea 9:15** | Every evil of theirs is in Gilgal; there I began to hate them [*metaphor for divorce*]. Because of the wickedness of their deeds. I will drive them out of my house. I will love them no more; all their princes are rebels.

Gilgal is where they rejected God as King and chose Saul. If you reject God's love, all that is left is God's wrath, and righteous hatred and indignation. Hate? But isn't it true that "God is love" (1 Jn 4:8)? God's love is spurned by Israel in exchange for idols. God's love now ends in some sense, says Hosea, not because God has ceased to love but because his love has been rejected.[85] It is also important to consider that the word hate here is being used as a metaphor for divorce (Deut 24:3). God explains when and where he began to consider divorcing his people: in Gilgal they rejected God as King and chose Saul (1 Sam 15:12-26).

Yet even in this warning God has a pattern of mercy. He threatens divorce so that they will repent and turn back to him. We see this right here in a couple more chapters:

> How can I give you up, Ephraim? How can I hand you over, Israel? ...My heart is changed within me; all my compassion is aroused. 9 I will not carry out my fierce anger, nor will I devastate Ephraim again. For I am God, and not a man— the Holy One among you. I will not come against their cities (11:8-9).

This pattern exists, Yahweh says, because "I am God, and not a man," that is, God's patience is a chief distinction between God and man. The book itself closes with a climax of God's solution to Israel's apostasy.

> I will heal their apostasy; I will love them freely, for my anger has turned from them (14:4).

They deserve hate, but God will give them love. God is saying: don't pass up my love!

The Blessing of God's Provision Removed (9:16a)

When a believer backslides, not only do they lose the experience of God's love but also his provision. Everything financially may begin to dry up.

> **Hosea 9:16a** | Ephraim is stricken [*blighted, withered*]; their root is dried up. They shall bear no fruit.

---

[85] Beeby. *Grace Abounding: Hosea*, 124.

Don't you know that every blessing and good "gift is from above and comes from the Father of lights" (Jas 1:17)? Forsake him, and he may remove your provision.

THE BLESSING OF GOD'S SEED REMOVED (9:16B)

Assyria was going to wipe Northern Israel out, and war means a great loss of children.

> **Hosea 9:16b** | Even though they give birth, I will put their beloved children to death.

What does this mean? It means that the Lord will allow the foreign armies to invade. Children will die in the Israel – Assyria will have no mercy. Both parents and their beloved children will be put to death by the Assyrian soldiers. God says, I will put them to death, because he is the Sovereign who sends the armies.

But understand, God did not order things this way. God desires "all people to be saved and to come to the knowledge of the truth" (1 Tim 2:4).

Israel chose to leave their children unprotected by choosing sin over God. Dear saints, don't think like your old life. You only thought of yourself. Married people, think of how important your marriage is to the testimony of the church and to your children. Work hard to give your children a godly environment where the Spirit of God is at work.

THE BLESSING OF A GOOD TESTIMONY REMOVED (9:17)

Instead of Israel proclaiming the good news to the nations, they are wanderers among the nations. They are the refugees!

> **Hosea 9:17** | My God will reject them because they have not listened to him; they shall be wanderers among the nations.

The prophecy of Deuteronomy 28:65's curses had comes to pass:

> And among these nations you shall find no respite, and there shall be no resting place for the sole of your foot, but the Lord will give you there a trembling heart and failing eyes and a languishing soul (Deut 28:65).

God rejects them (at least temporarily) since they have not listened to his Word and his prophets. No longer do backslidden believers give light to the nations. Instead they are "wanderers" among the nations.

SIN'S DEFEAT (COL 2:14)

We know in the New Testament that sin is defeated. Look what Jesus did for you on the cross! God made you alive together with him, having forgiven us all our trespasses, 14 by canceling the record of debt that stood against us with its legal demands. This he set aside, nailing it to the cross (Col 2:14). The reason that sin is so odious, ultimately is because it steals from God's glory. God created us for his glory. And Christ came into the world to "destroy the works of the devil" (1 Jn 3:8). He came to defeat sin.

Hosea 9 is not the end of the story for northern Israel. Jesus comes into the world and defeats sin on the cross. He specifically goes after northern Israel.

Jesus comes in the New Testament to rescue those remaining from the northern ten tribes of Samaria. One of the great stories is the Samaritan woman. She is the leftover of the northern kingdom. What happens? Jesus confronts her sins, and she tells her whole village about Christ. The ultimate solution to the great mess of Hosea's time is solved by the Messiah. This northern Israelite woman, like a New Testament version of Gomer: a woman who had five husbands is redeemed by Jesus. She proclaims him as Messiah. What does she do? She goes and tells the whole village who Jesus is! Many Samaritans from that town believed in him because of the woman's testimony, "He told me all that I ever did" (Jn 4:39).

Conclusion

Sin is defeated. Death is dead. Christ has won. God kept his promises not only to the Samaritans of Northern Israel, but to all of us today. Christ has defeated sin! He is the great Victor.

9 | HOSEA 10:1-15
THE TRUE VINE

Israel is a luxuriant vine that yields its fruit.
HOSEA 10:1

The heart of man is inexhaustible until we truly know Christ. Until that time, we are searching for something to fill it, and we fill it with idols. When we don't get our idols, we get angry, depressed, confused, messed up! We're not just a mess, but a hot mess!

Only Jesus Christ can fill and satisfy the human heart. Whether you are here saved or unsaved, you need Jesus. St. Augustine said it well: "You have made us for yourself, O Lord, and our heart is restless until it rests in you." God made food to remind us that Christ is our living bread (Jn 6:51). God made water to remind us that Christ is the living water who quenches our thirsty soul (Jn 7:39). Blaise Pascal famously said: "There is a God-shaped vacuum in the heart of each man which cannot be satisfied by any created thing but only by God the Creator, made know through Jesus Christ." [86]

This is the theological context of Hosea 10. Before we knew Christ, we were all so hunger, so desirous to be filled, and we could not find satisfaction till we met Jesus. He cleanses us, adopts us, empowers us, gives us a future and hope. Praise his name. What we find in Hosea 10

---

[86] Pascal, *Pensees*, 113.

is a very common theme in Scripture: No amount of riches, fame, pleasure, earthly comfort or even religious activity can ever come close to satisfying the human soul. Ancient Israel had all these things and was still empty. They had so much money and comforts at the time of the prophet Hosea, but they were so lost. All their earthly riches left them horrible enslaved to idols, with empty souls, broken homes. God was there with open arms, ready to cleanse them, forgive them, restore them, and bring them into his glorious Kingdom, but they wanted to fill their souls themselves. They got robbed as a result. Nothing on this earth, no matter how good or legitimate it is, can ever take the place of Jesus.

Are you in a place in your Christian walk, where you sense the fullness and satisfaction of your Lord and Savior? Are you drinking from the well that never runs dry? I think all too often we put up with idols in our lives that Christ died for. It ought not so to be. If there is anything keeping you from a full connection with Christ, be very open to the Holy Spirit. He's got an epiphany for you. He wants to cut into your heart. He wants to pour truth into you and open your eyes. Let the Spirit move deeply in you. Right now, open your heart. The people of Northern Israel had hard hearts. He tells them their great need verse 12.

> **Hosea 10:12** | Sow for yourselves righteousness; reap steadfast love; break up your fallow ground, for it is the time to seek the Lord, that he may come and rain righteousness upon you.

Instead of having a growing faith in Yahweh, the true and living God, the people of Israel were fascinated and thrilled with their earthly riches and worldly comforts. Their hearts were hard and cold, but they were keeping themselves distracted from their emptiness by all the gadgets and comforts of their time. In so many ways, they had the same disease that we in America have: affluenza, defined in the dictionary as:

> Affluenza: a psychological malaise supposedly affecting wealthy young people, symptoms of which include a lack of motivation, feelings of guilt, and a sense of isolation.

The people of Hosea's day were connected to so many superficial and meaningless, temporary comforts, that those very comforts left them completely disconnected from God.

DISTRACTED BY IDOLS AND DISCONNECTED (10:1-11)

How relevant the message of Hosea 10 is for us today. We are quite disconnected by a myriad of distractions. In order to get connected with Christ, we have to first evaluate how and why we are disconnected. A great example of this is ancient Israel. They perceived everything was fine because of their affluence. They were blinded by their prosperity and comfort.

The Perception (10:1)

> **Hosea 10:1** | Israel is a luxuriant vine that yields its fruit. The more his fruit increased, the more altars he built; as his country improved, he improved his pillars.

Our Lord Jesus was of course perfectly familiar with Hosea 10, where Israel is called a "luxuriant vine". He must have had this and other passages in mind when he said in John 15:

> I am the true vine, and my Father is the vinedresser. ² Every branch in me that does not bear fruit he takes away, and every branch that does bear fruit he prunes, that it may bear more fruit... ⁵ I am the vine; you are the branches. Whoever abides in me and I in him, he it is that bears much fruit, for apart from me you can do nothing (Jn 15:1-2, 5).

Israel's perception was dead wrong. They thought they had everything with their riches, but they actually had nothing of value. Do you know what all the riches of Israel amounted to? Nothing. They were without God. So all their riches, and their peace treaty with the pagan nations around them meant nothing. They were about to be smashed with the hammer of Assyria. They were about to lose their riches, their family members, their land, their identity, and most importantly, their protection from God. Jesus said it. You have to be connected to him. "Without me, you can do... nothing" (Jn 15:5).

The Problem (10:2)

What's the big problem? The heart of the problem is the problem with the heart.

> **Hosea 10:2** | Their heart is false; now they must bear their guilt. The Lord will break down their altars and destroy their pillars.

9 | HOSEA 10:1-15
The True Vine

Hosea addresses the primary problem with God's people: they have *a heart problem*. Outwardly, they are prosperous, but inwardly, their heart is "**false**" and divided. He later tells them to "break up the heard ground" of their hearts (10:12). Jesus says, "No one can serve two masters" (Mt 6:24). In order to serve Jesus, the true vine, we have to cut down all other allegiances that interfere with him. God promises to break down those false altars. That's a blessing.

The northern kingdom was so prosperous during this time, like a growing and spreading vine. They think they are ok, but God is going to destroy their golden calf Baal statues and break down their altars.

The altars to golden calf in Bethel and Dan were a form of Baal worship. The altar in Dan is still standing to this day. The golden calf altar in Bethel (house of God), here called Beth-aven (house of wickedness) is currently being excavated by archeologists. Below is a layout of the golden calf altar at Tel Dan which is likely identical to the one at Bethel. Much of the foundation for the temple for the golden calf and the altar at Tel Dan are still intact today. The sketch below illustrates what it might have looked like in the days of the prophet Hosea based on the most recent excavations.

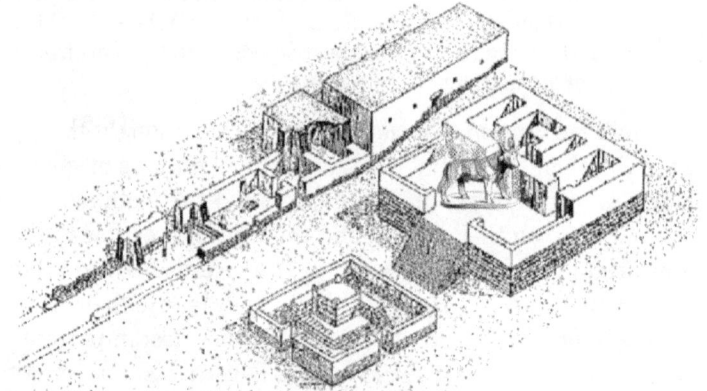

Figure of what the Golden Calf altars at Dan & Bethel might have looked like

The Platitudes (10:3)

There is a pattern of excuse making for those who are not connected to Christ. You may even fall back in some ways to your old life for a time even as a Christian, if you do not maintain your walk with Christ. Dear child of God, please listen to these warnings! In ancient

Israel, one of the reason they were not connected to God was a pattern of pious platitudes and excuse making. When Yahweh confronts Israel's divided heart, they basically say: "We are too far gone for repentance – we have no king because we did not fear the Lord." The king of Israel had no legitimate power. Everyone was living in the lap of luxury even though they

> **Hosea 10:3** | For now they will say: "We have no king, for we do not fear the Lord; and a king—what could he do for us?"

The monarchy of Israel is so far gone, but this is just an excuse. We do the same. We say, *"We can't live holy lives – look at our culture. Look at all the hypocrites in the churches Christian men are addicted to porn. Look at the women who constantly gossip. Once godly men are committing adultery. Godly pastors have been disqualified for their finances. If this is the case, then how can you expect my worship to be fervent?"* All that is just excuse making. Change your heart. Repent. Soften your heart to God. Come with true, fervent worship! He is worthy.

Who will stand up for Christ and live a holy life and stop making excuses? If you truly know God, you will worship and serve him no matter how perverse the culture is or how hypocritical the churches are. We worship God because he is worthy, not because his people are. Cut down all your excuse making and be grateful for the love of God even if you must stand alone. What are your excuses for not growing and changing in Christ? Why are you not a joy-filled Christian? What is taking away your peace? You might have some excuses.

"If I had more money, I'd give more sacrificially."

"If I had better health, I'd serve Jesus more."

The reason I'm not growing in Jesus is because of...

- My health problems
- My background and upbringing was really hard
- I have abuse in my past

Hosea 10 says the reason we don't serve Jesus and grow in him is because we have a heart problem. Until you recognize your sin and idolatry of putting your gaze on yourself and your circumstance instead of completely on Jesus, you are just making excuses. You know without Christ you can do... nothing!

Here's an excuse (anger): "I'm bitter because so and so hurt me." That's an excuse. God commands you to truly *love, do good, and speak blessings to the one who wronged you.* If you can't, then you are not maintaining your walk with Christ. Something is wrong. Get help. Without Christ we can do... nothing!

Another excuse (depression): "I'm so depressed, I'll just watch unfiltered movie and media. I deserve a break." Listen if that's you, something is wrong. You need help. Without Christ we can do... nothing!

Here's one (smokescreens): "I can't get to church service or prayer meeting. Or I can't get to this Bible study or connect with this person at church. I'm just too busy." Are you? Are you too busy, or is it just an excuse? You need the church. You need fellowship. Are you just using your busyness to hide? Come on out dear child of God. He loves you. Let God's people love on you. You need help. Without Christ we can do... nothing!

If you've fallen into a pattern of empty words and excuses, repent, get help, get right; get refocused on Christ! Get renewed. Bring your excuses and leave them at the foot of the cross. Whatever the wall you've hit, can't Jesus tear it down? "Behold, I am the LORD, the God of all flesh. Is anything too hard for me?" (Jer 32:27).

Without Jesus, you can do nothing, but with him, you can do anything he wants you to do. "With man this is impossible, but with God all things are possible" (Mt 19:26).

The Pattern of Empty Worship (10:4-8)

One of the greatest reasons a Christian might have any strongholds of sin in their life is simply because of empty worship. Worship of Christ, both privately and publicly should be so enriching that you don't need the idols of the world. Is the Spirit enriching you in personal, private worship of Christ? That's the core of your problem if you're not growing, or you are caught in some kind of a sin cycle or apathy about God or your marriage, or you church. Are you stuck in a "I don't care" mood? The diagnosis is always a hard heart that comes from empty worship! The idol worship that enslaved ancient Israel give us several principles about the nature of idol enslavement.

The Diminishing Principle (10:4)

The diminishing principle is simply this: idols crowd your heart so much, they choke real worship and make your heart small so that you our glorious God is boring to you.

> **Hosea 10:4** | They utter mere words; with empty oaths they make covenants; so judgment springs up like poisonous weeds in the furrows of the field.

It's like a person who fills themselves with cotton candy and lemon drops and is no longer hungry for a scrumptious dinner.

People put on words and even religious practices like a new set of clothes, but inside their heart is crowded with idols. They wear religion outwardly, but it is only superficial. Israel fell into this trap. The heart of a believer, not merely his words, is what God wants in prayer and any religious activity. As John Bunyan said, "When you pray, rather let your heart be without words than your words without heart."

Judgement was coming. Assyria would conquer Israel and be like a poisonous weed that would not satisfy. The people of Israel were careless with their hearts. When a farmer is not careful to cultivate his field, poisonous weeds easily grow there. So it is in the human heart. Hosea says these heartless prayers are like a judgment of poisonous weeds in the furrows of the field. A true born-again saint of God will instead cultivate his heart and delight in God's love in his inner person. Idols are like a poisonous weed that crowds out the heart. In the parable of the soils we read:

> The seed falling among the thorns refers to someone who hears the word, but the worries of this life and the deceitfulness of wealth choke the word, making it unfruitful (Mt 13:22).

Is your heart filled with weeds of worry or briars of bitterness? Are you crying out to God with your burdens in hope, or are you stewing on them with bitterness? Are you worrying about them? Root them up and give them to God.

One application of this diminishing principle of idolatry is how you see the practice of prayer. Do you see God as a Santa Claus, or vending machine? Or do you see him as your loving heavenly Father that wants to have a relationship with you? The first and most important thing in praying is not petition or supplication, but fellowship. Prayer is not mainly about getting good things. It's about getting the best thing: fellowship with God is your reward.

> Be still and know that I am God (Psa 46:10).
>
> I am your shield, your exceedingly great reward (Gen 15:1, NKJV).
>
> The LORD used to speak to Moses face to face, as a man speaks to his friend (Ex 33:11).

We have something so much greater than Moses. Prayer is more than petition and supplication: it's communion. That's why Paul says:

> Pray without ceasing (1 Thess 5:17).

Is your worship life filled and overflowing or is your heart crowded with idols? If not, you are missing out. There is nothing stopping you from full and sweet fellowship with the Lord if you are willing to worship him exclusively in your heart.

THE DEMAND PRINCIPLE (10:5)

The demand principle: when a good desire becomes a demand, it's become an idol. It's taken the place of God. It tears Christ off the throne of your heart. Most of the idols in our lives are actually desires for good things that we simply want too much. They are inordinate desires. We get fooled because they are good things. What you need is not idols. You need the all sufficient Christ.

> His divine power has granted to us all things that pertain to life and godliness, through the knowledge of him [Jesus] who called us to his own glory and excellence (2 Pet 1:3).

Hosea 10:5 | The inhabitants of Samaria tremble for the calf of Beth-aven. Its people mourn for it, and so do its idolatrous priests— those who rejoiced over it and over its glory— for it has departed from them.

The people of ancient Israel cry and fuss when the golden calf idol is taken away from them. Strong emotions occur when something you feel you cannot live without is taken away. That's how you know it's an idol. Something has displaced Christ on the throne of your heart. Christ alone is the only thing you cannot live without. Let me give you a couple principles about idol worship.

The golden calf worship was a form of Baal worship. The altar in Dan is still standing to this day. The golden calf altar in Bethel (house of God) is here called Beth-aven (house of wickedness). Look at how idols can destroy. For them, they had good desires to be taken care of, to be provided for. Those are good desires, but when they replace God and when they are demanded, they become idols. All our desires should be subject to the glory and honor and Lordship of Jesus. Nothing can compare to him.

> Everything else is worthless when compared with the infinite value of knowing Christ Jesus my Lord. For his sake I have discarded everything else, counting it all as garbage, so that I could gain Christ (Phil 3:8, NLT).

Some criteria to assess if your desire has becoming inordinate and enslaving: when it consumes and rules you, when you sin to get it, or when you sin if you don't get it.

How do I know if something is an idol? What makes you angry or sad if you don't get it? What do you punish someone for if they don't give it to you? Must you have your way? That's an idol.

What is now your identity? "I must have this job" or "I must be a parent" or "I must be married" or "I must have 'blank' to live a meaningful life." Or "If only 'blank' would change in my life, or about my spouse, I would be satisfied or content or joyful." That's a ruling desire. It's taken the place of Christ. Your identity is in Christ alone. If there is some other identity that has overtaken Christ, recognize it. Repent of it. Refocus on Christ's Lordship. You can be content with everything stripped from you as long as you have Christ.

Ancient Israel departed from worshipping the living God when they hoisted up a golden calf on their altar. It sure looked like a good thing, since the golden calf temples in Dan and Bethel were identical to the Solomonic Temple in Jerusalem. It looks like a good thing, but it's not a good thing. It's a *horrible thing*.

The Destruction Principle (10:6-8a)

The destruction principle: never put your hope and happiness in something God's not guaranteed. Idols are easily destroyed and taken away. Put your trust in Christ alone whose covenant love cannot be taken away. You should never let anything rule you that can be taken away. Find your contentment in Christ alone. Look at verse 6.

Hosea 10:6 | The thing itself shall be carried to Assyria as tribute to the great king. Ephraim shall be put to shame, and Israel shall be ashamed of his idol.

The final destruction of golden calf worship is prophesied. The golden calf idol would be carried away with their whole country to Assyria. That idol made the people feel good, but it wrecked their lives. I'll say it again: Never put your hope and happiness in something God's not guaranteed. Your identity is not your job, your single or marriage status, whether you are healthy or handicapped. Your identity and happiness and hope is in Christ. Everything else can and at some time will be stripped away.

The people of Samaria (the northern kingdom) had such confidence in their king, especially Jeroboam II. He had brought so much wealth and prosperity to the people of northern Israel. But the prophet reveals that he is just a puppet king, and he will perish by the Assyrians.

Hosea 10:7 | "Samaria's king shall perish like a twig on the face of the waters."

Their point was not that they literally were without anyone on the throne but that the king had no real legitimacy and little power or hope of success. Such a king is like a stick on water in that he can exercise no control over events. Just as their king is powerless, so their worship is powerless as well. The idols of Bethel and other shrines of false worship cannot help them. Hosea prophesies the future: thorns and thistles shall grow up on their altars, and that is exactly what happened.

Hosea 10:8a | The high places of Aven [wickedness], the sin of Israel, shall be destroyed. Thorn and thistle shall grow up on their altars...

The altar of the golden calf in Dan was left desolate for 2700 years as we mentioned until it was rediscovered in 1966 by renowned Israeli archaeologist Avraham Biran who mined the mound of Tel Dan during nearly thirty years of excavation. Truly thorns and thistles covered this altar for twenty-seven hundred years.

Hosea's complaint concludes with a promise that Bethel (here called Aven or "wickedness") and its associated shrines would be taken out of use. The designation "the sin of Israel" for the Bethel shrine is similar to the constant refrain in Kings that the shrines at Dan and

Bethel were the means by which Jeroboam son of Nebat "made Israel sin" (*cf* 2 Kgs 3:3).[87] It characterizes their lives as mired in the practice of sin and idolatry.

The Damnation Principle (10:8b)

The damnation principle: idols cannot save you; they can only pacify you till judgment day. When the Assyrians invaded northern Israel, their idols could not shelter them.

> **Hosea 10:8b** | ...they shall say to the mountains, "Cover us," and to the hills, "Fall on us."

Their cries are to no avail. "Cover us" and "Fall on us" are cries which the New Testament will take up twice: first to predict the still greater horrors awaiting the Jerusalem of ad 70 as the logical outcome of its Good Friday choice, and secondly to portray the terrors of the Last Judgment, with men of every rank and nation.

Idols cannot satisfy, and idols cannot save. If idols keep you from trusting in Christ, you will lose your soul. The idols you so needed will damn your soul to an eternity without Christ. There's coming a day when our friends and neighbors, and even some members of our own family will be...

> ...calling to the mountains and rocks, "Fall on us and hide us from the face of him who is seated on the throne, and from the wrath of the Lamb (Rev 6:16).

Of course, the destruction of northern Israel and later of the Temple are primarily pointing to the Last Judgment when Christ will come to destroy evil and set the world anew and aright. All the judgments of God that precede the Last Day are mercy cries. They are calls for repentance before that last great and terrifying day.

The Paradox (10:9-11)

The great paradox of all of this chapter, is that ancient Israel had everything from God. They were chosen by him. They were loved by him. They were given the Word of God and the prophets. They had everything in their favor. But they bypassed the Lord and became blinded.

---

[87] Ibid, 212.

A Double Iniquity

We are told they are guilty of "double iniquity."

> **Hosea 10:9-10** | From the days of Gibeah, you have sinned, O Israel; there they have continued. Shall not the war against the unjust overtake them in Gibeah? **10** When I please, I will discipline them, and nations shall be gathered against them when they are bound up for their double iniquity.

Yahweh reveals that Israel has nothing to look forward to but a complete military collapse. God's point in displaying his people's helplessness is for them to be able to see their own sin.

Gibeah? It was in Gibeah that we have the tragic story in Judges 19-20, when everyone did "that which was right in their own eyes". Sad. It was there in Gibeah that they began a civil war that nearly decimated the tribe of Benjamin. That's the result of doing that which is right in your own eyes. As a result, Israel is shameless, guilty of a double iniquity.

Double iniquity? In other words, Israel wasn't just like the other nations. They were not sinning in the darkness like pagans. They have the truth. They have the Word of God. Israel is sinning in the light.

A Doting God

Hosea then looks back at the sweetness of God's care for Israel when she was submitted to him. These verses return to the metaphor of Israel as a farm animal.

> **Hosea 10:11** | Ephraim was a trained calf that loved to thresh, and I spared her fair neck; but I will put Ephraim to the yoke; Judah must plow; Jacob must harrow [*make plow rows*] for himself.

At one time, Ephraim (northern Israel) was like a young calf who worked hard threshing grain. It had a natural life to her. She was alive like a young trained calf. God blessed her and didn't make her plow with a harness in the field. But now that Ephraim has lost that life, God puts the harness of affliction on her. Jacob (the name for the old life before he became Israel, prevailer with God). You are no longer worthy to be called Israel. You are Jacob.

What kind of yoke must this fair calf return to? The harness of the pagan nations. The nations will put Ephraim to the yoke – harnessed as captives of war with the Assyrians. It's often true for those who grow up in the light of the Gospel and depart from it, that there is a "double iniquity" and God must bring them back through a harsh yoke of affliction and difficulty. Some of you have that testimony.

For those who are not yet in Christ in this church, don't depart! Come to Christ now. Going after the world would be a "double iniquity". It's not just sinning in the darkness.

CONNECTED TO JESUS AND CONTENT (10:12-15)

Plow Your Heart (10:12)

To illustrate how to connect with the Lord and get rid of all idols, Hosea continues with the farming analogy. He says, you've got to plow up your hard heart.

> **Hosea 10:12** | Sow for yourselves righteousness; reap steadfast love; break up your fallow ground, for it is the time to seek the Lord, that he may come and rain righteousness upon you.

THE GOAL: PLANT RIGHTEOUSNESS (10:12A)

Something new and foreign needs to be planted in the soil of the sinner's heart. Something needs to be planted deep in our hearts: sow for yourselves righteousness.

> **Hosea 10:12a** | Sow for yourselves righteousness…

What is this righteousness? Paul tells us there is a righteousness apart from the mosaic law, that does not come from rule keeping, but directly from Christ by faith in Christ (Rom 3:21-26).

The Christian life is always a life of faith looking to the righteousness of Christ. Even the righteousness we do in our lives is a result of God's work in us.

> "…Work out your own salvation with fear and trembling, [13] for it is God who works in you, both to will and to work for his good pleasure" (Phil 2:12-13).

Sow, i.e. plant – cut open the hardened ground of your heart. Put in it the divine standard of righteousness found in Christ that you can never measure up to in yourself. Water it with weeping and mourning and repentance.

Paul made it crystal clear: he wanted to "be found in him, not having a righteousness of my own that comes from the law, but that which comes through faith in Christ, the righteousness from God that depends on faith" (Phil 3:9). Sow for yourselves. In other words, no one can do it for you. The pastor can't do it for you. Your spouse cannot do it for you. Only God can do it for you as you personally meet with him. You have to go to God yourself. The call to sow for yourselves is simply a call to faith in Christ's righteousness. Sow faith.

> "Circumcise therefore the foreskin of your heart, and be no longer stubborn" (Deut 10:16).

The Reward: Reap God's Covenant Love (10:12b)

Plant a righteousness apart from yourself or the law (Phil 3:9), a righteousness that comes from abiding in Christ by faith, and you will get a harvest: you will reap *hesed*: God's loyal, unrelenting covenant love.

Hosea 10:12b | ...reap steadfast love.

You will know the love of God. This divine love in Hebrew is called חֶסֶד (*hesed*). It is the merciful covenant faithful love of God.

If you want to get rid of all competing idols or things that rule you, like fear or anger or covetousness, then you need the love of God to possess you.

> "There is no fear in love, but perfect love casts out fear. For fear has to do with punishment, and whoever fears has not been perfected in love" (1 Jn 4:18).

The Process: Break Up Your Hard Heart (10:12c)

Hosea calls us to repentance. To turn back to God, you need to break up your fallow ground.

Hosea 10:12c | ...break up your fallow ground...

Instead of hardness, you need tenderness. Instead of excuses, you need to take responsibility. Repentance means we let the full conviction of the Holy Spirit come over us and we surrender to it. What does it look like to break up the hardened ground of your heart? It means to be cut to the heart by the Word, by the double-edged sword of the Spirit. It means you need to totally open your heart so the Lord can work. It means you turn away from your sin with great remorse, with the determination to utterly forsake it. The apostle Paul describes in detail what a true brokenness and repentance looks like.

The Moment: Now! (10:12d)

There is an urgency when it comes to your salvation. Though regeneration is a sovereign act of God on the human heart there is human agency. God never sets aside human responsibility. He places this duty upon every person and says, break up your fallow ground, for it is time to seek the Lord.

> **Hosea 10:12d** | ...for it is the time to seek the Lord...

The Lord says, "All day long I opened my arms to a rebellious people" (Isa 65:2a, NLT). The problem is not God. His arms are open wide to all. He is "not wishing that any should perish, but that all should reach repentance" (2 Pet 3:9). You must determine that the time is now. Seek the Lord, and he will be found.

> You will seek me and find me, when you seek me with all your heart (Jer 29:13).

The Blessing (10:12e)

There is a weather forecast: it's going to rain. Drops of God's righteousness are about to descend upon you (10:12d).

> **Hosea 10:12e** | ...that he may come and rain righteousness upon you.

The fruit of regeneration is just as St. Paul described it: "I have planted, Apollos watered; but God gave the increase" (1 Cor 3:6). Growth is the natural outcome when real life exists. All Christians are to "grow in the grace and knowledge of our Lord and Savior Jesus Christ" (2 Pet 3:18).

The glorious way forward is to be taken up in God's love. That's where genuine, meaningful, lasting transformation and growth come from in the Christian life.

Or Pay the Price (10:13-15)

If you decide you don't want to soften your heart, then what are the consequences? Jesus said,

> If anyone would come after me, let him deny himself and take up his cross and follow me. 35 For whoever would save his life will lose it, but whoever loses his life for my sake and the gospel's will save it. 36 For what does it profit a man to gain the

whole world and forfeit his soul? 37 For what can a man give in return for his soul? (Mk 8:34-37).

There are really only two choices: hold on to the world and lose your soul. Hold on to Jesus and gain eternal life.

> **Hosea 10:13-15** | You have plowed iniquity; you have reaped injustice; you have eaten the fruit of lies. Because you have trusted in your own way and in the multitude of your warriors, **14** therefore the tumult of war shall arise among your people, and all your fortresses shall be destroyed, as Shalman destroyed Beth-arbel on the day of battle; mothers were dashed in pieces with their children. **15** Thus it shall be done to you, O Bethel, because of your great evil. At dawn the king of Israel shall be utterly cut off.

These verses are obviously a prophecy of what is to come for northern Israel. They are the fulfillment of all that God had warned them about from the beginning. There is a tide of consequences from sin that cannot be stopped, but that God will most assuredly work for their good. It was this warning first sounded by Moses in Deuteronomy 28-29 of the blessings and cursings of the law. It was again reconfirmed by Joshua when he "read all the words of the law, the blessing and the curse, according to all that is written in the Book of the Law" (Josh 8:34). Israel had planted a harvest of human reasoning that is really rebellion.

SELF-INDULGENCE

Self-indulgence is at the root of every idol. The ancient pagans worshipped other gods for what those gods could give them. Truly all idolatry is a worship of self. This is what God is saying through Hosea. Self-indulgence is what you get from idolatry.

> **Hosea 10:13a** | You have plowed iniquity; you have reaped injustice...

The people of Israel thought they planted seeds of prosperity with the fertility cult. But it was nothing more than lawlessness. Iniquity means "lawlessness." They've done what they felt like. Their feelings, not God's law, has been their rule. It felt good. And what do they reap? Injustice. The idea is crime or vandalism of themselves. They were planting the seeds of their own destruction. "There is a way that seems right to a man, but its end is the way to death" (Prov 14:12). Self-indulgence leads to destruction! They are reaping a miscarriage of justice. They have served themselves and given their children to the Baals. Is there anything more unjust than to put the weak at risk?

Self-Deception

What is the fruit they eat? The false fruit of lies. They think their ways will make the prosper, but it leads them to lose everything.

> **Hosea 10:13b** | ...you have eaten the fruit of lies.

The fruit that Israel grows and eats is "false fruit."[88] It will not satisfy. The fruit is deceiving. It looks satisfying, but it is actually poisonous and inflicts disease. Look at the broken marriages. Look at the broken people addicted to substance or sex or self. They didn't mean to go down a road that would destroy themselves, but it happened. They were self-deceived. It's true that "sin will take you farther than you want to go, keep you longer than you want to stay, and cost you more than you want to pay." So why do people pay so much for sin? Because sin is deceptive. Sin always promises what it cannot deliver.

Self-Rule

People resist coming to Jesus because they love their own self-rule. For Israel that self-rule was through their **warriors**, that is their army. They were wrong to trust in their army. "Some trust in chariots and some in horses, but we trust in the name of the Lord our God" (Psa 20:7).

> **Hosea 10:13c** | Because you have trusted in your own way and in the multitude of your warriors.

The phrase "your own way" implies everything that Israel had built itself upon, including the fertility cult, political alliances, military fortifications, and raw violence. Above all, it was the pride and glory of their military.[89] Self-rule is the same as it always has been. Instead of surrendering to the lordship of Jesus, we choose to do "that which is right in our own eyes" (Jdg 17:6).

---

[88] Garrett, 217
[89] Ibid.

Self-Destruction

Living for self never ends well. "The wages of sin is death" (Rom 3:23a). Self-living always leads to self-destruction. "The soul that sins shall die" (Exo 18:20). There is no pathway to meaningful change except through Jesus. Trying to change ourselves is like performing heart surgery on ourselves. It is absolutely impossible and will lead to destruction. No one can continue in sin and succeed. Sin always leads to self-destruction as Israel was about to find out.

> **Hosea 10:14** | Therefore the tumult of war shall arise among your people, and all your fortresses shall be destroyed, as Shalman destroyed Beth-arbel on the day of battle; mothers were dashed in pieces with their children (10:14).

The tumult of war is what God uses to destroy all Israel's fortresses. The Assyrians had a sophisticated army. The problem is, Israel was blind to the possibility of Assyria's aggression. They thought that Assyria was their protector and friend, so this came as a deep shock to them. They did not believe God's warnings through Hosea.

Some have said that "Shalman" is the Assyrian king Shalmaneser, but it likely refers to the Moabite king on the list of those who paid tribute to Tiglath-pileser III, named, Salamanu. The prophet Amos records the horror stories that occurred in Gilead (*cf* 1:3, 13) documenting a similar account. The exact battle of Beth-arbel, a town in Galilee, while completely unknown to modern students, must have been well known to Hosea's hearers.[90] And it would have been something that would have gotten their attention. This king decimated the population as a warning sign and dashed the mothers and children of that town in pieces. Beth-arbel means "the house of God's court." The fall of "Beth-arbel" may be specifically cited here because the name sounds like "Bethel."[91] God sent a warning to Israel. Since they do not listen, what happens next?

> **Hosea 10:15** | Thus it shall be done to you, O Bethel, because of your great evil. At dawn the king of Israel shall be utterly cut off (10:15).

---

[90] Hubbard, 194.
[91] Garrett, 217.

God calls Israel by the name of her idolatrous town, Bethel. Bethel was once best known by the encounter Jacob had with God there (Gen 28:10-22), but now the city is infamous for deviant worship of the Baal calf god. It is now the "heart of Israel's darkness."[92] God says, be warned. The same shall be done to you. Because of their great evil, the king of Israel will be utterly cut off. The Lord even gives a time stamp: at dawn this will all occur. The king will be defeated very easily – at dawn, that is, at the very beginning of battle.[93] When we stand against God, there is no chance of victory. Israel of old needed to understand that God can use nations to carry out his will.

Has God sent you any warning signs? Have things gone wrong in your life? Do you get angry at those around you, or do you get humble before God? Break up your hardened heart. Soften your heart! You are not able autonomously to do so, but God can do it through his holy word, through fellowship, through prayer, and all the means of grace.

Do you have an unrepentant heart that needs to be plowed? What price are you willing to pay? Are you willing to cut into the soil of your heart and seek God's righteousness and kingdom? Cut into the soil of your heart. Plant the righteous presence of God. You will reap his love. You will produce a harvest of God's everlasting covenant love.

These closing verses are a prophecy of what is to come for northern Israel. They are the fulfillment of all that God had warned them about from the beginning. There is a tide of consequences from sin that cannot be stopped but that God will most assuredly work for their good. It was this warning first sounded by Moses in Deuteronomy 28-29 of the blessings and cursings of the law. It was again reconfirmed by Joshua when he "read all the words of the law, the blessing and the curse, according to all that is written in the Book of the Law" (Josh 8:34).

Israel had planted a harvest of human reasoning that is really rebellion. At the end of the day, following idols may seem right, but it leads to destruction.

> There is a way that seems right to a man, but its end is the way to death (Prov 14:12).

If you decide you don't want to soften your heart, then what are the consequences? Jesus said,

---

[92] Ibid.
[93] Ibid.

> If anyone would come after me, let him deny himself and take up his cross and follow me. 35 For whoever would save his life will lose it, but whoever loses his life for my sake and the gospel's will save it. 36 For what does it profit a man to gain the whole world and forfeit his soul? 37 For what can a man give in return for his soul? (Mk 8:34-37).

There are really only two choices: hold on to the world and lose your soul. Hold on to Jesus and gain eternal life.

Conclusion

Today so many people are connected. We are more connected than ever, yet more disconnected than ever. Our connections are superficial. I recently saw a placard that said: Look at faces not at devices! It reminds me the most important face to look at: Jesus! Connect to Jesus! He will satisfy you. Idols destroy. Jesus delights! Easy choice. Die to self! Live to Christ! Christ left his throne to connect with you. He came to take you dead and unplugged and unite you and plug you into himself. At the end of the day, Jesus is the true vine. You can't tape fruit to yourself and say you are connected to Jesus.

> Jesus said, "I am the true vine... I am the vine; you are the branches. Whoever abides in me and I in him, he it is that bears much fruit, for apart from me you can do nothing" (Jn 15:1a, 5).

10 | HOSEA 11
GOD'S LOVE IN CHRIST

How can I give you up, O Ephraim? How can I hand you over, O Israel? ...My heart recoils within me; my compassion grows warm and tender. I will not execute my burning anger... for I am God and not a man, the Holy One in your midst, and I will not come in wrath.
HOSEA 11:8-9

I love the words of Francis Chan who said, "Many Spirit-filled authors have exhausted the thesaurus in order to describe God with the glory he deserves. His perfect holiness, by definition, assures us that our words can't contain him. Isn't it a comfort to worship a God we cannot exaggerate?"[94] God's love cannot be exaggerated! You can express it with the highest superlatives, and it will never be described adequately. All eternity will not be sufficient to adequately speak of his everlasting love he has displayed through the priceless death of his Son for you. Oh, how good God is!

In theology proper, we often speak of the attributes of God. Hosea 11 is one of those chapters in the Bible where we see one of the most brilliant of his attributes: his love. When we speak of God's love, it is

---

[94] Francis Chan. *Forgotten God Reversing Our Tragic Neglect of the Holy Spirit* (Elgin, IL: David C. Cook Publishing, 2009), 179.

not worldly love in any way. Worldly love is self-serving. God's love is sacrificial, generous, and indiscriminate. No matter what your objection, Hosea 11 is clear that God is no respecter of persons in demonstrating his love. The nation of Israel was the most unlovable and undeserving, yet Yahweh loved them. He did this to prove that he desires to give his love to the most unworthy. This is good news for everyone. Beginning with this chapter and continuing to the end, a new emphasis on the sovereign and ultimately triumphant love of God can be found in this book of the Bible.

In this, the prophecy of Hosea comes full circle and parallels in its structure the story of the marriage on which it is built. The story of the marriage had three phases. There was an initial period of love and happiness. There was the period of Gomer's unfaithfulness in which the course of her life was continually downward. During this phase, Hosea continued to love his wife and provide for her, but her dissolute and promiscuous life led her into increasing poverty and eventually into slavery. The third phase is seen in Hosea's act of redemption in which he purchased his wife in the slave market and thereby made her his forever. He said in that day,

> You are to live with me many days; you must not be a prostitute or be intimate with any man, and I will live with you (3:3).

On the basis of that analysis, we may say that the last four chapters of Hosea correspond to stage three. The love of God has been present all along, but from chapters 4 to 10 the notes of discipline and judgment predominate. Now, although judgment is still present, the emphasis falls on God's prevailing and unquenchable love. What an amazing love this is! In chapter 11 Hosea writes of the love of God in reference to Israel's past, present, and future. But in each case, there are surprises.[95]

GOD'S LOVE IS FOUND IN CHRIST (11:1-4)

In the beginning after the fall of man, God promised a deliverer, a Savior of the human race. Who would it be? God chose Abraham, Isaac and Jacob. Jacob's people, the people of Israel, were enslaved in Egypt for 400 years. They started there favored under Joseph, one of Jacob's sons, who was the prime minister of Egypt. But after Joseph, the people

---

[95] Boice, 87.

were enslaved by the Egyptians. What began as a blessing became a terrible situation.

An Unexpected Love

> **Hosea 11:1** | When Israel was a child, I loved him, and out of Egypt called my son.

Before Israel was a nation God, when they were just a child, God says, "I loved him" and called his son out of Egypt. God turned that terrible situation of slavery was then turned around. God raises up Moses. Through Moses God tells Pharaoh: "Let my people go." And out of Egypt came God's son, Israel.

Interestingly, the New Testament quotes this verse in Hosea and applies it to Jesus Christ. What we find is that Israel pre-figures the true promised Son. The hope of the world is not the nation of Israel, or the king of Israel, but the true Israel and the true King of all kings: Jesus, God's beloved Son. Matthew makes a theological point by quoting this verse in Hosea.

> Now when they had departed, behold, an angel of the Lord appeared to Joseph in a dream and said, "Rise, take the child and his mother, and flee to Egypt, and remain there until I tell you, for Herod is about to search for the child, to destroy him." [14] And he rose and took the child and his mother by night and departed to Egypt [15] and remained there until the death of Herod. This was to fulfill what the Lord had spoken by the prophet, "Out of Egypt I called my son" (Mt 2:13-15).

Here's the theological point: Our Savior, our King, our true Israel entered into our world, was incarnated and put on human flesh. He went into Egypt for us! If you want God's love, you get it through the one who came into this world to reconcile and restore your relationship with God.

An Undeserved Love

> **Hosea 11:1** | When Israel was a child, I loved him, and out of Egypt called my son.

When the Lord says, "When Israel was a child, I loved him," He is referring to a passage in Deuteronomy 7, where we read:

> The Lord did not set his affection on you and choose you because you were more numerous than other peoples, for you were the fewest of all peoples. But it was because the Lord loved you and kept the oath he swore to your forefathers that he brought you out with a mighty hand and redeemed you from the land of slavery, from the power of Pharaoh king of Egypt" (Deut 7:7-8).

What claim did Israel have on God? None at all! That is what these verses teach. Israel was not more numerous and therefore useful. He was not more moral or devoted. There was nothing in Israel that in any way made his superior or more desirable to God than the other nations round about. So the explanation of God's electing love is to be found in the love itself and in no other place. He loved them because he loved them. That is all.[96]

The passage before us is remarkable. The portrayal of God as a Father calling and caring for his Son is so tender in its detail that it is hard to imagine anyone (particularly a Jew) reading this and not personally feeling great joy being the object of such divine compassion when they deserved divine retribution. God's love is an unimaginable, shocking love. Look at the relentlessness of God's love in the midst of their rebellion:

> **Hosea 11:2** | The more they were called, the more they went away; they kept sacrificing to the Baals and burning offerings to idols.

God says: In spite of my deep kindness to them, they kept loving idols. Yet God's love for Israel is not based on their worthiness or behavior. God's election of Israel as a nation is based on God's kindness alone.

This is sovereign love based on his own patient and forgiving character. The more the prophets called the people to the Lord, the more they went astray. God's love is personal. St. Augustine said, "God loves each one of us as if there were only one of us to love." God elected you based on his free love. It is not because we chose him that he loves us.

St. Augustine also said, "God chooses us, not because we believe, but that we may believe."

Paul describes this undeserving sovereign choice.

---

[96] Ibid., 87-88.

> But we ought always to give thanks to God for you, brothers beloved by the Lord, because God chose you as the first fruits to be saved, through sanctification by the Spirit and belief in the truth (2 Thess 2:13).

We don't know why he chose us. Yet he did. Ephesians 1:4-6, says:

> ...he chose us in him before the foundation of the world, that we should be holy and blameless before him. In love he predestined us for adoption as sons through Jesus Christ, according to the purpose of his will, to the praise of his glorious grace, with which he has blessed us in the Beloved (Eph 1:4-6).

Israel was called to come to Christ. Some in Israel were chosen. How do you know you are chosen? Those who trust in Christ and call on him in repentant faith will be saved.

Don't trample on his love. Don't take his grace for granted. Turn to him! And if you have turned to him, cut off the world, and walk with God as your Father. You are reconciled. Walk moment by moment in prayerful fellowship with him. Grow understanding your good Father in heaven.

A Tender Love

We see again the tender love of God for Israel (and us!) where the father-son picture continues to be painted.

> **Hosea 11:3** | Yet it was I who taught Ephraim to walk; I took them up by their arms, but they did not know that I healed them.

The metaphor of teaching to walk appears to relate to Israel's walking out of Egypt.[97] The picture is of a father teaching his child to walk; the father does this by bending over and holding the child's arms, not by picking up the child. God's election is displayed in great tenderness. He took up his child by the hands with the simple trust of a child learning to walk. Israel trusted God, and because of that, they walked right out of Egypt. Indeed, God has taught each one of us to walk out of Egypt. We are to have nothing to do with loving the world "or the things in the world. If anyone loves the world, the love of the Father is not in him" (1 Jn 2:15).

The great tragedy is that though God healed them, they were blind to who supplied their strength. God brought them out of Egypt and

---

[97] Garrett, 223.

healed them from the disease of slavery, but they did not know that God healed them. God's electing love guided them even though they were unaware of it.

Now we see another illustration of love, not of a father, but of a human deliverer. This brings us back to when God's people were four hundred years in Egypt, and God sent his human deliverer to rescue them: Moses. Moses did not elect Israel. He was merely the human instrument that led them out of slavery. Notice how God lovingly talks to his people:

> **Hosea 11:4a** | I led them with cords of kindness, with the bands of love.

The cords of kindness or literally "a man" are such as those with which men, especially children, would be led, as opposed to ropes, with which animals are tied. In this illustration, gentle treatment is sweetly implied. God treats us like a mother who ties a cord around her child's arm, so that he or she does not get lost. He never straps us in like an animal. He takes off the horrible bands of the slave master (as in Egypt) and he gives us loving leaders (like Moses) to lead us with cords of kindness, with the bands of love. Where in your life are you resisting the Spirit's bands of love?

Now we see the illustration of a farmer who eases the harness on the jaws of his ox. He loves his people like a compassionate farmer loves his animals. He takes the harness off and feeds that animal gently by his own hand.

> **Hosea 11:4b** | And I became to them as one who eases the yoke on their jaws, and I bent down to them and fed them.

When the world straps us in like an animal, even in our suffering, God will open up our jaws like that of an animal so that we may eat conveniently. God does not give us what we deserve. We deserve ropes of condemnation, but God gives us cords of kindness. God throws over us the cords of love even today, when he calls us through the preaching of his word, gives us his sacraments, promises and supplies us with every good thing, and visits us with precious afflictions: so we would pray that God would draw us further still after himself.[98] This is the love that we are called to receive from God as Christians. This is also

---

[98] Lange & Schaff, et. el, *Hosea*, 88.

the love we are to display. Much of the time our love is unrequited. Our love as Christians is not based on whether or not a person loves us in return. Our love, like God's love, is selfless.

God's Love Found in Christ Alone

Look at the love of God! It can only be truly demonstrated in his beloved Son was incarnated and had to flee to Egypt as a child.

God called him into and out of Egypt. He came to our Egypt. Lived in our Egypt. And God calls him out of Egypt to die: not in Egypt. It wasn't the world that crucified the Savior. Sure, their were Romans involved, but the Roman magistrate Potius Pilate washed his hands of Jesus' death. His people killed him. You killed him. I killed him. Our sins put him there. What love that Christ would willingly, lovingly give his life for us. That's why God's love can only be found in Christ.

GOD'S LOVE IS EXPERIENCED IN THE HEART (11:5-7)

The Bible teaches us in the New Testament book of Romans 8:28-30 that in the full salvation that God gives us, all who are justified will be conformed to the image of God's dear Son. In this next section of Hosea (11:5-7), we see that the bliss of Israel's infant years will now be replaced with brokenness and emptiness. There is a pprice of rejecting God. Instead of God as King, their greatest hope is Assyria's king.[99] God sends pain and suffering to his beloved people to grow them and conform them to his image.

The Price of Not Knowing God

> **Hosea 11:5-6** | They shall not return to the land of Egypt, but Assyria shall be their king, because they have refused to return to me. **6** The sword shall rage against their cities, consume the bars of their gates, and devour them because of their own counsels.

They don't go back to Egypt, but to a new kind of slavery. Theologically this is a prophecy of the Assyrian captivity for northern Israel. But on a more practical level, this is also a principle of blessing or loss. The people of Israel will not trust God with their heart. "They have refused to return to me" (11:5). They reject God and lose everything. A life without Christ is so vain, superficial, and meaningless.

---

[99] Ibid., 89.

The northern people of Israel lose their country and king. Why? Because they refused to return to the Lord. Simple right? They could have had it all. They wanted protection, pleasure, and provision. They trusted in themselves and forsook the Lord. Bad choice, right? What was their problem? They thought they knew God but didn't.

The Blessing of Knowing God

God says:

> **Hosea 11:7** | My people are bent on turning away from me, and though they call out to the Most High, he shall not raise them up at all.

Blessing can only come when you turn your heart to God. Israel refused to turn. So God refuses to help them or hear them. Whoa, wait a minute. They call to God, but he won't hear them? He won't answer them? That doesn't sound like our loving and merciful God. I thought we were learning about the unrelenting love of God in Hosea. The principle here is simple: God will not help Israel or anyone if your heart is turned away from him. Had they turned to him, he would have delivered them.

Is your heart turned to the Lord? Is your heart bent on turning to God in all your trials and tribulations? Who do you turn to when you are wronged? Do you gossip. Put off gossip and turn to Christ. The people of Israel were bent on turning away from God, but we are bent toward serving God.

> But now that you have been set free from sin and have become slaves of God, the fruit you get leads to sanctification and its end, eternal life (Rom 6:22).

GOD'S LOVE IS RELENTLESS (11:8-12)

Tim Keller says: "You get down to Hosea 11:8, and suddenly we hear the most amazing noise in the Bible. God crying."[100]

---

[100] Timothy J. Keller. "A Strong Love in the Same Direction" (October 18, 1992), sermon. *The Timothy Keller Sermon Archive*. New York City: Redeemer Presbyterian Church.

God's Compassion (11:8)

God has been comparing himself to a man, a human father. He has spoken of his love and the ingratitude and irony of having Israel go her own way rather than remain with him. It is a striking image, but in the back of our minds we are always thinking that it is, after all, an image and not to be pressed too far. God loves us, yes! But surely not with the full emotions that a human father would have at the rebellion of his son! No? Yet that is what God says in verses 8 and 9. And not only this, he also portrays himself as being inwardly divided—uncertain what to do, vacillating.[101] Can this be God saying:

> **Hosea 11:8** | How can I give you up, O Ephraim? How can I hand you over, O Israel? How can I make you like Admah? How can I treat you like Zeboiim?

God is relentlessly loving, and his love won't let his people go. Although, because he is Holy, God does have to judge and punish us – he also, by the power of his Holy Spirit, lovingly works in our hearts and patiently waits for us to humbly turn back to him. He speaks to us and gently persuades us to come back to him, promising us his hope and his safety and renewing his promise to us to enter into a new intimate relationship with him - by his relentless love, time and time again.

We deserve wrath. Israel's sin has brought her to the brink of irrevocable judgment, the very theme that has occupied the center section of the book (chs. 4–10). "Giving them up" and "handing them over" refer to total destruction. Admah and Zeboiim were two of the cities of the plain destroyed when Sodom and Gomorrah were also destroyed (*cf* Gen 14:2, 8; 19:19; Deut 29:23). Their names stand for swift annihilation. But on the brink of such judgment it is God rather than Israel who hesitates. "How can I do it?" he says, as wrath against sin and love for the people do battle within him. Then comes God's tender tears:

> **Hosea 11:8b** | My heart recoils within me; my compassion grows warm and tender.

This is the most amazing noise, as Keller says, in all the Bible! God's heart is wrenched. His heart is warm and tender. Our Lord would later weep over Jerusalem, but here weeps over Israel.

---

[101] Boice, 89.

When the hearts of God's people are hard, God's heart remains soft. When our actions and guilt cry out for hell, God in grace cries for mercy and compassion. The warmth and tenderness of God's tears will be the atmosphere of heaven.

God's Mercy (11:9)

At last the answer comes:

> **Hosea 11:9** | I will not execute my burning anger; I will not again destroy Ephraim; for I am God and not a man, the Holy One in your midst, and I will not come in wrath.

God is not a man. He is not capricious. He is not impulsive or out of control. He is not a tyrant. He is compassionate. God will never give up on you. He says, "I will never leave you nor forsake you" (Heb 13:5). The author of Hebrews is quoting Deuteronomy 31:5, "Be strong and courageous. Do not fear or be in dread of them, for it is the Lord your God who goes with you. He will not leave you or forsake you."

God's Roar (11:10-11)

God's love is compared to a lion's roar.

> **Hosea 11:10-11** | They shall go after the LORD; he will roar like a lion; when he roars, his children shall come trembling from the west; **11** they shall come trembling like birds from Egypt, and like doves from the land of Assyria, and I will return them to their homes, declares the LORD.

For both those who are faithful, and those who are going astray, God has a promise. He will conform them ultimately to "their homes." He will bring peace. Here Yahweh takes upon himself the ferocity of the lion, not to destroy Israel but to restore it. The image, like many in the prophets, is disorienting: a lion roars, but birds come to it rather than flee.

Hosea's point here is that there is to be a new exodus in which God will again play the part of the lion and deliver his people from their enemies and into a new Promised Land.[102] Let me say that the New Promised Land is not fulfilled in the time of Ezra or in the time of King Herod. All the building back of their homes and of the Temple did not restore the peace of God.

---

[102] Garrett, 229.

His children come "from the west." Without trying to stretch this text too far, I am reminded of the words of Jesus – that this is not just referring to ethnic Jews, but also to his people among the Gentiles. We read in Luke:

> You will see Abraham and Isaac and Jacob and all the prophets in the kingdom of God but you yourselves cast out. 29 And people will come from east and west, and from north and south, and recline at table in the kingdom of God. 30 And behold, some are last who will be first, and some are first who will be last (Lk 12:28-30).

God's View (11:12)

Hosea 11:12 | Ephraim has surrounded me with lies, and the house of Israel with deceit, but Judah still walks with God and is faithful to the Holy One.

Though the northern kingdom is being judged, Judah (southern Israel) at the time of Hosea's writing is seeing fidelity to God through the rule of King Hezekiah. God sees Judah trying to be faithful. That's important. Under Jeroboam II, northern Israel was prosperous and very committed to their pagan idols like Baal and Asherah mixed with worship to Yahweh. God says that kind of syncretism is filled with lies and deceit. How refreshing it is to know that God sees us. He sees the true reality. The north believes they are ok, but they are not. They are wretched, and God sees their wretchedness. The south is trying to walk with God in humility, and God sees! That's encouraging.

> Search me, O God, and know my heart! Try me and know my thoughts! 24 And see if there be any grievous way in me, and lead me in the way everlasting! (Psa 139:23-24)

Conclusion

This week I was in Mexico with a bunch of people training to give their lives away and be sent to the hardest places in the world. Fifty young people with college degrees in every profession were enrolled in cross-cultural training, ready to give the rest of their lives to people in the hardest, most difficult and unreached places in the world.

They were there purposely without internet or a lot of modern conveniences, training themselves for hardship. They were training themselves to be uncomfortable in this world, but so so comfortable in the love of Jesus. Why would they do this? Because the love of Jesus is worth laying your life down for. It's the deep, infinite love of Jesus. What a powerful, unrelenting love God has. Let's share it with the world. Hallelujah!

11 | HOSEA 12

PRESSING INTO GOD

In the womb he took his brother by the heel, and in his manhood he strove with God. He strove with the angel and prevailed; he wept and sought his favor. He met God at Bethel, and there God spoke with us—the Lord, the God of hosts, the Lord is his memorial name: "So you, by the help of your God, return, hold fast to love and justice, and wait continually for your God."

HOSEA 12:3-6

I've experienced an increasing uneasiness in my own life and the life of our church and in the culture of the American church regarding prayer. The very touchstone of Christianity is union with Christ, and the outflow of your union with Jesus is a life of weakness and total dependence on Christ through prayer.

Can I say something controversial? Biblical principles but they alone cannot change people. You can give Biblical principles, and very often and dead people stay spiritually dead. What's the difference? Prayer. God must move, and he chooses to move through weak, dependent, desperate praying people. You're learning so much, but if knowledge takes away your desperation for God, then you are headed in the wrong direction. Don't let anything take away your sense of neediness for Jesus. Satan is happy if you keep learning stuff and you don't depend on God. Information does not necessarily equal life transformation. You need the Spirit; and the only way to the Spirit is humility.

> God resists the proud, but gives grace to the humble (1 Pet 5:5).

There are only two categories of Christians - you're either desperate or you're deluded. God's wants us desperate, not deluded. If you think you are strong, you are deluded. The measure of how you view your weakness is your desperation in prayer, to press into God. How weak are you? Look at your prayer life. Prayer is our lifeline that connects us to God.

In Hosea 12, the Lord retells the story of Jacob and how he came to be known as Israel. He went in as a proud prayerless man, and he came out of that wrestling match with a great limp as one of the greatest prayer warriors in the Bible. Do you have a limp when you walk? Are you fully aware of just how weak you are? Jesus said, " My grace is sufficient for you, for my power is made perfect in weakness" (2 Cor 12:9). Paul replies, "Therefore I will boast all the more gladly of my weaknesses, so that the power of Christ may rest upon me...when I am weak, then I am strong" (2 Cor 12:10).

Understand this dear saint. You are weak. You will always be weak. When hard times come, you are either going to press into the world or press into God.

WHY PRESS INTO GOD (11:12; 12:1-2)

At the end of Hosea 11 into chapter 12, we see how incredibly important a communion with God is. Israel of old had forgotten God. No fellowship. No prayer. Lots of money. Lots of comfort. They were deceived. They thought comfort equals communion.

> **Hosea 11:12** | Ephraim has surrounded me with lies, and the house of Israel with deceit, but Judah still walks with God and is faithful to the Holy One.

Consider Hosea 12:8. Israel was so far from God, but they thought they were perfectly fine.

Hosea 12:8 | Ephraim has said, 'Ah, but I am rich; I have found wealth for myself; in all my labors they cannot find in me iniquity or sin.

Israel was feasting on meals of vanity.

Hosea 12:1 | Ephraim feeds on the wind and pursues the east wind all day long; they multiply falsehood and violence; they make a covenant with Assyria, and oil is carried to Egypt.

They think because they have outward comforts that their inner relationship with God is ok. They confuse comfort with holiness.

Here the people of Israel were being pressed in by the world. They turned to the nations to provide them with comfort. They needed relief. They felt the pressure. Instead of being pressed into God, they were pressed into the world. That's the great choice: press into the world or press into God.

A Warning from God

Look at God's indictment. The world will eat you for lunch.

Hosea 12:2 | The LORD has an indictment against Judah and will punish Jacob according to his ways; he will repay him according to his deeds.

God says: you want the world: you can have it. God repays his people by giving them what they want. The nations of Assyria with an assist from Egypt destroy both Judah and Israel. You don't want the world. Without an intervention from God, Ephraim just keeps feeding on the wind.

Hosea 12:1 | Ephraim feeds on the wind and pursues the east wind all day long...

But there is an application to God's true people today. Don't let the pressure of life press you into the world. The world promises *big pleasure* with small consequences. When in reality there is little pleasure with *gigantic* consequences. Listen to God's indictment: the world will hang you out to dry. You could lose your own soul, thinking you know Christ, but you have no real walk with him. If you let yourself get pressed into the world, it's like thinking you are eating at Maggiano's Little Italy, when you're really eating from that other "M" place. Not McDonald's but the dumpster behind McDonald's!

WHY PRAY?

So why press into God? Why pray? Why put the world behind you? Why refuse to be fed by the world and be fed by God? Why pray and commune with the living God?

1. Some things come about only by prayer and fasting.

> This kind can come out by nothing but prayer and fasting (Mk 9:24).

Remember the disciples were struggling with a child whose father had brought them his demon possessed boy. They said: why couldn't we cast out the demon? It was because of prayer and fasting. Prayer changes things.

Now God is immutable. He doesn't change. But he chooses to exercise his omnipotent power through praying people. All his decrees come from necessary means. That means God uses human beings who pray. Amen!

Think about our brother Ahmed (a member of our congregation) from Saudi Arabia. Why did he come to Christ in Auckland, New Zealand? Why not here? There was a group of dedicated people that were praying and fasting for another person to be added to their group. They had seen Muslims from Egypt, Syria, and Dubai saved, but no one from Saudi. They were fasting and praying for a Muslim from Saudi to come to Christ. So God moved there in time and space. That's how it works.

What is God doing here? Is he doing anything? Pray and fast and watch him work. You need to get desperate and remember nothing's happening unless God moves.

> Unless the Lord builds the house, they labor in vain who build it (Psa 127:1a).

2. We're commanded to pray!

> Pray without ceasing (1 Thess 5:17).

Communion is a command, but it's also a privilege.

> Colossians 4:2, 12, "Continue earnestly in prayer, being vigilant in it with thanksgiving... v. 12 Epaphras, who is one of you, a servant of Christ, greets you, always laboring fervently for you in prayers, that you may stand perfect and complete in all the will of God."

Here's an example of prayer. Here's a man who is laboring in the power of the Spirit in prayer. The Spirit is flowing through him. That's a big part of this church standing mature and complete in all the will of God. This is not an immature church. Why? Because Epaphras is praying.

3. Prayer shows you haven't forgotten who really has the power.

Remember Jehoshaphat's prayer:

> O, our God, will you not judge them? For we have no power against this great multitude that is coming against us; nor do we know what to do, but our eyes are fixed on you (2 Chron 20:12).

God commands Jehoshaphat to pray and for the priests to sing. So the Kohathite priest being to lift up their voice and praise the Lord, and God fights for them!

4. Because when you live for Christ you're going to war!

> For we do not wrestle against flesh and blood, but against the rulers, against the authorities, against the cosmic powers over this present darkness, against the spiritual forces of evil in the heavenly places. 13 Therefore take up the whole armor of God, that you may be able to withstand in the evil day, and having done all, to stand firm.... 18 praying at all times in the Spirit, with all prayer and supplication (Eph 6:12-13, 18).

Life is war. Principalities and powers from hell are warring against you. You want to give Satan an open invitation to your life? Stay away from praying and watch your life and your ministry dry up. Without prayer you don't have the words people need. You are not going to be reaching them at the right time, because you can't hear the Spirit. You need prayer. It's a covering in spiritual warfare. You need to have people praying for you. You are in a war. Don't go unarmed.

5. Prayer gives you a holy boldness and the very words to say.

How many times there is something you need to say to someone to help them grow, but you don't have the words to say. You know what you need to say, but you're staying quiet. How are you going to get the holy boldness to speak? Prayer! You better be praying when you get ready to do or say a hard thing. Remember Esther? She wasn't supposed to speak to the king. She knew there was risk. But she said to her people, "I need you to fast for me." Listen to her:

> Esther 4:16, "Go gather all the Jews who are present in Shushan, and fast for me; neither eat nor drink for three days, night or day. My maids and I will fast likewise. And so I will go to the king, which is against the law; and if I perish I perish!"

Are you willing to speak the truth in love to people even if they get spitting angry at you? How are you going to have the power to do that? Sometimes you are the only person that's not only willing to speak the truth, but you're one of the very few people who even has the truth!

Do you lack courage to help others grow and change? Are you in your fleshly, protected isolation? How can you get the courage? Prayer. Fellowship. Communion.

6. Prayer gives you discernment.

So many times I come to a situation, and I say, "Lord I have no idea what to do!" Saints, where can we get wisdom and discernment?

> If any of you lacks wisdom, let him ask of God, who gives to all liberally and without reproach, and it will be given to him (Jas 1:5).

> For the Lord gives wisdom; from his mouth come knowledge and understanding; he stores up sound wisdom for the upright (Prov 2:6-7).

He's got it stored up for those walking with him. You will not have wisdom unless you are walking with God. You don't need just biblical principles. That's good, but you need wisdom to know how to apply the Word, when to apply it. When you are praying, God will just lay out a hard situation before you.

7. Prayer breaks through strongholds.

People can't just repent any time they want to. God must grant repentance. - Never forget that repentance is a gift from God!

> And a servant of the Lord must not quarrel but be gentle to all, able to teach, patient, in humility correcting those who are in opposition, if God perhaps will grant them repentance, so that they may know the truth, and that they may come to their senses and escape the snare of the devil, having been taken captive by him to do his will (2 Tim 2:24-26).

Prayer breaks through strongholds. People in their own strength do not even have the will to change and please God! People like change. They do! This is what people say:

"Lord, change my spouse."

"Change my boss."

"Change my child."

But you know what we need to be praying: "Lord change me!" You need to ask God to change you.

> Work out your own salvation with fear and trembling; for it is God who works in you both to will and to do for his good pleasure (Phil 2:12b-13).

It's not about you working: it's about God working! Here's a good prayer to pray. Ask God to soften and incline your heart to him.

> Incline my heart to your testimonies, and not to covetousness (Psa 119:36).

Do you want to change? You've got to become desperate and not deluded. Only God can change you. Ask God to move on your heart and incline your will to his Word.

HOW TO PRESS INTO GOD (12:3-6)

The Wrestling Match

The diagnosis is clear and Hosea 12:3-5. Jacob is a sinner from the womb, just like all of us. But he took the opportunity when cornered and brought low to wrestle with God in his manhood. God often gets worldliness out of us by humbling us like Jacob.

> **Hosea 12:3-5** | In the womb he took his brother by the heel, and in his manhood he strove with God. **4** He strove with the angel and prevailed; he wept and sought his favor. He met God at Bethel, and there God spoke with us— **5** the Lord, the God of hosts, the Lord is his memorial name.

JACOB THE SCHEMER

Jacob had the reputation from birth of being a schemer, a supplanter, and a trickster. "In the womb he took his brother by the heel" (12:3a). He was always cutting in line taking advantage of everyone around him, beginning with his brother Esau.

Jacob, as all men are, was "dead in his sins" (Eph 2:1-3). Though Jacob was the grandson of Abraham, he was "a lost sheep." And so it is with us before we know Christ. We have no power within ourselves.

Without God, Jacob was a schemer. He was always the smartest one in the room, and that's not a compliment. He had plan A, B, and C. He didn't depend on God. He had some great plans too. Remember, he cheated his brother Esau out of the birthright and the blessing. Esau gave up his birthright for a mess of lentil soup. And remember how he tricked his blind father into thinking he was the oldest – Esau – when he was the youngest. He even put on the furry hand costume. Wow. He had schemes. Jacob the schemer.

But maybe the best thing for you is for God to put you in a place of total disaster and crisis, like Jacob. Jacob was positive Esau was going to kill him for stealing the blessing. Jacob had put all his servants and family in front of him when he fled for his life. He made sure he was good and hidden in the back, behind everyone else. He weighed everything and made sure he had no liabilities or vulnerabilities.

God made him desperate. He finally came to the place where he gave up. He gave up scheming. He gave up planning. He just went to God and said, I'm done. I need your blessing. The greatest disaster in your life right now is probably the greatest blessing. That disaster is God showing you how weak you are. What you need to know is if you belong to Christ, all things are working for your good, whether they are trouble or blessing (Rom 8:28-30).

Israel the Wrestler

Jacob goes from being a schemer to a wrestler, one of the greatest wrestlers in the history of the planet. Who's ever wrestled God and won? Jacob. He gets a new name as a result.

> **Hosea 12:3b-4a** | In his manhood he strove with God. ⁴He strove with the angel and prevailed; he wept and sought his favor…

As Jacob was fleeing from Esau after his father's death he came to a place where God renewed the covenant with him. Finally, later at Penuel (Face of God), Jacob realized that he could not depend on his wit or strategies to get him out of his troubles but that he must call on his God! He then began to call out to God in earnest prayer, paralyzed with anxiety through the night (Gen 32:9-12). When Jacob had finished his strategizing, God stepped in. The scripture says, Jacob was left alone; and there wrestled a man with him until the breaking of the day!

Who was Jacob wrestling with? A Christophany: a pre-incarnate appearance of Jesus. The Bible does not reveal the identity of the man here, but Jacob later stated that he had seen God face to face. Jacob saw God, later referred to as the Messenger or Angel of the Lord. Who is our Messenger, but the Word of the Father? As Jacob wrestled with the man it appears that none was gaining control of the contest; as the day began to break the Angel of the Lord touched the hip joint of Jacob's thigh so that it became dislocated. Despite this however Jacob hung on to the man. This was one battle that Jacob was not going to lose! He wanted God's blessing so bad. He would not let go till God blessed him, and God did: giving him a new name: Israel (Prevailer with God).

God says to his people in Hosea's day: wrestle with me again! Prayer is the pathway to repentance, transformation, and lasting change!

JACOB THE DREAMER

Twenty years before Penuel, God made a promise to Jacob. He saw the ladder to heaven, a type of Christ.

Hosea 12:4b | ...He met God at Bethel, and there God spoke with us.

At Bethel he saw a ladder and stairway to heaven – a shadow of Christ who is the ladder between heaven and earth – the way to "eternal life." But 20 years would pass, and Jacob would still be on the run.

God reminded Jacob again of his memorial name.

Hosea 12:5 | ...the Lord, the God of hosts, the Lord is his memorial name.

The Lord, YHWH is his memorial name means that YHWH is the name by which Israel was to remember him.[103] He is the "God of hosts" or God of the armies of heaven and earth. YHWH "commands the forces of heaven, both visible and invisible, rules with unrestricted omnipotence on earth as well as in heaven (*cf* 1 Sam 1:3)."[104] These people

---

[103] Lange & Schaff, et. el, *Hosea*, 90.
[104] Keil & Delitzsch, *Hosea*, vol 10, 96-97.

were trusting in foreign powers to protect them, not realizing these nations get their power from the Lord.

In other words: Prayer opens heaven where the God of all the armies of heaven are. He commands the angel armies, and he will open up ways of fellowship, communion, and fruitful ministry, if you will seek him like Jacob.

How Do We Get There?

You might say, "I can't repent." No one can on their own. That's why the Bible refers to faith as a "gift of God" (Eph 2:8-10) as is all of our salvation. If you lack repentant faith, you need merely to ask God for it. Indeed, this is what Hosea says to God's rebellious people. How can they do something they have no power to do?

> **Hosea 12:6** | 'So you, by the help of your God, return, hold fast to love and justice, and wait continually for your God.'

So what does God want from Israel, and what does God want from us? God says, "*Hold on to me! I will not let you go!*" Hold on to God's unrelenting, unconditional love. We are imprinted with God's heart. The idea of justice is turning back to that which is right. That's the fruit of repentance and humility. We are to wait continually for God. This is an expression of living out our faith.

You cannot do this alone. You can only "return" "by the help of your God." Even repentance is impossible without the divine grace that enables it.[105]

God will help you. If you are without Christ, he will enlighten your mind to come to Christ in repentance and surrender. Come!

HOW CAN YOU AS A CHRISTIAN TAP INTO PRAYER?

1. You should walk with God daily.

> Daniel 6:10, "When Daniel knew that the document had been signed, he went to his house where he had windows in his upper chamber open toward Jerusalem. He got down on his knees three times a day and prayed and gave thanks before his God, as he had done previously."

---

[105] Ibid., 218.

Pray for circles of influence, spouse (if married). Pray Scripture. Pray for wisdom. Praise God and commune with him in the Psalms. Sing to God. Make up songs. Some of you introverted people just had a panic attack. You can do this. If you are alive and you have a pulse, you need to get the refreshment of the Lord.

A great time to pray is when you don't know what to do. Pray when you can't sleep. It's amazing. God gives his beloved sleep. But sometimes God gives you sleeplessness because he wants you to pray. You need to see your God! You need to see him high and lifted up.

2. Pray for people in your circle of close spiritual influence.

Who's your Paul, your leaders? Are you praying for your pastors? Are you praying for your elders, your deacons? Are you kids praying for your youth leaders? Who's your Timothy? Who are you discipling? Are you praying for them? Who's your Barnabas?

3. Pray for those around you each day.

Are you praying with your family? Are you praying with your friends? Co-workers? Neighbors? Are you inviting the Almighty presence of God into your spheres of influence? Do those around you know that you don't walk alone?

Do you know a 1-minute prayer can be life changing for your lost neighbor? They're hurting. Don't worry about what they think. What's the worst that can happen? You may get hit in the eye. So what. They need to know that you are talking to Someone who is alive and on his throne. You can introduce them to the King of kings.

4. Pray during every life situation.

The king says, "What do you want me to do for you?" So Nehemiah prayed...

> So I prayed to the God of heaven. And I said to the king... (Neh 2:4-5).

Send up 'flare prayers'. God gave Nehemiah the words that changed the course of a nation because he prayed!

5. Pray when you are saying goodbye to people.

You want prayer to be the bookends that sandwich everything you're doing.

- Touch them if possible. Hold their hand. Put your hand on their shoulder.
- Praise and encourage them and affirm them in the prayer.
- Acknowledge what God is doing in their life right then and there.
- Pray Scripture.

Ephesians 3:20, "Now to him who is able to do exceedingly abundantly above all that we ask or think, according to the power that works in us."

Jeremiah 29:11, "For I know the plans I have for you, declares the Lord; plans for welfare and not calamity, to give you and future and a hope."

WHAT'S STOPPING YOU FROM PRESSING INTO GOD (12:7-9)

This life of prayer, demonstrated by Jacob seems so far from Israel, who is lost and blinded by their prosperity. They're already manufacturing their own blessings.

Comfort Might Be Stopping You

Hosea 12:7 | A merchant, in whose hands are false balances, he loves to oppress.

The word "merchant" could also be translated "Canaanite!" He's calling out the people of Israel – that they are just like the inhabitants who they were to conquer. Ephraim has the heart of a lost and unregenerate Canaanite, comforting himself with money. Israel can't see how desperate they should be, so instead, they are deluded.

Hosea 12:8 | Ephraim has said, 'Ah, but I am rich; I have found wealth for myself; in all my labors they cannot find in me iniquity or sin.

Israel's task was to make Canaan Israel. What happened? Canaan made Israel Canaan.[106] How sad it is that the world is now evangelizing the church. The solution for many churches to day for church growth is to put on a better show than the world. David F. Wells in his book *No Place for Truth*, describes how pragmatism has replace the truth of Christ in our churches today:

---

[106] Boice, 98.

> "When we listen to the church today, at least in the West, we are often left with impression that Christianity actually has very little to do with truth. Christianity is only about feeling better about ourselves, about leaping over our difficulties, about being more satisfied, about have better relationships, about getting on with our mothers-in-law, about understanding teenage rebellion, about coping with our unreasonable bosses, about finding greater sexual satisfaction, about getting rich, about receiving our own private miracles, and much else besides. It is about everything except truth, embodied in Christ."[107]

We need the Gospel of the old rugged cross. Jesus never told us to get good and comfortable in this world. He tells us to pick up an instrument of death and die. We are to die and get good and uncomfortable in this world, knowing Christ and making him known. So comfort is the number one reason Christians don't pray.

Have you ever considered that your outrageous prosperity may be robbing you of what your soul really longs for: to know Christ more deeply?

It's Not God Stopping You

This is his promise if we wrestle with God: he will bring them to a place of celebration, like in the fall feasts of Israel. The "appointed feast" is specifically referring to one of the most joyous feasts in Israel: the feast of Tabernacles.

> **Hosea 12:9** | I am the LORD your God from the land of Egypt; I will again make you dwell in tents, as in the days of the appointed feast.

This refers to the Feast of Tabernacles or Booths.[108] This was the annual holy week in which Israel memorialized the wilderness wandering by leaving their homes and spending a week in tents or in hastily constructed, temporary lean-to shelters (Lev 23:33–44).[109]

The verse looks ahead to Israel's Diaspora. They would become, like their ancestors, homeless wanderers. Yet it is better to have nothing but God than to gain the whole world and lose your own soul.

---

[107] David Wells. *No Place for Truth Or, Whatever Happened to Evangelical Theology?* (Grand Rapids: Eerdmans, 1993).
[108] Ibid.
[109] Andersen and Freedman, *Hosea,* 618.

How long has it been since you've been in the place of celebration? Where you feel at home with God? We are not of this world. We are passing through. We are God's guest, but this world is not our home. Philippians 3:20 says that "our citizenship is in heaven, and from it we await a Savior, the Lord Jesus Christ." Let each day be a pilgrim feast for us! We ought not feast on the world!

THE PRIZE OF PRAYER (12:10-14)

God promises two great rewards in coming to him: prophecy and his power. He's going to speak to and enable everyone who comes to him.

God's Word and Spirit

Abruptly, Hosea switches his focus from the patriarchs to the ministry of the prophets. Look at how God wants us to commune with him. He sends prophets to convince Israel, but they reject God's Word.

> **Hosea 12:10** | I spoke to the prophets; it was I who multiplied visions, and through the prophets gave parables.

Wow, can you imagine? I've never had a vision. God gave visions to the prophets and the people, but they did not respond. The prophets had to hide God's powerful message in parables. That's the thing about prayer: the more you do it, the more you want to do it. The more you don't do it, the more you don't want to do it.

God's given us something more than visions: he's given us a "more sure Word of prophecy" (2 Pet 1:19) – the 66 books of your Bible. And you have something better than temporary visions, though people can have those, but you have something better: the ministry of the Holy Spirit.

God bids us to commune with him today. He calls us through his Word and Spirit to commune with him. He doesn't have to multiply visions to us, though he can. But we have something better. We have the Word and the Spirit.

God's Awesome Power in Our Weakness

What do you get with prayer? God's awesome power in our weakness. Yet the people didn't listen. He tells them to go back to the beginning to Gilead and Gilgal. Remember God's grace there. He says, go back and remember when you as a nation were weakest: it was then you were strongest.

> **Hosea 12:11a** | If there is iniquity in Gilead, they shall surely come to nothing:

Gilead is the first of the Promised Land that Israel conquered, still under Moses' leadership, before his death. Gilead is the area once ruled by Sihon, King of the Amorites and Og, King of Bashan – their kingdoms straddling the Jordan River (*cf* Num 21). So Gilead is really the land of victory! . Gilead is the only victory Moses had in the Promised Land. How great a victory that was. It's celebrated in many places of the Bible (Psalm 135:11; 136:20; Neh 9:22). But if there is iniquity, literally wickedness (*aven*), then this victory shall surely come to nothing. We need to go back to Gilead, or we'll have nothing to show for our lives. Then Hosea talks about Gilgal.

> **Hosea 12:11b** | ...in Gilgal they sacrifice bulls; their altars also are like stone heaps on the furrows of the field.

Gilgal is the land of worship. If you go to Gilgal today, it is not far from Gilead. Gilgal is the place where Joshua gathered his troops to worship before conquering the Promised Land. God told them to place twelve stones there at the entrance of their place of worship, and those twelve stones are still there to this very day. I saw them in January 2018. It is Gilgal where Joshua set up the Tabernacle for a time. It is here in the land of victory and worship that Israel's false worship is taking place. Gilgal is the land of victory because Israel had nothing but God. That's all they had. They knew: "Unless the LORD builds the house, those who build it labor in vain" (Psa 127:1a). They were desperate and that desperation gave them incredible spiritual and national success. Let's get back to the glory cloud leading us!

JACOB'S WEAKNESS

Suddenly Hosea goes back to the story of Jacob to demonstrate weakness.

> **Hosea 12:12** | Jacob fled to the land of Aram; there Israel served for a wife, and for a wife he guarded sheep.

Remember how weak Jacob was? He didn't care much about God at that time he fled to Syria (here called by it's ancient name: *Aram*).

He love a girl. Waited for her for fourteen years. But God made him the father of the twelve tribes of Israel. You see what God can do with weak people?

Moses' Weakness

Hosea 12:13 | By a prophet the LORD brought Israel up from Egypt, and by a prophet he was guarded.

God uses a weak prophet named Moses who can't talk very well to deliver a nation of two million people from Egypt, the powerhouse of the ancient world. When we are weak, we can say, because of Christ, we are strong! God's strength is made perfect in weak vessels.

Israel's Weakness

Hosea 12:14 | Ephraim has given bitter provocation; so his Lord will leave his bloodguilt on him and will repay him for his disgraceful deeds.

What was the ultimate conclusion for Israel? God has to show them how weak they are. He's got to repay him by showing how weak and sinful they are. The story of ancient Israel is such a tragic story, because instead of pressing into God, they pressed into the world. The world didn't help them but destroyed them.

My prayer is that we will believe God that we can change our world. Even Jesus, the Almighty Son of God needed prayer as part of his constant communion with God. He was always getting away from the crowds to pray. If Christ had to pray for power, so do we! Are you ready to make prayer a priority in your family and in your church?

Conclusion

Most people inside and outside the church think of prayer as a harmless but necessary starting pistol that shoots blanks and gets things going. Satan knows that prayer is a deadly weapon that binds hell and invites heaven to do the impossible. Harmless but necessary: hey we prayed, not we can really get to the important stuff. No prayer is the important stuff. Satan is fine if you do all your spiritual activity, but he just doesn't want you to pray. He doesn't want you to go to God in desperation and dependence.

12 | HOSEA 13

THE DEATH OF DEATH

I shall ransom them from the power of Sheol; I shall redeem them from Death. O Death, where are your plagues? O Sheol, where is your sting? Compassion is hidden from my eyes.

HOSEA 13:14

Death is devastating. In our congregation alone, I have done so many funerals. Yet for the Christian, this life is as bad as it gets. We all face the death of loved ones and friends, and one day we will face our own mortality.

Death has had a major impact on my life from an early age. When I was 15 years old, just after I came to know Christ, I came face to face with death. It was New Year's Eve, 1989, and I heard my sister cry out from my mother's bedroom: "Matt, there's something wrong with Mom!" I went back to see my mom lying there. Here hand was still warm to the touch. She seemed like she was in a coma. I said a brief prayer before the paramedics burst it. My Mom died that night at age 49 of a massive heart attack.

Have you ever had to face death? No doubt most of us have seen the death of a loved one or friend or even faced death ourselves. Hosea 13 prepares us to face death. Christians know that once we come to know Christ, death no long has any power. We look forward with joy to seeing Jesus face to face! This world is not our home.

We see this victory over death taking place in the 13th chapter of Hosea. Remember God loves Israel. But Israel is spiritually dying. And God has to let Israel die, so he can raise this nation again when Christ comes. The popular verse in Romans that really summarizes the Hosea 13 just perfectly.

> "For the wages of sin is death, but the gift of God is eternal life in Christ Jesus our Lord" (Rom 6:23).

This is the message of Hosea 13: because of Jesus being our sin bearer, death is defeated. Death is dead!

THE DEATH OF A NATION (13:1-3)

To say that God is contrasting Israel's former days of youth and health with her present old age is technically inaccurate since Israel is already dead. But it is a strange death. We need to follow the hand of the divine surgeon as he conducts a spiritual autopsy. In medicine an autopsy is conducted to determine the cause of death and establish the condition of the corpse for the record. God does this in the first three verses of chapter 13.

An Autopsy Report

> **Hosea 13:1** | When Ephraim spoke, there was trembling; he was exalted in Israel, but he incurred guilt through Baal and died.

A summary of charges against Israel. This is what you've done. This is what you deserve. This is an autopsy report: a devastating review of Israel's history. You started off strong. Nations trembled before you. Remember the pillar of smoke, the glory cloud that went before them. No one wanted to contend with Israel. Kings and nations trembled before them. They were an incredible super power on the world stage that came out of nowhere.

Then they started worshipping Baal, and died (13:1). It wasn't an immediate death, but their death as a nation was certain.

Consider how exalted Israel was in the days of Solomon. Financially, militarily, and in every way, they were the picture of strength. But by the time of Hosea, they were almost dead.

Cause of Death: Idols

What a sad report we hear in the time of Hosea:

Hosea 13:2-3 | And now they sin more and more, and make for themselves metal images, idols skillfully made of their silver, all of them the work of craftsmen. It is said of them, "Those who offer human sacrifice kiss calves!" **3** Therefore they shall be like the morning mist or like the dew that goes early away, like the chaff that swirls from the threshing floor or like smoke from a window.

Israel was willing to participate in human sacrifice to get what they wanted. The nature of Baal worship was to offer a little baby to the bull god so that he might bless with material, agricultural or other forms of prosperity. They looked at the Baal as Yahweh's footstool. They were mixing Baal worship with worship of the true God. How confusing! Because Israel is neck-deep in idolatry, like the morning dew or the dry chaff, they will be burnt up and obliterated by the heat of judgment.

God had promised the Messiah to come through Israel. Jesus is the hope of the world. God's assessment is that Israel is dead by idols. She sold her soul to the world like Gomer earlier in the book.

WHY DID ISRAEL DIE?

Why did Israel die? It's the same reason anyone perishes. They would not trust in the Lord, their Helper. They walked right past the Way, the Truth, and the Life. Look how sad their lives are without the Lord. How sad would your life be without the Lord?

REMEMBER GOMER?

Do you remember Gomer? In the first three chapters, she is the wife of the prophet. But this dignified wife turns to prostitution. Remember what it was like when you were lost and dead in sin in the world? We were all Gomers. Remember she had sold herself to her lovers and ended up for sale in the slave market. We were all there once. Gomer needed a Savior, and her husband the prophet Hosea was a type of Christ, wasn't he? He paid with his own money, 30 pieces of silver, to purchase her back. He loved her, welcomed her, and received her back as his wife.

Before Hosea received her back, she was on the trading block at the slave market: for sale. Worthless. As good as dead. That's where

Israel is. What a mess. Israel is dead. Israel is like the chaotic mass of earth and water that God created in the beginning.

> The earth was without form and void, and darkness was over the face of the deep. And the Spirit of God was hovering over the face of the waters (Gen 1:2).

It looks like there is no hope.

GOD LOVES SAVING PEOPLE FROM DEATH (13:4-6)

Who is the source of the prophesied destruction? Some, wishing to preserve the name of God from any imagined tint of dishonor, speak as if death is merely a product of mother nature. This is not what Hosea says or what the Bible as a whole teaches. Hosea says that God sends death. The Almighty is the destroyer.[110]

But first he reminds them, that even though he is destroying their nation, he loves them, and he will never stop loving them. He takes away their nation in order to bless them. God always has good purposes when he takes thing from us.

> "The Lord gives, and the Lord takes away. Blessed be the name of the Lord" (Job 1:21).

He Saved His People in the Exodus

Here we see an historical reminder of the deliverance of the people from Egypt by God's hand.

> **Hosea 13:4** | But I am the LORD your God from the land of Egypt; you know no God but me, and besides me there is no savior.

Israel is neck-deep in idolatry. And why do they serve idols? Can they actually do anything. Remember the glorious feat of rescuing them from Egypt? They left with no weapons, only the pillar of God's presence in front of them. He carried them on eagles' wings, and brought them out of Egypt and through the Red Sea (Exo 19:4).[111]

God tells them plainly: "besides me there is no savior." Why is this important? Because God is telling them: you are dead, but I can raise those who are as good as dead.

---

[110] Boice, 105-106.
[111] Mackay, 344.

He Saved His People in the Wilderness

The tender words of God continue to tell us that he has an absolutely perfect record. The passage continues with a reminder of the care God gave during the days of the people's desert wanderings. It was not God who abandoned Israel, but Israel who forgot God.

> **Hosea 13:5-6** | It was I who knew you in the wilderness, in the land of drought; **6** but when they had grazed, they became full, they were filled, and their heart was lifted up; therefore they forgot me.

God was such a glorious provider for them in the wilderness. Remember God's assessment at the end of Deuteronomy?

> "I have led you forty years in the wilderness. Your clothes have not worn out on you, and your sandals have not worn off your feet" (Deut 29:5).

God was really generous to Israel. He fought for them. He provided for them. He taught them. He made them noble and strong. At this point, God's people should have responded with worship and gratitude, but instead they became proud about God's provision thinking they were better than others, and they forgot God and became self-reliant.

They were so filled and satisfied, they forgot it was God who blessed them. Beware of prosperity and comfort saints. Your blessing might not be a blessing. Your biggest blessing might just turn your heart away from God.

When you wonder why you have so many incredible judgments in the Old Testament, you must understand that it is very dangerous for God to bless sinful people. It's not until the New Testament that you have the new birth and the gift of the Holy Spirit that people can understand the bigger picture. But we're not there yet in the time of Hosea. God actually has to allow the nation of Israel to die.

Let's also remind ourselves that if we have a selfish attitude even as Christians, God's material blessings might hurt us far more than they could help us. When we go through trials, let's remember that God knows what he's doing.

> "...he who began a good work in you will bring it to completion at the day of Jesus Christ" (Phil 1:6).

Sometimes the greatest blessing God can give us is a devastating trial or difficulty that makes us draw near to him. He's doing a work. He had to crush Israel in order for them to know him.

My heart is "Lord whatever it takes. Do whatever it takes for me to know you and then to know you more."

DEATH IS WORSE THAN YOU THINK (13:7-13; 15-16)

Death without God is far worse than you can imagine. Israel forgot God. Because of their backsliding, in this passage, he gives two images that picture the destruction of the nation and the discipline of God's people.

God's Warning

> "The wages of sin is death..." (Rom 6:23a).

God wants Israel to know that this is not some passive judgment. Their death comes by his hands. They reject him as Savior and Lord, and therefore, they cannot be saved. There is no other way of salivation. Because of Israel's sin, the Lord will attack them like those animals that are the sheep's natural enemies:

> **Hosea 13:7-9** | So I am to them like a lion; like a leopard I will lurk beside the way. **8** I will fall upon them like a bear robbed of her cubs; I will tear open their breast, and there I will devour them like a lion, as a wild beast would rip them open. **9** He destroys you, O Israel, for you are against me, against your helper.

Ok, the devastation in these verses is incredible and frightening. He uses the most frightening animals to portray what's going to happen to them by the nations and ultimately eternal damnation. He doesn't say, "Assyria will be like a lion" but "I am to them like a lion...a leopard...a bear robbed of her cubs, a wild beast" who rips them open.

This passage is speaking of Israel's earthly destruction, but I believe it also points to the eternal damnation of the lost among them. Israel was asleep to their damnation, and I believe there are many who are asleep in the church today, riding their pew to hell. And that has everything to do with us today. There may be lost people in our church at this moment.

WHAT ABOUT HELL?

So we have to ask, what about hell? This verse gets at the heart of the doctrine of eternal damnation. If you reject God as your helper, there is no help for you. If God is not your helper, he is your enemy.

I have had conversations with people in our congregation through the years who were not sure of their salvation. Many have been very disturbed about this, but some shockingly, are completely undisturbed and even cavalier.

> Jesus himself warned, "Do not be afraid of those who kill the body but cannot kill the soul. Rather, be afraid of the one who can destroy both soul and body in hell" (Mt 10:28).

Be afraid! Be very afraid. If you don't know Christ, you will be separated from God in everlasting torment forever and ever. God uses this fearful imagery here in Hosea as a mercy to warn us.

Listen to the Lord in Revelation 21:6-8

> And he said to me, "It is done! I am the Alpha and the Omega, the beginning and the end. To the thirsty I will give from the spring of the water of life without payment. 7 The one who conquers will have this heritage, and I will be his God and he will be my son. 8 But as for the cowardly, the faithless, the detestable, as for murderers, the sexually immoral, sorcerers, idolaters, and all liars, their portion will be in the lake that burns with fire and sulfur, which is the second death." (Rev 21:6-8).

How awful is hell. Remember the rich man who went to the underworld, and he said:

> "Have mercy on me, and send Lazarus, that he may dip the tip of his finger in water, and cool my tongue; for I am tormented in this flame" (Lk 16:24).

Don't reject God as your Savior and Helper. Take God up on his salvation. You may be dead in your sins, but we serve a God that knows the way out of the grave.

Man's Responsibility

The second image in these verses is of an unborn child, a fetus, who refuses to be born. It speaks of our deep need to respond to God.

Hosea 13:10-13 | Where now is your king, to save you in all your cities? Where are all your rulers —those of whom you said, "Give me a king and princes"? **¹¹** I gave you a king in my anger, and I took him away in my wrath. **¹²** The iniquity of Ephraim is bound up; his sin is kept in store. **¹³** The pangs of childbirth come for him, but he is an unwise son, for at the right time he does not present himself at the opening of the womb.

God's given Israel a way to escape death. They didn't need an earthly king, like Saul. They needed God's king. David was just a type of God's king, but not a very good type. The true king they needed to be waiting for was Messiah: Jesus, God's Son.

They need to be alive to this, but instead, when the time came for them to be alive to God and trust in him, they were like a stillborn child. They would not come out and live. They were responsible to respond to God and draw near to him and worship him, but they never came out and lived.

Israel's Death

So what do we say to all this? Will Israel as a nation die? Yes. Northern Israel will be taken captive by Assyria. Judah will be enslaved by Babylon. But that's not the end.

God is the God of new beginnings. Do you believe that? There is death on the horizon for every one of us. Ten out of ten people die.

We are all born dead in our sin, but God, rich in mercy saved us (Eph 2:1-10). What a glorious God. Were it not for grace we would be doomed.

The final image is one that would be well understood by the inhabitants of Palestine: a destructive wind from the desert. It represents the invasion that was to come from Assyria that would absolutely put Israel as a nation to death, so to speak.

> **Hosea 13:15-16** | Though he may flourish among his brothers, the east wind, the wind of the LORD, shall come, rising from the wilderness, and his fountain shall dry up; his spring shall be parched; it shall strip his treasury of every precious thing. **¹⁶** Samaria shall bear her guilt, because she has rebelled against her God; they shall fall by the sword; their little ones shall be dashed in pieces, and their pregnant women ripped open.

Countryside and city, agriculture and culture, all will be ruined. This is actually what happened when Assyria became the wind, historically speaking. But to linger over that would be to fall prey to a facile form of reductionism, for the wind's first cause was the Lord—the ambivalent Lord. The same Lord who once nourished his people *in* the wilderness now brings terror and mortality *from* the wilderness. [112]

The result of the Assyrian "east wind" invasion is the slaughter of so many in Israel. It is so cruel and ugly at the time it happened, but it ultimately results in good for the overall plan of God. We must die before we can be raised from life. Israel would need to suffer the deaths of the most vulnerable through war and terrorism: their little ones and infants as well their pregnant wives.

The death of Israel will be devastating and awful. Life and eternity without God will be more awful than anyone can imagine!

THE DEATH OF DEATH (13:14)

Now we come to one of the Mount Everests of verses. Here God declares that death is dead. There is a ransom coming that will purchase God's people from the power of death. Indeed, because of this ransom, death has no sting.

The Old Testament Promise

God has to allow the nation of Israel to die essentially in order for the true Redeemer to come and purchase the true Israel back with his own blood. Because of this ransom, death is dead!

> **13:14** | I shall ransom them from the power of Sheol; I shall redeem them from Death. O Death, where are your plagues? O Sheol, where is your sting? Compassion is hidden from my eyes.

Here is death's obituary! Here is the death of death. Israel has to go into captivity and be "put to death" so that Christ can come and conquer death. Therefore, when it comes to Israel, God says, "Compassion is hidden..." I'm going to let Israel be cut down. But out of that cut down nation is going to come a sprout, a Branch, named Jesus.

The New Testament Redeemer

This verse is pointing directly to the New Testament Redeemer, Jesus Christ. He is the one who with his own blood ransoms Israel, and the true Israel of Jews and Gentiles together (Rom 11:17-24). Because of Christ's ransom, death is dead and the people of God of all ages are

---

[112] Beeby, 173–174.

ransomed and redeemed. God promises a resurrection to Israel. God can restore that which has died.

The Apostle Paul has therefore very properly quoted these words in 1 Corinthians 15:

> "Death is swallowed up in victory." "O death, where is your victory? O death, where is your sting?" (1 Cor 15:55).

Israel must "die" to come alive again. Therefore, Yahweh says, "Compassion is hidden from my eyes" (13:14b). The death and destruction of the nation is inevitable that the soul of the nation would be saved.

We need to see our need of Christ. We are as good as dead without him. As he says in John 15:5, "Without me you can do nothing." Because of the ransom of Christ's blood, we can live. Death has no sting and no power over anyone who trusts in Christ.

> By dying on the cross for our sins, Jesus actually struck a deathblow to sin, death, and the devil. Now the outcome of the battle between the two kingdoms is certain. All that remains is for God to liberate the captives of Satan's kingdom and bring them into the kingdom of His Son. ~Phillip Ryken

Death now has no sting! This has to do with a sting of a bee, stinger of a bee or a poisonous serpent. After that day that Christ took the sting of death, death has no sting for the Christian. The stinger's removed. You know, frankly, for the Christian, in the truest sense, when death plunged its stinger into Christ at the cross, it left its stinger there. And Christ bore the whole sting of death for us so that death for us has no sting. It's still an enemy; it still buzzes around and makes you dodge a lot. But it can't sting anymore. It left its stinger in Jesus Christ, and it's been flopping around in the throes of death ever sense.

Death doesn't harm us in any meaningful way. It invades our world, and we have to dodge a little bit, we have to recover from what it does, but it doesn't ever really harm us unless there is sin there. The sting of death is sin. But if you are in Christ, he's taken your sin from you.

> Death in its substance has been removed, and only the shadow of it remains... Nobody is afraid of a shadow, for a shadow cannot block a man's pathway for even a moment. The shadow of a dog can't bite; the shadow of a sword can't kill. ~C. H. Spurgeon

God put death to death by the death of his Son on the cross.

> For He made Him who knew no sin to be sin for us, that we might become the righteousness of God in Him. (2 Cor 5:21).

Conclusion

The great turning point in the whole long biblical story is Christ's resurrection. It is there that Jesus defeated death. He overcame death. Never did I see this more powerfully than in my friend's dad, Ralphie John Castine, Sr. We called him Big Ralph because he was so tall, and he was a large man. My dad called him "Ralph the Mouth," but I would never dare call him that because I liked living too much. Ralph Sr. worked at a paper factory during the night shift, so I'd see him when he came home around 10am in the morning. I'd be playing in the backyard on a summer day, and he'd yell out, "Matt the rat!" I loved him very much despite his sarcastic humor.

I moved away for eight years to Louisiana, then moved back to my childhood home after my mom died. My best friend was still Ralph Jr., and I was shocked to hear that his dad was dying of Leukemia. I didn't know what do to do but pray for Ralph Sr. to come to know Jesus. Not much time passed and I was invited to Ralph Sr.'s funeral. I wasn't sure how I would handle it if Ralph Jr. asked where his dad's soul was. I'd have to tell him I didn't think it was with the Lord. I was devasted. I had prayed daily for Ralph Sr. to be saved, and it felt like I had no power to help him know Jesus, and now he was dead.

I went to the funeral, and Ralph Jr. introduced me to his uncle, who was a wrestler. Now a little side note – one of my favorite things about Ralph Jr. was that he was a lot shorter than me, and I loved to wrestle him and destroy him any chance I could. That is, until he visited me in Louisiana one day and he literally lifted me up and body slammed me. I said, to Ralphie: "Where did learn that?" He told me his Uncle was an Olympian wrestler. I never messed with Ralphie John again. I showed him due respect!

Back to the funeral. I finally get to meet his Olympian uncle who Ralphie tells me also now works for Athletes in Action. He's a born again Christian. His uncle tells me that he's reading the Bible every day for three months with Ralph Sr., and that about two months ago, Ralph Sr. gave his life to Jesus Christ. Whoa! I jumped so high I almost put a hole in the ceiling at the funeral home. Because of the Gospel, this funeral home was a launching point of eternal life for Ralph Sr. Death is defeated, and Ralph Sr. has eternal life!

Listen, that's true for anyone who trusts in Jesus. Because of Jesus, death is dead. The devil has been stripped of his power. Hell is defeated! Christ is risen from the dead. Now he lives in you and me! And one day, Jesus will come again and my mortal body will put on immortality. Death is conquered. Death is now a portal to a life I cannot even now imagine. Life without pain, without sin, without despair. Truly we can sing: *Death is dead, love has won, Christ has conquered!*[113] If you are without Christ, come to the one who overcame death for you today. Don't wait! Don't hesitate!

---

[113] Keith Getty. *See What a Morning*. Hymn.

13 | HOSEA 14
GOD'S GARDEN OF LOVE

I will heal their apostasy; I will love them freely, for my anger has turned from them. I will be like the dew to Israel; he shall blossom like the lily; he shall take root like the trees of Lebanon; his shoots shall spread out; his beauty shall be like the olive, and his fragrance like Lebanon. They shall return and dwell beneath my shadow.

HOSEA 14:4-7

The message of Hosea 14 is one of such transcendent hope that the contrast with Hosea 13 is like travelling from one age to another, or even from one world to another. We have become accustomed to Hosea juxtaposing good news with bad news. But nothing quite prepares us for the quick transference from the darkness of chapter 13 to the warm and brilliant light of chapter 14.[114] Like so many of the prophets (Isaiah, Ezekiel, Amos, etc.), Hosea saves the best news for last.

Here is the good news: God invites wretched sinners to come to know him intimately and forever. He invites us to his garden of love. We come right back to the Garden of Eden, but this time, it's Paradise restored. It's the Garden Temple where we worship God.

---

[114] Beeby. *Hosea*, 177.

13 | HOSEA 14
God's Garden of Love

We are in the midst of an incredible panic in our country (with the Coronavirus pandemic). People are looking for answers, and we are in an unprecedented time of where people aware of their need for help and hope than perhaps any time since 9/11. People need hope! And Hosea 14 delivers. In Hosea 13, we are faced with the devastation of death, and all the woes of broken planet earth. It's very much like the fear and panic we've experienced this week. There seems to be no hope.

But at the end of chapter 13 of Hosea, we get a glimpse. God says: I know all you see is death and devastation, but I'm coming to kill death. I'm coming to put death to death. Jesus, our great Champion, as God puts on human flesh and has a wrestling match with death. And it's a match to the death. We know the end of the story: Jesus wins! Death is dead! Love has conquered!

Hosea 14 is like a new honeymoon. Remember Hosea begins with a love story gone terribly wrong. Hosea is told by God to marry a woman who becomes a prostitute. You know the story. She becomes penniless. Worthless. Her beauty gone. No one could love her. No one wants her. She's put up for sale. The holy prophet goes to the slave market. There's his disgraced, unfaithful wife. He buys her back for the equivalent of 30 pieces of silver. Despair is turned to hope. Beauty is turned to ashes. God restores the years that the locusts had eaten. Death is defeated. Gomer, for all intents and purposes is resurrected from the burial of her own sin.

It's it amazing saint, that God brings every child of God to this point? We were dead in trespasses and sins, but God, rich in mercy, raises us from death to life! Glory to our risen King!

Hosea 14 is like the marriage celebration. It's where God invites his people into his honeymoon Garden, the restored Paradise. He renews his love to Israel and to us. In Hosea 14, we have not only Garden of Eden language, but we have Song of Solomon language. We are invited into God's Garden to experience his love and care and healing.

If I could put a New Testament verse as the main point of this message, it is this:

> "Where sin abounds, grace super abounds" (Rom 5:20).

But you might ask: how do I get there? I want that super abounding grace! I want that unshakable hope. We all know we can't find it here on this earth. We can't even find toilet paper or bottled water.

What Jesus offers to each of us, indeed, to the whole world today is an unshakable hope: eternal life with him in Paradise Restored. Christ is returning at any moment in his Second Coming. He could come before this service ends. When that happens, he's going to wipe away every tear and restore peace on earth.

At that moment, everything and everyone will bow at his feet. Sin and iniquity and evil will raise the white flag of sufferer. Every disease, including the Coronavirus will be banished forever from earth. Satan, the one who is utterly and completely depraved and all his evil demons will bow and be confined to hell. And death, yes death will see Christ and will bow as a defeated foe.

But Christ promises peace not only when we see him face to face, but here and now when we "walk through the valley of the shadow of death" we have nothing to fear! He is with us!

RETURN TO THE LORD (14:1-3)

You say, how do I get that? Hosea 14 is the answer.

The Call to Return (14:1)

> **Hosea 14:1** | Return, O Israel, to the LORD your God, for you have stumbled because of your iniquity.

Return. That's not hard to understand. Stop sinning and return to me, God says. You need return. Jesus says, "Come to me, all who labor and are heavy laden, and I will give you rest" (Mt 11:28). That's what God says here. He's holding out his arms to you. Return! Come back sinner! Now this is written to proud Israel. They were not following God. I believe this is a call for repentant faith. Return. Stop your sinning. Turn back to me.

For Israel, they were holding on to their **iniquity**. Lawlessness. They knew what they were doing was wrong, breaking God's law, but they felt like they had no choice.

In order to repent, open your heart to God's Word. Let the conviction of the Holy Spirit come. Believe God for forgiveness. Trust in his mercy through Jesus. Come to Jesus!

The Words to Return (14:2a)

God even tells them how to approach him in prayer. Turn your heart to me with sincere words!

Hosea 14:2a | Take with you words and return to the LORD; say to him, "Take away all iniquity..."

We must not merely assume that God knows of our repentance, though he does if we are repentant. Rather, we must express our repentance verbally.[115] Words are nothing unless they come from the depths of the heart.[116]

> John Bunyan said, "When you pray, rather let your heart be without words, than your words without heart."[117]

The Spirit of God alone can teach such words as we need. Sincerely come to God and confess you sin to him. Turn to him in prayer filled with sincere repentance.

We need to ask God to "take away all iniquity." This is key to godly repentance. We must be radical in returning to God. You can't serve two masters. It's all or nothing.

The Cost of Returning to God (14:2b)

Some people try to repent with half-hearted repentance. There are various responses to sin that stand in the way of true repentance. We don't want to ask God to "take away all iniquity." We want to keep a bit of iniquity by making excuses. Instead God says to be all in and take full responsibility for our own waywardness and depravity.

Hosea 14:2b | ...Take away all iniquity; accept what is good, and we will pay with bulls the vows of our lips.

When David repented of his sin of pride in numbering his vast army, he repented by purchasing what is today the Temple Mount. It was offered to him for free, but David says:

"I will not offer burnt offerings to the Lord my God that cost me nothing" (2 Sam 24:24).

Repentance is costly. Hosea says that there is a specific cost in repentance. Solomon names the specifics. We have to bring something beyond bulls and lambs and goats. We need to bring a repentant heart.

"Whoever conceals his transgressions will not prosper, but he who confesses and forsakes them will obtain mercy" (Pro 28:13).

---

[115] Boice, 112.
[116] Lange & Schaff, et. el, *Hosea*, 100.
[117] John Bunyan. *Works*, vol 1, from "Bunyan's Autobiography" (London: Blackie and Son, 1850), 63.

The cost of repentance is that we confess and forsake our sins and make no excuses. We bring it all out. We hold nothing back. Many are not willing to pay the price. The sewers need to open up. You need be radical in your repentance.

Reject False Saviors (14:3)

> **Hosea 14:3a** | Assyria shall not save us; we will not ride on horses; and we will say no more, 'Our God,' to the work of our hands.

Forsake False Saviors (14:3a)

"We will not ride on [military] horses" is the graphic way of denouncing all trust in military might for survival or expansion (*cf* 8:14; 10:14).[118]

> "Some trust in chariots and some in horses, but we trust in the name of the LORD our God" (Psa 20:7).

There is only one true Savior – Yahweh, Almighty God. No foreign nation could ultimately deliver them. No army, even riding on horses could save them.

If you are married, your spouse is a terrible savior. Your job, your money, your bank account: are all lousy saviors. Don't depend on your blessings and gifts as if they were God.

> Jesus said, "I am the way, the truth, and the life, no one comes to the Father except through me" (Jn 14:6).

Jesus is the only Savior. Trust in him alone.

Find Shelter in the Father's Love (14:3b)

Here we see the plentiful mercy of God towards those who acknowledge their helplessness.[119]

> **Hosea 14:3b** | ...in you the orphan finds mercy.

The point of Hosea's prayer is that the people of Israel have become orphans. Their adulterous mother, the idolatrous worship of Israel, will be dead; their father, Baal, will have given them no help. But this fatherless people will turn back to their one true Father, the refuge of orphans, and find shelter in him. They will be taken into captivity

---

[118] Garrett, 240.
[119] Ibid.

and there return to Yahweh. They will return to the land, no longer orphans, but as the "elect of God." When that happens, Not-my-people will become the sons and daughters of the living God.[120] In repentance, we return to our God, and we are no longer orphans! We are sons and daughters of the most High God!

REJOICE IN GOD'S GARDEN (14:4-8)

This is where the whole book comes to a glorious crescendo and God promises to fully restore his love to Israel and to us.

The God of the Garden Returns to Us

> James says, "Draw near to God, and he will draw near to you" (Jas 4:8).

When you return to God, he returns to you. That was true for Israel. From the ruins of judgment, like plants or trees in a burnt forest, rising above the destruction, the people would again begin to grow under God's divine presence and blessing.[121]

The greatest loss in Eden was that Adam and Eve were ushered away from God's presence, from the Tree of Life. He sent them out of the Garden of Eden...

> He drove out the man, and at the east of the garden of Eden he placed the cherubim and a flaming sword that turned every way to guard the way to the tree of life (Gen 3:24).

The greatest loss in Eden for Adam and Eve as their loss of God's presence, from the Tree of Life. Their fellowship with God was broken. He sent them out of the Garden of Eden...

But here in Hosea 14:4, God returns. He comes back to Israel and begins to offer these great Edenic promises of a Paradise restored.

God's Heals

This is incredible. Israel had fallen away, but if they were willing to return and trust in him by faith, he would completely heal their apostasy.

Hosea 14:4a | I will heal their apostasy; I will love them freely,

---

[120] Ibid., 272.
[121] Boice, 113.

Apostasy occurs when someone knows the truth of salvation and walks away from it. Apostasy is a very difficult disease to heal. It's one thing to sin in the darkness, like the unbelievers. It far more damning to sin in the light. The hardness that comes to the heart from knowingly rejecting the truth seems impossible to break through. But God can do it. He promises to anyone who has apostatized that he will heal them. When we come to Christ, the Holy Spirit changes the nature of our heart as Ezekiel 36:26 says. He puts his Spirit in us. He loves us freely. I've seen God heal so many apostates that are now serving God in our local church. Kids who grew up in Christian homes, who sinned in the light, and knowingly rejected salvation in Christ alone have turned back to God and are now serving Jesus Christ.

Dear saints, you who are in Christ, don't settle for the Baal gardens of your former lives. We need to be done with those gardens. Baal gardens are like plastic inflatable trees. They give instantaneous relief from the sun, but there is no fruit on them. And they wither quickly in the blistering heat. They are gone before we know it. God's garden offers us the "oaks of righteousness" that can endure the storms. It can give us the fruit we need. It does not stink with sin and death like Baal's garden. God's garden emanates the life-giving aroma of life in Christ!

God's Forgives

We read in Hosea (8:5), that God's "anger" was "kindled against" his people, but now in chapter 14, there has been a great change in God's disposition toward his people.

Hosea 14:4b | ...for my anger has turned from them.

Isn't it amazing? When we come to God through Christ, he forgives us all our sins!

> As far as the east is from the west, so far does he remove our transgressions from us (Psa 103:12).

Justification in Christ means it's not only just as if I've never sinned, but just as if I had obeyed God's law perfectly. When we trust Christ, it's the great exchange: my sin for Christ's righteousness. My record of sin is obliterated on the Cross. And Christs record of righteousness is written down for me in the book of life. My sin is placed on Christ, and I'm robed in his righteousness. That's the only reason God's anger can turn away from us. We deserve hell. But Christ's death and perfect obedience satisfy God's just wrath against us.

The Beauty of the Garden Is Restored

The amazing beauty of God's garden is restored! It's breathtaking! Can it be that God would be so kind to such horrible sinners like those in Israel? How about sinners like you and me? This is what Christ gains for us: restored fellowship in this picturesque garden of God's love.

Fellowship Restored (Like Dew)

Now God begins to describe his garden of love.

Hosea 14:5a | I will be like the dew to Israel...

God promises his fellowship to be like the dew to us. He will be like the early dew of morning—quiet but ever present and effective. The "dew" (14:5) signifies a return of God's favor. Dew is gentle (unlike a downpour, which can become a flood), but agriculture in Israel cannot survive without it. The evening dew waters the earth most copiously when it is most needed, in the summer, in time of greatest heat.[122]

God is your dew, child of God. When hand sanitizers and social distancing cannot help you, the Lord will never fail.

Fruitfulness Restored

Hosea 14:5b | ...he shall blossom like the lily.

Oh, the ugliness of the fall. We were cursed physically. We all turn into raisins and die. But in Christ, death is defeated. Of course, when Christ comes, we'll have a new body, but here and now God makes our wilderness to bloom. God can restore beauty to our wilderness places. He restores "the years that the locust has eaten" (Joel 2:25).

"Where sin abounds, grace super abounds" (Rom 5:20).

If you've wasted your life, why waste any more? Just know that when you give your life to Christ, he will make you a fruitful vine.

> I am the true vine, and my Father is the vinedresser. ² Every branch in me that does not bear fruit he takes away, and every branch that does bear fruit he prunes, that it may bear more fruit. ³ Already you are clean because of the word that I have

---

[122] Garrett, 274.

spoken to you. 4 Abide in me, and I in you. As the branch cannot bear fruit by itself, unless it abides in the vine, neither can you, unless you abide in me. 5 I am the vine; you are the branches. Whoever abides in me and I in him, he it is that bears much fruit, for apart from me you can do nothing (Jn 15:1-5).

FAITHFULNESS RESTORED

Hosea 14:5c | ...he shall take root like the trees of Lebanon...

This passage is very similar to what God promises us in Isaiah 61,

> ...to grant to those who mourn in Zion— to give them a beautiful headdress instead of ashes, the oil of gladness instead of mourning, the garment of praise instead of a faint spirit; that they may be called oaks of righteousness, the planting of the LORD, that he may be glorified (Isa 61:3).

God wants us to be "rooted and grounded" in the love of Christ (Eph 3:17). Some of the trees of Lebanon were palm trees that could bend in the fiercest storms without breaking. This is a picture of the saint of God who is rooted by streams of water (Psa 1:1-3).

INCREDIBLE FRUITFULNESS

Hosea 14:6-7 | ...his shoots [*branches*] shall spread out; his beauty shall be like the olive, and his fragrance like Lebanon. 7 They shall return and dwell beneath my shadow; they shall flourish like the grain; they shall blossom like the vine; their fame shall be like the wine of Lebanon.

God's garden is towering branches and sweet aroma. Like a tree with a great harvest of fruit, the believer's godly character will blossom. Lebanon (14:5, 6, 7), the land of thick green forests and rivers, is the final word in each verse and symbolizes the overflowing fertility of God's garden in dramatic contrast to the bleak, almost treeless terrain of Palestine in Hosea's day.[123] He speaks of the...

"trees of Lebanon" (14:5)
"fragrance like Lebanon" (14:6)
"wine of Lebanon" (14:7)

---

[123] Hubbard, 242.

So much of the imagery is identical to the Song of Solomon, that it is likely the allusion is to the love ballad of Solomon for the poor Shulamite farm girl.

Solomon's song is about the love he shares with a peasant girl who becomes his princess. This girl was not someone who should have been on the radar of a great king. The Shulamite girl was so poor that her brothers made her a shepherdess—"they made me keeper of the vineyards" (Song 1:6). This was not a flattering vocation for a girl. Not much was on her side. She was impoverished and without striking natural beauty. Yet Solomon loved her and wrote this letter as the standard for marital love in the Bible.

Everything about Solomon seeking a poor peasant farm girl to marry is meant to tell the greatest love story ever told. This is the story of how God can love the most unworthy people. God takes impoverished sinners and pursues them. He overcomes them with his relentless love. Lebanon's prominence in Solomon's Song is evident: once they are married, Lebanon is the lover's favorite romantic getaway (Song 4:8) known for its streams (4:15), wood (3:9), mountain (7:5; lit. 'tower'), cedars (5:15), and fragrance (4:11; *cf* 14:6) and gardens.[124]

What incredible fruitfulness we have in Christ! Psalm 1 tells us all about the blessed man...

> He is like a tree planted by streams of water that yields its fruit in its season, and its leaf does not wither. In all that he does, he prospers (Psa 1:2).

The Protection of God's Garden (14:7)

Hosea 14:7 | They shall return and dwell beneath my shadow...

In all this foolishness and fear that we are going through in our country, of course we want to be wise, but child of God you must remember something: the safest place to be is in the center of God's will.

God's garden is our protection. When we return to God, we have the security of dwelling beneath his shadow and care.

> Those who live in the shelter of the Most High will find rest in the shadow of the Almighty (Psa 91:1).

---

[124] Burroughs, ibid.

We are tended to by God himself. God is the vine dresser, our divine and perfect Gardener. People can see the difference in those who are cared for and tended to by God.

The Source of Fruitfulness (14:8)

> **Hosea 14:8** | O Ephraim, what have I to do with idols? It is I who answer and look after you. I am like an evergreen cypress; from me comes your fruit.

God has absolutely nothing to do with idols. As a good gardener, he has lots of tools in his pouch, and all other masters will no longer enslave you if you turn to Christ.

We are compelled to give all glory and honor to God for any fruit and progress we have made in the Christian life. In case we have forgotten, which we often do, God reminds us: from me comes your fruit. Jesus words are familiar: "Without me you can do nothing" (Jn 15:5).

REHEARSE GOD'S PROMISES (14:9)

> **Hosea 14:9** | Whoever is wise, let him understand these things; whoever is discerning, let him know them; for the ways of the LORD are right, and the upright walk in them, but transgressors stumble in them.

There are two types of people: those who follow God in the right way, and those who stumble over what God says. These are the humble and the proud. Remember:

> "God resists the proud but gives grace to the humble" (1 Pet 5:5).

The Humble are Established

The world is going to try to flood you with fear because that's all they know. But if you are wise, you will turn your eyes to Christ and to his promises.

There's something worse than the coronavirus and cancer and death! There is an eternity without Christ. That's wisdom. Be wise in this world. Love your neighbor. Do good during this time of testing.

Find someone to bless and pour out the wisdom and rich oil of Christ. Give the aroma of life to those around you. This is your time to shine.

How many of you can testify this morning with David?

> I waited patiently for the Lord; And He inclined to me, and heard my cry. ² He also brought me up out of a horrible pit, out of the miry clay, and set my feet upon a rock, *and* established my steps. ³ He has put a new song in my mouth— Praise to our God; many will see *it* and fear, and will trust in the Lord (Psa 40:1-3).

The Proud Stumble!

The essence of verse 9, is that you must have a regenerated mind to understand all God's ways.

> **Hosea 14:9b** | ... but transgressors stumble in them [God's words].

Without the new birth, sinners will stumble and trip up over God's words and truth.

> The natural person does not accept the things of the Spirit of God, for they are folly to him, and he is not able to understand them because they are spiritually discerned (1 Cor 3:24).

A.W. Pink defined the new birth. He said:

> Regeneration consists in a radical change of heart, for there is implanted a new disposition as the foundation of all holy living; the mind is renovated, the affections elevated, and the will emancipated from the bondage of sin.[125]

In your testimony of salvation, how did you know you were regenerated? Dear saints, we need to offer this lush and fruitful garden of God to the world.

Conclusion

When I was a kid, we used to boat on Lake Ponchatrain. One time it was really stormy. We were out there on the Lake, and the waves were 10 feet high and we thought we were going to be carried away to the ocean. We headed back to the calm waters of Tickfaw River. Brothers and sisters, Christ is our calm water. He is our place of Refuge.

Jesus brought us that place of refuge when he came to this earth, and he went to his favorite place to pray: the Garden of Gethsemane. It was there he accepted the cup of suffering from the Father. Remember what he said: "not my will, but yours be done." From there he went to the cross and died for our sins. And he didn't stay dead, did he? He rose

---

[125] A.W. Pink. *Studies in the Scriptures, Volume 7* (Lafayette, IN: Sovereign Grace Publishers, 2001), 72.

the third day, defeating death, sin, and hell. Now we can say, "There is no condemnation to those of believe in Christ Jesus!"

There is coming a day when God brings us to his final Garden Temple, the New Earth where heaven and earth is one. Though we are not there yet, the place of peace is here.

Dear child of God because the King of all kings died for you, there is now a restored place of fellowship and forgivingness and rest and peace: God's garden of love. Amen!

Leave the gardens of Baal! Come into the love, and nourishment and protection of Yahweh's garden of love. Be rooted in Christ! Be grounded in him! Emanate his aroma! Let the fame of his wine and joy be your testimony! As we close this prophecy of Hosea, remember God's love is relentless! I will love you *unrelentingly*! Hosea 14:4a, "I will love them freely."

In some ways, Hosea ends as it began. Hosea was commanded to marry Gomer who became a prostitute, in order to illustrate God's great love to Israel. You and I are the prostitute in the story. We have been lavished with such love, but we often renege on it and betray our loving God. Yet, he keeps calling us back to his garden of love. Let us find rest and security through faith in him. His love is everlasting. His grace abounds to wretched sinners. What a great, merciful and loving God we serve!

You may obtain this and many other fine resources made available by Proclaim Publishers by contacting us:

Web:
proclaimpublishers.com

Email:
contact@proclaimpublishers.com

Postal Mail:
Proclaim Publishers
PO Box 2082
Wenatchee, WA 98807

Soli Deo Gloria

www.ingramcontent.com/pod-product-compliance
Lightning Source LLC
Chambersburg PA
CBHW022000100426
42738CB00042B/1019